JOURNAL FOR THE STUDY OF THE NEW TESTAMENT SUPPLEMENT SERIES
77

JSOT Press
Sheffield

Redemptive Almsgiving in Early Christianity

Roman Garrison

Journal for the Study of the New Testament
Supplement Series 77

Published by JSOT Press
JSOT Press is an imprint of
Sheffield Academic Press Ltd
343 Fulwood Road
Sheffield S10 3BP
England

Typeset by Sheffield Academic Press
and
Printed on acid-free paper in Great Britain
by Biddles Ltd
Guildford

British Library Cataloguing in Publication Data

A catalogue record for this book is available
from the British library

ISBN 1-85075-376-8

CONTENTS

PREFACE

This work is the product of my doctoral research at the University of Toronto. I was privileged to have Peter Richardson as my supervisor and I gratefully acknowledge his gracious and instructive guidance throughout the academic and political maze of graduate school.

Peter's own enthusiastic interest in early Christianity inspired my readings of the Apostolic Fathers and my returns to the New Testament. He helped to shape the focus of my study: the theological and social forces that brought about the idea of redemptive almsgiving in early Christianity. His integrity and sense of humour added both depth and joy to our working relationship which has become a treasured friendship.

I recognize an even greater debt to my wife, Evann, who has given of herself in order that this work might be completed and has been a continual source of encouragement and support. Not only has she sacrificed time and energy but she has willingly, lovingly, set aside her own needs, hopes and ambitions in order that I would achieve my goals.

ABBREVIATIONS

AJT	*American Journal of Theology*
ATR	*Anglican Theological Review*
BR	*Biblical Research*
CAH	Cambridge Ancient History
CBQ	*Catholic Biblical Quarterly*
CTM	*Concordia Theological Monthly*
ExpTim	*Expository Times*
GRBS	*Greek, Roman, and Byzantine Studies*
HTR	*Harvard Theological Review*
HUCA	*Hebrew Union College Annual*
IB	*Interpreter's Bible*
JBL	*Journal of Biblical Literature*
JPSV	*Jewish Publication Society Version*
JQR	*Jewish Quarterly Review*
JRH	*Journal of Religious History*
JTS	*Journal of Theological Studies*
NEB	*New English Bible*
NovT	*Novum Testamentum*
NTS	*New Testament Studies*
SJT	*Scottish Journal of Theology*
SR	*Studies in Religion*
TDNT	G. Kittel and G. Friedrich (eds.), *Theological Dictionary of the New Testament*
TS	*Theological Studies*
VC	*Vigiliae christianae*
ZNW	*Zeitschrift für die neutestamentliche Wissenschaft*
ZTK	*Zeitschrift für Theologie und Kirche*

Chapter 1

INTRODUCTION

The present research has grown out of an interest in early Christianity's developing conception of 'entrance requirements' for the kingdom of God. Several enter/inherit traditions are introduced with phrases such as 'do you not know?' or 'do not be deceived',[1] and some standards are regarded as incredible or even unintelligible.[2] In two references, Paul specifies what the kingdom of God is *not*,[3] and there is an implicit warning that 'misconceptions' of the kingdom constitute a grave danger.[4]

The economic status of the individual was, at one time, a condition which either guaranteed or virtually prohibited entrance into the kingdom.[5] This eventually gave way to an accommodation of the wealthy and a 'readjustment' of kingdom standards. Another major conflict of interpretation concerns the issue of whether baptism guarantees entrance into the kingdom,[6] or whether individuals' subsequent conduct (or misconduct) could jeopardize their inheritance.[7] This is the apparent context of the caution in *Barnabas*: 'Let us never rest as though we were called and slumber in our sins, lest the wicked ruler gain power over us and thrust us out from the kingdom of the Lord' (4.13).

The tension is apparent even within New Testament writings. On

---

1. 1 Cor. 6.9-10; Eph. 5.5-6; *Ign. Eph.* 16.1; *Ign. Phld.* 3.3.
2. Mk 10.23-26; Jn 3.3-9; cf. 1 Cor. 15.50-51.
3. Rom. 14.17; 1 Cor. 4.20; cf. Clement of Alexandria, *Rich Man* 21.
4. Cf. Gal. 5.19-21.
5. Lk. 6.20; Jas. 2.5; Mk 10.25.
6. Cf. Jn 3.5; *Herm. Sim.* 9.16.1-4.
7. Such a study lies outside the focus of this volume, but the above claim is a provisional conclusion of my earlier research. For the importance of good works as an entrance requirement of the kingdom, see again 1 Cor. 6.9-10; Gal. 5.19-21; Mt. 25.31-46; *Herm. Sim.* 9.13.1-3; 9.15.1-3; 9.29.1-2.

the one hand, the tradition despairs of human effort, maintaining that it is possible to enter the kingdom only by God's power;[1] yet, on the other hand, early Christianity demands a high standard of personal 'righteousness' and virtue that will merit entrance into the kingdom.[2] The latter principle is expounded in a variety of ways in the first several centuries of Christian literature, but it is the pronouncement of John Chrysostom (c. 400 CE) that captured my attention and redirected my interest. In his *Homilies on St John* he writes, 'It is impossible, though we perform ten thousand other good deeds, to enter the portals of the kingdom without almsgiving'.[3] Chrysostom further claims that while baptism provides the initial cleansing from sin, almsgiving is the foremost means of 'wiping off the filthiness' of post-baptismal sin.[4]

Here I was forcefully introduced to the doctrine of redemptive almsgiving, that almsgiving not only wins favour with God, earning the individual entrance into the kingdom of God, but even merits the forgiveness of sin. Redemptive almsgiving as a doctrine functions for the theological benefit of the rich but for the material benefit of the poor. It was the rich who struggled to gain entry into the kingdom. My provisional definition of *redemptive* almsgiving has been that the giving of alms provided a ransom for sin.[5] How and why did early Christianity come to adopt a doctrine of redemptive almsgiving? This question became the focus of my research. A tradition that once ridiculed the idea that a wealthy man could enter the kingdom of God[6] actually came to regard wealth as a blessing, a potential means of

1. Mk 10.26-27; cf. *Diogn.* 9.1.
2. Mt. 5.20; cf. *2 Clem.* 9.6; 12.1.
3. *Homily* 23.
4. *Homily* 73; cf. Cyprian, *On Works and Almsgiving* 2.
5. The concept of ransom is not explained in the earliest sources; it seems to have been adopted from previous tradition. Within the Christian context, one of the most primitive of the ransom formulae is found in Mk 10.45 where it is claimed that the life of the Son of man is a ransom for many (λύτρον ἀντὶ πολλῶν). Implicit is that the 'ransom' is paid to God. F. Buchsel, 'λύτρον', *TDNT*, IV, pp. 341-44. J. Jeremias, 'Das Lösegeld für Viele (Mk 10, 45)', *Judaica* 3 (1948), pp. 262-64. (For the idea of almsgiving as a *loan* to God, see Prov. 19.17.) Later Christian tradition interpreted the ransom as paid to the devil. See Origen, *In Matthaeum* 16.8, quoted in G. Aulen, *Christus Victor* (New York: Macmillan, 1969), p. 49.
6. 'It is easier for a camel to go through the eye of a needle...' (Mk 10.25; cf. Lk. 12.32-33).

redemption: 'He has made you rich, that you may assist the needy, that you may have release of your own sins, by liberality to others. He has given you money, not that you may shut it up for your destruction, but that you may pour it forth for your salvation'.[1]

My present research[2] has been provoked by a related concern. The early Christian belief that the death of Jesus is the unique atonement for sin seems to be incompatible with the doctrine of redemptive almsgiving. The two interpretations collide.

> For what else could cover our sins but his righteousness? In whom was it possible for us, in our wickedness and impiety, to be made just, except in the son of God alone? O the sweet exchange, O the inscrutable creation, O the unexpected benefits, that the wickedness of many should be concealed in the one righteous, and the righteousness of the one should make righteous many wicked! (*Diogn.* 9.3-5)

> O splendid trading! O divine business! You buy incorruption with money. You give the perishing things of the world and receive in exchange for them an eternal abode in heaven. Set sail, rich man, for this market, if you are wise. Compass the whole earth if need be. Spare not dangers or toils, that here you may buy a heavenly kingdom[3] (Clement of Alexandria, *Rich Man* 32).

It is my thesis that the New Testament writings provide a foundation for both these interpretations; the former is particularly evident in Hebrews and the letters of Paul,[4] while the latter is *implicit* in the teachings of Jesus and other New Testament traditions. The clear emergence of the doctrine of redemptive almsgiving in the Apostolic Fathers is partly to be explained by texts such as 1 Pet. 4.8, but certain identifiable social and theological issues promoted the doctrine so as to raise doubts about the all-sufficiency of Christ's death as an atonement for sin. Why this happened is the principal interest of my research.

1. Chrysostom, 'On the Statues', *Homily* 2.18-20.
2. It has been necessary to restrict the focus of my research to the earliest development of the doctrine in Christianity.
3. Cf. G.E.M. de Ste. Croix's description of this passage: 'Clement puts most eloquently the argument that almsgiving can actually purchase salvation', in *The Class Struggle in the Ancient Greek World* (London: Gerald Duckworth, 1981), p. 435.
4. Cf. A.D. Nock, 'Hellenistic Mysteries and Christian Sacraments', in *Essays on Religion and the Ancient World* (Cambridge, MA: Harvard University Press, 1972), II, pp. 806-807; and 'Early Gentile Christianity and its Hellenistic Background', in *Essays on Religion*, I, p. 83.

a. *The Problem*

The so-called letter to the Hebrews boldly expresses the belief of early Christianity that the death of Jesus provided an abiding sacrifice for sin that made the cultic ritual of Judaism obsolete.[1]

> But in these sacrifices there is a reminder of sin year after year. For it is impossible that the blood of bulls and goats should take away sins (10.3-4)... When Christ appeared as a high priest... he entered once for all (ἐφάπαξ) into the Holy Place, taking not the blood of goats and calves but his own blood, thus securing an eternal *redemption* (αἰωνίαν λύτρωσιν, 9.11-12)... And every priest stands daily at his service, offering repeatedly the same sacrifices which can never take away sins. But when Christ had offered for all time a single sacrifice for sins he sat down at the right hand of God... For by a single offering he has perfected for all time (μιᾷ γὰρ προσφορᾷ τετελείωκεν εἰς τὸ διηνεκές) those who are sanctified (10.11, 12-14).

The author goes on to claim that the prophetic vision of Jeremiah has been fulfilled in the new covenant (cf. Heb. 8.7-13) and he draws specific attention to the Lord's promise, 'I will remember their sins and their misdeeds no more' (10.15-17). The significant claim is then made: 'there is no longer any offering for sin' (10.18). While such a conclusion is theologically consistent, it has promoted an intolerance and a hopelessness for Christians who were guilty of post-baptismal sin.[2]

The dominant, though not exclusive, New Testament view of the death of Jesus is in harmony with the letter to the Hebrews. According to 1 Corinthians, Paul maintained that it is of high priority for the gospel that 'Christ died for our sins' (15.3). Elsewhere Paul argued that if justification[3] were possible by any other means, including the Law, then Christ's death served no purpose (Gal. 2.21). Martin Hengel has recognized here 'a fundamental break with the atoning and saving significance of sacrifice in the worship of the Temple in

---

1. Unless otherwise noted, biblical quotations are taken from the Revised Standard Version. Quotations from the Apostolic Fathers generally follow the translation of Kirsopp Lake.
2. Heb. 10.26-29; cf. 6.4-6. *Herm. Man.* 4.3.1-2.
3. No attempt can be made here to deal adequately with Paul's understanding of justification.

Jerusalem'. Early Christianity had the 'revolutionary insight' that the crucified Messiah had borne the curse of the Law, offering himself as the ultimate sacrifice for sins: 'The death of the Messiah Jesus on Golgotha had brought once and for all...universal atonement for all guilt'.[1] There are several passages in the New Testament writings that claim the death—indeed the very blood—of the Christ has redeemed and secured the forgiveness of those who believe (cf. Mt. 26.27-28; Eph. 1.7-8; 1 Pet. 1.18-19), even the whole world (1 Jn 2.2). It can be argued that the cross makes the temple ritual unnecessary.[2]

It is a natural expectation, then, that in the interests of propaganda (and evangelism), early Christian literature might exploit the destruction of the Temple by the Romans in 70 CE. Yet, while a 'prophecy' of the Temple's destruction is found in the Gospels, the New Testament contains no historical references to its fulfilment.[3] Even the so-called Apostolic Fathers virtually ignore the fall of Jerusalem.[4] This is an intriguing reluctance to capitalize on the collapse of the Jewish sacrificial cult. More problematic, however, is the remarkable fact that, following the destruction of the Temple, early Christianity wavered in its belief that the death of Jesus was a 'once for all' atonement for sin such that no other offering was necessary. The doctrine

1. M. Hengel, *The Atonement* (Philadelphia: Fortress Press, 1981), pp. 44, 47. For a different perspective, see W.D. Davies, *Paul and Rabbinic Judaism* (London: SPCK, 1948), p. 259.

2. Ethelbert Stauffer summarizes the New Testament view with the startling claim, 'Good Friday is the atonement day for the history of the whole cosmos', *New Testament Theology* (London: SCM Press, 1955), p. 145. Jeremias comments that for the authors of the New Testament the death of Jesus is 'the sum and the end of all sacrifices prescribed by the Old Testament ritual. It is the one sacrifice for the sins of all mankind', *The Central Message of the New Testament* (Philadelphia: Fortress Press, 1965), p. 36.

3. J.A.T. Robinson calls this a 'significant silence' which suggests that the books of the New Testament were all written before 70 CE. It is a fascinating thesis (*Redating the New Testament* [Philadelphia: Westminster Press, 1976], p. 13). Also, G.W.H. Lampe, 'AD 70 in Christian Reflection', in E. Bammel and C.F.D. Moule (eds.), *Jesus and the Politics of his Day* (Cambridge: Cambridge University Press, 1984), pp. 153-91; B. Reicke, 'Prophecies on the Destruction of Jerusalem', in D.E. Aune (ed.), *Studies in New Testament and Early Christian Literature* (Leiden: Brill, 1972), pp. 121-34.

4. *Barn.* 16.4 is the most notable exception. Striking for its ambiguity is *Ign. Eph.* 9.2.

of redemptive almsgiving, understandable within the context of post-70 Judaism, emerges unchallenged in early Christianity. Such a development is unexpected. While the destruction of the Temple and the consequent loss of the sacrificial cult provide some explanation for rabbinic Judaism's acceptance of redemptive almsgiving,[1] a crisis of similar magnitude in early Christianity is not easily found.

The belief prevails in rabbinic literature that giving money to the poor or works of loving-kindness atone for sin.[2] We shall see that it is significant that this idea is already implicit in the New Testament collection of writings,[3] but it is the Apostolic Fathers who boldly advocate a second means of redemption: almsgiving provides a ransom[4] for sin:

> Almsgiving is therefore good as repentance from sin. Fasting is better than prayer, but almsgiving is better than both. Love covers a multitude of sins but prayer from a good conscience rescues from death. Blessed is every man who is found full of these things for almsgiving lightens sin (*2 Clem.* 16.4).

> Do not be one who stretches out his hands to receive, but shuts them when it comes to giving. Of whatever you have gained by your hands, you shall give a ransom for your sins (*Did.* 4.5-6).

> You shall remember the day of judgment day and night and you shall seek the face of the saints either labouring by speech and going out to exhort, and striving to save souls by the word, or working with your hands for the ransom of your sins. You shall not hesitate to give and when you give you shall not grumble... (*Barn.* 19.10).

These texts from the period 70–135 CE[5] raise significant questions for the student of early Christianity. Several issues emerge with theological, historical and sociological dimensions. The central problem to be considered is how, and then why, early Christianity came to

---

1. Cf. *ARN* (version 1) 4, 11a. Cf. J. Neusner, *Judaism in the Beginning of Christianity* (Philadelphia; Fortress Press, 1984), pp. 95-99; also, A. Cronbach, *Philanthropy in Rabbinic Literature* (Cincinnati; UAHC, 1939), p. 6.

2. See *b. B. Bat.* 9a, b, 10a; *b. Suk.* 49b; *Midr. Ps.* on 50.8; cf. A. Cronbach, 'The Me'il Zedakah', *HUCA* 11 (1936), pp. 513-15, 528-29.

3. See below, Chapter 4.

4. A ransom (λύτρον) becomes necessary despite the eternal redemption (αἰωνίαν λύτρωσιν, Heb. 9.12) of Jesus' death!

5. This is of course only an estimation of the period in which these writings were composed.

hold and endorse a belief in redemptive almsgiving, that is, that money given to the poor earns the forgiveness of sins.

Both the New Testament and the Apostolic Fathers maintain that Jesus the Christ suffered 'for us', that he died 'for our sins', and that this sacrifice was sufficient to redeem humanity.[1] From a theological standpoint, then, an early Christian appeal to almsgiving as a further offering for sin is not only unexpected, but it also seems to be a virtual denial that the death of Jesus has made full atonement for sins. These unusual statements in the Apostolic Fathers warrant investigation; their appearance on the horizon of early Christian soteriology is confusing at the least.

To regard almsgiving as redemptive is to grant considerable theological prestige to this specific act of charity. Almsgiving provides a ransom for sin. Within early Christianity such a doctrine appears inconsistent with the belief in the 'once for all' atonement through the death of Jesus. This tension within early Christian tradition prompts my interest in the theological aspects of the subject.

The issue of redemptive almsgiving is critical in the development of ante-Nicene Christianity and affects discussions of wealth and penance in the early church. Clement of Alexandria and Cyprian give considerable attention to the role of almsgiving in the achievement or guarantee of salvation. The roots of the doctrine in early Christian literature go back at least as far as the Apostolic Fathers.

Within rabbinic Judaism there was a parallel belief in the meritorious, indeed redemptive, value of almsgiving. Historical questions might focus on the mutual interests and common sources of early Christianity and Tannaitic Judaism which promoted the doctrine of redemptive almsgiving. For my purposes, however, particular attention is to be given to the passages cited above from the Apostolic Fathers. Again, I am primarily interested in the issue of how and why the early church adopted such a belief. Interpretation and exegesis will depend on the recognition of certain conflicts within Christian

---

1. For the Apostolic Fathers see *1 Clem.* 7.4; 12.7; 16; 21.6; *Ign. Rom.* 6.1; *Ign. Smyrn.* 2.1; 7.1; *Phil.* 8.1; *Barn.* 5.1; 7.3. Cf. W.K.L. Clarke, *The First Epistle of Clement* (London: SPCK, 1937), p. 27: 'Clement has a devotion to "the blood of Christ"'. Also J. MacKinnon, *The Gospel in the Early Church* (London: Longmans, Green & Co., 1933), p. 263.

communities and a reconstruction of the emerging theological need for a doctrine of redemptive almsgiving.

Finally, almsgiving, particularly as a community ethic, has an obvious function within a given society and where this service is sanctioned and even institutionalized by an identifiable group, then certain sociological principles are at work. Max Weber observed that 'the giving of alms is a universal and primary component of every ethical religion, though new motivations for such giving may come to the fore'.[1]

It is these 'new motivations' which bear on the social significance of almsgiving in early Christianity. We should not simply assume that redemptive almsgiving within the Christian tradition was an idea advocated by the needy members of the community anxious for the material support of their wealthy brothers. Inasmuch as that same tradition reported that Jesus had declared, 'How hard it will be for those who have riches to enter the kingdom of God' (Mk 10.23), it is surely worth considering the possibility that wealthy Christians sought to rationalize their possession of property. They could appeal to the merit and reward they achieved through almsgiving. And beyond the issues related to wealth there remains the question—why is *redemption* promised to the one who gives alms? Why is this offered as motivation?

Early Christianity holds incompatible views on wealth. Within the New Testament there is an utter rejection of those who are wealthy: 'Woe to you that are rich for you have received your consolation' (Lk. 6.24). Yet the New Testament reveals a clear attempt to accommodate the wealthy. In 1 Tim. 6.17-19 the author warns that rich Christians are not to be haughty (ὑψηλοφρονεῖν)[2] nor to build their hopes on their wealth. Rather, they are encouraged 'to do good, to be rich in good deeds, liberal and generous, thus laying up for themselves a good foundation for the future so that they may take hold of the life which is life indeed'.

Hengel finds the roots of this 'religious justification' of the use of property in both Stoic and Jewish teaching, the latter being based on

---

1. M. Weber, *The Sociology of Religion* (Boston: Beacon, 1922), p. 212.

2. 'Haughtiness' apparently characterized many Christians (see *Did.* 3.9; *Barn.* 19.6) and perhaps especially the wealthy, *Herm. Sim.* 8.9.1.

the principle that 'all good gifts come from God himself'.[1] It is equally possible, however, to discern a development that is open to sociological analysis.

> The attitude of the *Jesus movement* to possessions and riches was ambivalent. On the one hand there was criticism of riches, and on the other the movement profited from them... This ambivalence can be seen as a sign of the lack of principle in the Jesus movement: renunciation of riches was not an essential condition of salvation, but it could be required in particular instances. This position can also be derived from the social situation of the Jesus movement: wandering charismatics without possessions could make a credible condemnation of riches; but as charismatic beggars they were also concerned that they should have their share of the produce of the land. The two things went well together. The generosity of many rich people could be encouraged by playing on their consciences over their riches. In any case these were the hated rich, tax-collectors, prostitutes, outsiders, whose riches had been gained by questionable means. Of course their generosity also benefited the poor.[2]

Theissen's reference to the wealthy as a despised and dishonest group is an unwarranted generalization but his comments are nevertheless suggestive. The poor, even as they might criticize wealth, were in fact dependent on the continued affluence (and generosity) of the rich. Understandably, the poor might attempt to motivate charity. The wealthy, for their part, in the face of criticism of their possessions (whether they were obtained honestly or not) might seek to justify their continuing financial security. Redemptive almsgiving could be advocated by the poor hoping to prompt charity, or it might be promoted by the wealthy attempting to rationalize their bounty as an invested treasury for the poor. Indeed, such a doctrine could well have had the support of both rich and poor Christians. Evidence for an emerging attitude which reflected both the concerns of the needy and the interests of the wealthy is found in the *Shepherd of Hermas*:[3]

---

1. M. Hengel, *Property and Riches in the Early Church* (Philadelphia: Fortress Press, 1974), p. 20.

2. G. Theissen, *The Sociology of Early Palestinian Christianity* (Philadelphia: Fortress Press, 1978), pp. 37-39.

3. See C. Osiek, *Rich and Poor in the Shepherd of Hermas* (Washington, DC: Catholic Biblical Association of America, 1983).

> ...instead of lands, purchase afflicted souls, as each is able, and look
> after widows and orphans. Do not despise them... For this reason the
> Master made you rich... Blessed are they who are wealthy and under-
> stand that their riches are from the Lord, for he who understands this will
> also be able to do some good service (*Herm. Sim.* 1.8-9; 2.10).

The issue of redemptive almsgiving invites a study of the social (or more precisely, socio-economic) factors which shaped early Christian communities. Unfortunately, the various theological, historical and sociological questions relevant to this doctrine in early Christianity have received little attention in any of those fields of research. The questions not only remain unanswered, they are unasked. There is a genuine need for a study of the dramatic emergence of this idea within Christianity in the period 70–135 CE.

I intend to approach this subject primarily from a literary-historical point of view, yet with a principal interest in the developing social relationships between rich and poor Christians, particularly in the Corinthian and Roman communities. Such a perspective gives priority to the understanding, appreciation and interpretation of the primary sources within their own historical setting. This is the evidence which is most available to us. The texts from the Apostolic Fathers determine the focus of my inquiry; questions or issues relevant to the exegesis and interpretation of these passages will determine its extent. Any analysis of this literature ought to recognize the theological concerns that dominate the authors. Sociological insights are more likely to be legitimate when the historical and theological issues are also considered. Finally, I acknowledge that my own training has prepared me to work more effectively, and so to make a more significant contribution, where I give greater attention to the literary and historical tasks at hand.

At the present nothing exists that could be described as a scholarly consensus on the topic of redemptive almsgiving in early Christianity. This void is both an impetus to and a justification for the development of a thesis.

b. *Relevant Literature*

The immediate context for a discussion of redemptive almsgiving in early Christianity is the issue of wealth in the church during the first two centuries CE. From one perspective, the 'best recent book from the continent of Europe'[1] on this topic is that of Martin Hengel, *Property and Riches in the Early Church*. For our purposes, however, it is unfortunate that Hengel makes virtually no mention of almsgiving in general and the theme of redemptive almsgiving receives no treatment at all, despite the fact that both Clement of Alexandria and Cyprian are considered.[2] Hengel's silence is particularly striking because both these early Christian authors attribute great significance to the redemptive power of almsgiving.

Gerhard Uhlhorn's work, now over one hundred years old, *Christian Charity in the Ancient Church*,[3] is a very comprehensive treatment of its subject, and the author makes a few comments on redemptive almsgiving. The issue, however, is not given the attention it deserves, and Uhlhorn simply dismisses the doctrine: 'Justification by faith being no longer understood, the forgiveness of sins was soon made dependent on the fulfillment of the Divine commands'.[4]

Uhlhorn's suggestion is developed into a harsh polemic by T.F. Torrance in *The Doctrine of Grace in the Apostolic Fathers*[5] (see below). Yet neither makes any constructive attempts to account for early Christianity's 'misunderstanding' of justification by faith; redemptive almsgiving is treated merely as an aberration from New Testament soteriology.

A. Harnack's study, 'The Gospel of Love and Charity', in volume I of *The Mission and Expansion of Christianity in the First Three Centuries*,[6] is an excellent summary of the primary source material on the topic of charity in early Christianity. While Harnack is aware of the significance of redemptive almsgiving, he chooses to ignore the

---

1. L.W. Countryman, *The Rich Christian in the Church of the Early Empire* (New York: Edwin Mellen, 1980), p. 17.

2. Hengel's only significant comment on the issue is on p. 82: 'The idea of merit, taken over from Judaism and to be found above all in Hermas, Tertullian, and Cyprian, may be seen as a theological regression but it was this that provided a strong motive for concrete social and philanthropic action' (cf. p. 66). We will find this brief analysis of Hengel's to be inadequate. Far from being a mere 'theological regression', redemptive almsgiving in early Christianity evolved as a solution to critical social and theological problems. This thesis will be developed in much of what follows.

3. New York: Charles Scribner's Sons, 1883.

4. *Christian Charity*, p. 211.

5. London: Oliver & Boyd, 1948.

6. London: Williams & Norgate, 1904.

topic: 'It is not our business to follow up this aspect of almsgiving, or to discuss the amount of injury thus inflicted on a practice which was meant to flow from a pure love to men'.[1] It is the explicit purpose of the present research to investigate that feature of almsgiving in early Christianity which Harnack neglects.

Countryman's investigation, *The Rich Christian in the Church of the Early Empire*, relates more directly to my particular interests and is a helpful survey of early Christian attitudes towards the use of wealth. Of particular value are his studies of Clement of Alexandria and Cyprian, two significant advocates of redemptive almsgiving. Countryman does not focus on the doctrine in the Apostolic Fathers. While he recognizes the potential theological difficulty that redemptive almsgiving could create, he does little to trace its development, much less its necessity, for early Christianity other than to remark on its probable Jewish origins.

Countryman's most significant insights are related to the critical interdependence between social relationships and theology in early Christian communities. It is his thesis that the divergent attitudes towards wealth were shaped by

> the requirements of the early church's social life, in which rich laymen played an essential role but also gave rise to a variety of problems... The social importance of the rich within the church was as fundamental in determining attitudes toward wealth as was any preconceived doctrinal position.[2]

The one work which discusses the pertinent texts from the Apostolic Fathers is that of T.F. Torrance.[3] Unfortunately, Torrance too often is critical of the Apostolic Fathers for their 'fall from grace' rather than sympathetic to—or even interested in—the purpose and function of their writings. Thus the *Didache* is condemned: '...there can be no Christian explanation of the unevangelical nomism that runs through the whole writing'.[4] *Barnabas*, likewise, is repudiated: 'There could be nothing more crass than the words, "By thy hands thou shalt work for the redemption of thy sins"'.[5] Torrance is sharply critical of

1. *Mission and Expansion*, p. 192.
2. *Rich Christian*, pp. 34, 121.
3. *Doctrine of Grace*.
4. *Doctrine of Grace*, p. 37.
5. *Doctrine of Grace*, p. 108.

2 Clement for its several 'heresies' including the doctrine of redemptive almsgiving. Torrance labels the homily 'the least evangelic of all the writings of the so-called Apostolic Fathers'.[1] Among these early Christian advocates of almsgiving as a means of redemption, only Polycarp is spared such a harsh rebuke, but even he is regarded as misguided.[2]

John Lawson has pointedly criticized Torrance's analysis. He writes that Torrance's work is 'a good example of the neo-Reformation attack upon the ancient Church'.[3] Lawson maintains that from Torrance's perspective

> We must apply to the Fathers the Reformation formula 'justification by faith *alone*'. This is the anachronism which can easily vitiate modern thought upon the ancient writers. We are sometimes not sufficiently willing to let them express themselves in their own way, and ourselves to judge them by the canons of their own time.[4]

It must be said, however, that Torrance has contributed to the objectives of our research by drawing attention to the unusual development in early Christian soteriology found in the Apostolic Fathers. His reaction is indeed prejudiced and judgmental, but his lack of objectivity has provoked him into renouncing a clear divergence from the New Testament's emphasis on Christ's death as the ransom for sin. And he renounces what he first recognizes. The development is to be acknowledged, but at the same time we must bear in mind the historical, theological and social conditions that shaped this evolution. To his credit Torrance has made some attempt to explain, to account for, what he regards as a 'corrosion of the faith'. Unfortunately, he does little more than vaguely accuse Judaism and Hellenism (!) and the use of the Septuagint in the early church for corrupting the 'original' gospel.[5] Torrance fails to provide a constructive analysis for the doctrine of redemptive almsgiving in early Christianity, and he would

---

1. *Doctrine of Grace*, p. 132.
2. *Doctrine of Grace*, pp. 94-95. See *Phil.* 10.2.
3. J. Lawson, *A Theological and Historical Introduction to the Apostolic Fathers* (New York: Macmillan, 1961), p. 15.
4. *Historical Introduction*, p. 16; cf. H.E.W. Turner's remarks in *The Patristic Doctrine of Redemption* (London: Mowbray, 1952), p. 24.
5. *Doctrine of Grace*, pp. 133-37.

surely resist any suggestion that the New Testament itself may implicitly sanction such a doctrine.[1]

Ultimately, Torrance's work is little more than an evangelical renunciation of the doctrine of grace found in the Apostolic Fathers. Yet his bias and consequent caricature of these early Christian authors show the need for a balanced, historical study of redemptive almsgiving in the late first and early second century of primitive Christianity.

More recently, Redmond Mullin's *The Wealth of Christians*[2] and Charles Avila's *Ownership: Early Christian Teaching*[3] have added to the understanding of Christian attitudes toward property in relation to contemporary Graeco-Roman views.[4] Neither study, however, offers a specific analysis of almsgiving and neither focuses on the redemptive nature of charity other than to note the role of almsgiving as a form of penance.

The most stimulating work in this area has been initiated by Klaus Berger. In his article, 'Almosen für Israel',[5] Berger has given attention to the significance of almsgiving as an act of community solidarity whereby an individual demonstrates his goodwill, empathy and identification with a particular group. More specifically, Berger is interested in the so-called Pauline collection ('alms for my nation', Acts 24.17) as a theologically and sociologically motivated effort to establish the legitimacy of the Gentile mission as well as to relieve the needs of the saints. Through their generosity to the community in Jerusalem, Gentile believers justified their inclusion among the people of God.

Berger finds implicit support for this interpretation in the traditions about Cornelius in Acts 10 and about the captain in Capernaum reported in Luke 7. Both men, clearly described as Gentiles, prove themselves to be deserving of God's grace (through the gospel) because of their kindness to the people of Israel. Luke claims that Cornelius 'gave alms liberally to the people' (Acts 10.2). Berger correctly draws attention to the fact that Cornelius was generous to

---

1. This vital question is explored below, see Chapter 4.
2. Maryknoll, NY: Orbis Books, 1984.
3. Maryknoll, NY: Orbis Books, 1981.
4. The classical description of Graeco–Roman views is found in H. Bolkestein, *Wohltätigkeit und Armenpflege im vorchristlichen Altertum* (Utrecht: A. Oesthoek, 1939).
5. *NTS* (1977), pp. 180-204.

the Jews, to the people of Israel, and for this reason his almsgiving was 'remembered before God' (Acts 10.31; cf. 10.4). Similarly, in Luke 7, the elders of the Jews take up the concern of the captain who comes to Jesus for help: 'he is worthy to have you do this for him for he loves our nation and he built us our synagogue' (vv. 4-5). Significantly, Matthew's parallel tradition lacks this reference (8.5-13). Whether or not the special Lukan material is to be traced to an early source, it serves Luke's purpose, a purpose Berger has recognized.

Berger regards Cornelius and the centurion as concrete examples which illustrate the principle underlying Paul's concerns about the collection, namely that Gentile believers demonstrate their solidarity with the chosen people of God through almsgiving. Of particular value for my own research is Berger's section on the redemptive character of almsgiving in Judaism and early Christianity.

Berger maintains that in the Wisdom literature, almsgiving is regarded as a means of atonement available to Gentiles, provided that the recipient of the alms is from among the people of Israel. Although this is in part accurate, almsgiving is actually prescribed as the duty of all Jews and it has redemptive power for any who practise it.[1] Berger is too strict in his interpretation that almsgiving is meritorious as an atonement for sin only for uncircumcised Gentiles.[2] Furthermore, alms are sometimes to be given even to the undeserving; presumably this could include Gentiles.[3]

The doctrine of redemptive almsgiving was taken up by early Christianity apparently without objection in the church. This tradition stood unchallenged even in the face of the distinctive and emphatic Christian teaching of atonement through the sacrifice of Christ.

> On the one hand are statements where God's love is especially related to atonement and forgiveness of sins. On the other hand there are also many texts (seemingly untouched at all by the typical Christian concept of the atonement of sins through the death of Jesus) according to which love or alms 'cover' sins or atone. The unevangelical nature of this tradition ought not to be weakened exegetically; rather it becomes clear how little the early Christian authors were interested in a consistent Christianisation of Jewish traditions when adopting paraenetic materials.[4]

1. See Chapter 3, section B.
2. Berger, 'Almosen', p. 183.
3. Sir. 4.1-6, 8; 7.32; 29.8-9.
4. Berger, 'Almosen', pp. 185-86.

This is the most intriguing feature of redemptive almsgiving in early Christianity. How and why did it come to be sanctioned by a religion which gave high priority to the belief that Jesus died for sins (cf. 1 Cor. 15.3)? Even if—as we may find—the doctrine were to some degree implicit in Paul's theological understanding of the collection, why is the idea not only retained but developed by the Apostolic Fathers and made explicit? Why did these early writers not feel the obvious tension? Are we to assume simply that they were carelessly disinterested as they adapted 'Jewish paraenetic materials'?

Berger insists that 2 *Clem.* 16.4 warrants the 'strongest attention'. He makes several provocative comments about the theological/ soteriological equivalence of repentance and almsgiving in this passage. 'Above all, alms have the same effect as turning away from sin. This is noted right away in the first sentence that means: in a way that *metanoia* normally effects forgiveness of sins, so also alms can have the same result.'[1] Berger rightly concludes that it is astonishing that 'the function of the *metanoia*—conversion—so central to Christian thought—can be replaced by almsgiving'. In 2 *Clem.* 16.4, almsgiving 'takes over the soteriological function of repentance'.[2]

These phenomena occasion my own research. Berger, for the purposes of his article, must be content to leave it as a remarkable development; the purpose of the present research is to begin to trace, examine and understand the evolution of redemptive almsgiving in early Christianity.

Berger gives close attention to New Testament texts because he is prompted by an interest in the sociological dimension of early Christian almsgiving, or more specifically, where theology and group behaviour intertwine.[3] However, within the article he does not address the critical issue of why early Christianity came to endorse redemptive almsgiving. Berger's perspective is, nevertheless, illuminating for the interpretation of passages such as Mk 9.41/Mt. 10.42, Lk. 19.8, and Mk 10.17-22: '...the Jewish custom of "alms to Israel" is being transferred in ever-changing variations to the relationship of new converts or sympathizers to the community or to the poor... In the

---

1. 'Almosen', p. 186.
2. 'Almosen', p. 186.
3. 'Almosen', p. 192.

Gospels the depicted tradition is only presupposed...'[1]

It is the New Testament's implicit understanding of almsgiving that is more enigmatic. This material may assume the doctrine of redemptive almsgiving as later Christian authors find plausible prooftexts in the Gospels to support the belief. Yet the prevailing view that the sacrifice of Christ is the atonement for sins suggests that the New Testament authors in general may not have taken for granted such a high view of almsgiving. The bold emergence of passages such as *2 Clem.* 16.4 is in fact astonishing, as Berger claims, because of the New Testament's apparent silence on the issue of redemptive almsgiving.

Berger's initiative is welcome as an instructive study on the sociological and theological interpretations of almsgiving which informed and motivated Paul's objectives in the collection. The Jewish roots of this tradition, particularly in connection with the theme of community-solidarity on the part of the Gentile believers, are vital to the appreciation of Paul's attitude. A more extensive investigation of redemptive almsgiving in early Christianity is needed to complement Berger's suggestions.

My own concern, then, is to explore the background of redemptive almsgiving in early Christianity and to investigate the theological, historical and sociological issues relevant to its abrupt appearance in the Apostolic Fathers. I am persuaded that Berger's approach is constructive, seeking to understand developments within the thought of early Christianity. By contrast, I regard Torrance's analysis to be prejudiced by a standard of theological purity which prohibits an interest in the how and why of the doctrine of redemptive almsgiving. The purpose of my research is to raise the legitimate questions that Torrance neglects.

c. *Social Stratification in Rome and Corinth in the Early Empire*

The early history of Christianity is Roman history, and I should claim that Roman history itself needs the collaboration of those who try to relate the Christian movement to the whole life of the Empire, not explaining everything Christian in Roman terms or everything Roman in Christian terms but trying to understand identities, similarities, and differences.

---

1. 'Almosen', p. 195.

Otherwise, Roman history fades away with the past, and Christian history remains a myth.[1]

This strong claim justifies interest in the influence of social stratification within the Roman Empire, and especially the disparity and consequent hostility between the upper classes and the poor, and its effect on Christian communities in the first and early second centuries CE. The development of the doctrine of redemptive almsgiving in this period of Christianity is directly related to this context.

Berger's analysis is accurate when he states that almsgiving in early Christianity takes on a soteriological/theological function derived from Judaism where 'theological aspects and concrete group behaviour intertwine'.[2] That 'group behaviour', however, occurs in a Graeco-Roman setting. Attention must be given to the 'altered socioeconomic, socio-ecological, and socio-cultural conditions' which Christianity 'encountered in the urban Hellenistic world'.[3]

Within this Hellenistic setting, we have chosen to focus on Rome and Corinth, not only because of their prominent Christian communities, but particularly because much of the early church's literature which bears on the question of redemptive almsgiving is associated with one or the other (or even both) of these cities.[4]

My survey of the social stratification in the early empire actually begins in the middle of the first century BCE. For our purposes it is both convenient and reasonable to take into consideration two events which occurred during the career of Julius Caesar. The first is the Catilinarian conspiracy of 63 BCE in which the tensions between the poor and the affluent citizens of Rome were exploited. Secondly,

1. R.M. Grant, 'Introduction', in S. Benko and J.J. O'Rourke (eds.), *The Catacombs and the Colosseum* (Valley Forge, PA: Judson, 1971), p. 24.

2. 'Almosen', p. 192; cf. p. 186.

3. This is not Theissen's precise point, but his observation is relevant here. G. Theissen, *The Social Setting of Pauline Christianity* (Philadelphia: Fortress Press, 1982), pp. 39-40, cf. pp. 106-107.

4. Paul's letters: Rom. 1 and 2 Corinthians; New Testament writings thought to be connected with Rome: Hebrews and 1 Peter; from the Apostolic Fathers: *1 Clement*, the *Shepherd of Hermas* and perhaps the most significant, *2 Clement*. Note Theissen's comment on Corinth and Rome (*Social Setting*, p. 146).

Julius Caesar ordered the rebuilding of the city of Corinth[1] in 44 BCE and it became the capital of the province of Achaia.

1. *Rome*

During the time of the late republic, in 63 BCE, Catiline initiated a conspiracy that threatened to bring about revolutionary change in the city of Rome. S.A. Handford accurately and humorously characterizes the early Catiline as 'merely an ambitious careerist who in spite of a taste for dissipation and homicide had something likeable about him'.[2]

Catiline, embittered by his narrow defeats in 64 and 63 when he sought to be elected as consul, attempted to take power through violence. Having announced his intention to cancel all recorded debts, he hoped to enlist the support and allegiance of the lower classes. Denouncing those who held office, Catiline appealed to the poor:

> Can anyone who has the spirit of a man endure that they should have a superfluity of riches to waste in building out into the sea and levelling mountains, while we lack means to buy necessities? They have two, three, or four houses joined together, when we have not a home to call our own... For us there is destitution at home and debts everywhere else; misery now, and a still worse future to look forward to; we have nothing left, in fact, save the breath we draw in our wretchedness.[3]

Sallust, who reports the speech, indicates that it was specifically addressed to 'men who were afflicted with manifold misfortunes and had nothing good to enjoy or to hope for'; Catiline's words 'reminded them of their needy condition'.[4] According to Sallust, the conspiracy won the loyalty of the lower classes: 'poverty has nothing to lose'.[5]

While the genuineness of his concern for the poor has been questioned,[6] there can be no doubt as to the social stratification or the hostility of the poor towards the wealthy that Catiline intended to

1. The city was destroyed by the Roman consul Mummius in 146 BCE because of its rebellion against Rome.
2. Sallust, *Jugurthine War, Conspiracy of Catiline* (trans. S.A. Handford; Harmondsworth: Penguin, 1969), p. 163.
3. Sallust, *Conspiracy of Catiline*, 20.
4. Sallust, *Conspiracy of Catiline*, 23.
5. Sallust, *Conspiracy of Catiline*, 37.3.
6. H.H. Scullard, *From the Gracchi to Nero* (London: Methuen, 1976), p. 114; cf. Cicero, *Against Catiline* (First Oration).

exploit. Sallust himself testifies that as wealth became the distinguish-
ing feature of status and power, morality was disregarded. 'Poverty
was now looked on as a disgrace and a blameless life as a sign of ill
nature. Riches made the younger generation a prey to luxury, avarice,
and pride.'[1] The animosity between the affluent and the lower classes
cannot be denied. Still the conspiracy failed.[2]

Whatever Julius Caesar's sympathies may have been toward
Catiline,[3] during his administration Caesar found it both necessary and
expedient to continue the free corn policy despite its tremendous
burden on the state treasury. Caesar initially 'inherited the unpleasant
responsibility' of providing grain for close to two-thirds of Rome's
free inhabitants. While he was able to reduce the number of recipi-
ents, he still maintained 150,000 on the rolls. The large-scale problem
of poverty was overwhelming. 'Free corn may well have meant the
difference between life and death from starvation to many of the
poverty-stricken inhabitants of Rome's teeming tenements.'[4]

These overcrowded and dangerous living quarters for the poor
stood in stark contrast to the elaborate homes and gardens of the
wealthy.[5] The obvious social stratification within Rome during the late
republic promoted a deep hatred between the rich and the poor of the
city. The injustices of the society, the gross inequalities which existed,
were direct causes of crime and dangerous conditions. The streets
were not safe.[6]

This stratification was characteristic of the early empire as well.
Under Augustus, 200,000 were registered for free grain and the
number steadily grew.[7] The animosity and resentment between the
classes increased. Honour and prestige became associated with wealth.
It was a principal basis for *dignitas* and the legal system in Rome
'favoured the interests of the higher orders in Roman society'.

---

1. Sallust, *Conspiracy of Catiline* 12.
2. Scullard, *Gracchi to Nero*, pp. 112-14.
3. S.A. Handford, 'Introduction', Sallust, *Conspiracy of Catiline*, pp. 164-68.
4. F.R. Cowell, *Cicero and the Roman Republic* (Harmondsworth: Penguin, 1956), pp. 327-28.
5. Scullard, *Gracchi to Nero*, pp. 186-87.
6. Scullard, *Gracchi to Nero*, pp. 182, 187.
7. Dio Cassius 45.10; cf. G. Edmundson, *The Church in Rome in the First Century* (London: Longmans, Green & Co., 1913), p. 3.

Economically, politically and legally, wealth aggravated the tensions between rich and poor citizens.[1]

At the root of this conflict lay two common assumptions: (1), that poverty is disgraceful, and (2), that wealth *by itself* earns respect.[2] Juvenal mocks these attitudes and exposes the corruption of Rome:

> A man's word is believed in exact proportion to the amount of cash which he keeps in his strongbox. Though he swear by all the altars of Samothrace or of Rome, the poor man is believed to care naught for gods and thunderbolts.

> Of all the woes of luckless poverty none is harder to endure than this, that it exposes men to ridicule.

> It is no easy matter, anywhere, for a man to rise when poverty stands in the way of his merits, but nowhere is the effort harder than in Rome.

> Who but the wealthy get sleep in Rome?[3]

Musonius Rufus also speaks out on the vanity and misuse of wealth. He encourages the 'true lovers of philosophy' to escape from the evil influences of the city 'which are an obstacle to the study of philosophy'.[4] Musonius deplores the extravagant buildings and furnishings of the wealthy. He ridicules the delicate tastes and the eating habits of the upper classes who 'make the act of swallowing more enticing', and he repudiates the widespread vices of gluttony and luxurious living.[5]

Throughout the first century of the empire and into the reigns of Nerva and Trajan poverty was a serious problem in Rome and there was mutual contempt between the rich and the poor. During the rule of these two emperors even greater measures were taken to ease the

---

1. P. Garnsey, *Social Status and Legal Privilege in the Roman Empire* (Oxford: Clarendon Press, 1970), pp. 258, 270, 277. Cf. de St. Croix, *Class Struggle*, pp. 425-26.

2. R. Macmullen, *Roman Social Relations* (New Haven: Yale University Press, 1976), pp. 116-17. See also M.I. Finley, *The Ancient Economy* (Berkeley: University of California Press, 1973), pp. 35-36.

3. Juvenal, *Satire*, 3.143-46, 152-53, 164-66, 235; cf. 10.23-25; 14.173-76.

4. From 'What Means of Livelihood is Appropriate for a Philosopher?', in C.E. Lutz, 'Musonius Rufus, "The Roman Socrates"', *Yale Classical Studies* 10 (1947), p. 85.

5. 'On Food', 'On Clothing and Shelter', 'On Furnishings', in Lutz, 'Musonius', pp. 113, 115, 117, 119, 123, 127.

burden of the needy, especially in the capital, in order to relieve some of the ever-increasing unrest.[1] Social stratification within Rome, the tendency of the wealthy to despise the poor, and the hostility of the impoverished towards those of affluence and authority all shape the environment of the Christian community in Rome during the first and early second centuries CE. Unfortunately, we lack direct evidence for the formative years of Christianity in the city.[2]

The Apostle Paul's letter to the Romans is our earliest source regarding that congregation.[3] Edmundson claims that the letter is evidence for the existence of a 'distinguished and well-established Christian church in Rome...in 57AD'.[4] There is some dispute as to Paul's specific knowledge of the community,[5] but the letter itself at least reveals a clear concern that the more affluent members provide for the poorer members. Paul was certainly aware of social stratification within the Roman congregation.[6]

Chs. 12 and 13 reveal the social distinctions in the church. The apostle encourages liberality, sharing and hospitality; he calls on the wealthy to be humble and to identify with the lowly (12.3-16).[7] This is set in a context of a strong love ethic: 'Let love be genuine...love one another with brotherly affection; outdo one another in showing honour... He who loves his neighbour has fulfilled the law' (12.9-10; 13.8-10). The use of κοινωνοῦντες in 12.13 (cf. 2 Cor. 8.4; 9.13) stresses that generosity is an expression of fellowship. The verb suggests 'sharing' rather than 'contributing'. Within the community, social stratification must be overcome; the needs of even one are the concern of all and the bounty of one is to be enjoyed by all.[8] This unity of compassion

1. CAH, I, pp. 211-14; G. Downey, 'Who is my Neighbor? The Greek and Roman Answer', *ATR* 47 (1965), p. 13.
2. R.E. Brown and J.P. Meier, *Antioch and Rome* (New York: Paulist Press, 1983), p. 92.
3. W.A. Sanday and A.C. Headlam, *The Epistle to the Romans* (New York: Charles Scribner's Sons, 1905), p. xiii.
4. *The Church in Rome*, p. 14.
5. Brown and Maier, *Antioch and Rome*, pp. 105-11.
6. P. Lampe, *Die stadtrömischen Christen in den ersten beiden Jahrhunderten* (Tübingen: Mohr, 1987), p. 63.
7. Lampe, *Die stadtrömischen Christen*, p. 64.
8. J. Knox, *The Epistle to the Romans* (New York: Abingdon Press, 1954), p. 590.

and empathy is all-embracing: 'Rejoice with those who rejoice; weep with those who weep' (12.15). The letter to the Romans establishes for that community the high priority of ἀγάπη as the standard of Christian behaviour. Hospitality, humility and mutual respect for others, as well as generosity to the poor, are to be essential features of that love. Paul intends that they break down the barriers of social stratification through a 'participation in the experience of others'.[1]

The epistle commonly called *1 Clement* was probably written from the Roman community to the Corinthian congregation about 96 CE.[2] As evidence of conditions in both churches, it is striking that in the epistle Clement himself draws attention to the similarities between problems in the communities: 'Now, all this is not being written as a warning to you alone, beloved, but for a reminder to ourselves as well, because we too are in the same arena and have the same conflict before us' (7.1). Surely this common arena is not the crisis over deposed elders; there is no reason to believe this was an issue in the Roman congregation. I will argue that Clement is alluding to the animosity between believers, particularly between the rich and the poor, in both Corinth and Rome.

In *1 Clem.* 37.1–38.2 the author reveals his concern for resolving social tensions within the church.

> For the great cannot exist without the small, nor the small without the great. Every organism is composed of various different elements; and this ensures its own good. Take the body as an instance; the head is nothing without the feet, nor are the feet anything without the head. Even the smallest of our physical members are necessary and valuable to the whole body; yet all of them work together and observe a common subordination, so that the body itself is maintained intact.
>
> In Christ Jesus, then, let this corporate body of ours be likewise maintained intact, with each of us giving way to his neighbour in proportion to our spiritual gifts. The strong are not to ignore the weak, and the weak are to respect the strong. Rich men should provide for the poor and the poor should thank God for giving them somebody to supply their wants.

It is clear that Clement is aware of conflicts between the 'great' and the 'small'. His advice is not merely directed to the Corinthians; he reflects on the needs of his own community.[3]

1. Lampe, *Die stadtrömischen Christen*, p. 64.
2. For a discussion of the dating of the epistle, see Chapter 5, Section A.
3. Cf. Lampe, *Die stadtrömischen Christen*, p. 69; R.M. Grant, *Early*

That Clement is aware of serious cases of poverty in his own church is indicated in 55.2, 'As for our own people, we know that many have surrendered themselves to captivity as a ransom for others, and many more have sold themselves into slavery and given the money to provide others with food'. The economic need of the poor Christians in Rome was apparently so great and the wealthy unable or unwilling to provide for them, that 'Christians who could sell nothing but themselves did so in order to help out poor brethren'.[1]

It is here that the *Shepherd of Hermas* provides sharp references to the social injustice that prevails in the Roman congregation. Hermas indicts the wealthy for their neglect of the poor and he seeks to prod the rich into responsible community service to the needy. Angry that the affluent are double-minded, distracted by business, and 'superficial in their Christianity', Hermas issues a call for a second repentance. Lampe makes the significant point that 'the theology of a second repentance has an unmistakable social function'.[2] (It is important to note that a parallel development is reflected in *2 Clem.* 16.4, where almsgiving is 'as good as' repentance.)[3]

Finally, Ignatius's letter to the Romans demonstrates the presence of wealthy and influential members in that congregation. He fears that these persons will intervene on his behalf and rescue him from martyrdom. He pleads for them not do so (1.2; 2.1-2; 4.1; 7.2; 8.1-3). Ignatius's constant and repeated appeal that the Romans should not keep him from dying makes sense only if he believed they could exercise influence at his trial. He is aware of 'socially high-placed influential brothers'.[4]

There is sufficient reason, then, to believe that the social stratification that characterized the city of Rome was also reflected in the membership of the Christian community in the capital. Along with the disparity and inequality between rich and poor Christians there were natural tensions and hostility. Paul, Clement and Hermas each sought to promote harmony within the body of Christ. Along this

Christianity and Society (New York: Harper and Row, 1977, p. 130.
   1. Lampe, *Die stadtrömischen Christen*, p. 69.
   2. *Die stadtrömischen Christen*, pp. 71-76. For a more detailed look at Hermas, see below, Chapter 5, Section B.
   3. Again cf. Berger, 'Almosen', p. 186.
   4. Lampe, *Die stadtrömischen Christen*, pp. 70-71; R.A. Aytoun, *City Centres of Early Christianity* (London: Hodder & Stoughton, 1915), p. 217.

trajectory we will find that an original emphasis on the ethic of love (or love-patriarchalism)[1] was gradually superseded by the doctrine of redemptive almsgiving. The parallel developments in the Corinthian community are of vital importance.

2. *Corinth*

Poverty was a critical problem throughout the Empire and particularly in urban areas. By no means was Rome the only city where social stratification led to conflict between classes.[2] It is worth noting Theissen's observation that the Christian communities in Corinth and Rome exhibit the sharp disparity among their members that is reflected in their broader social context.[3]

From the eighth to the second centuries BCE Corinth had been a significant polis of Greece.[4] Benefited by her location, the city became quite prosperous. 'Corinth's position on the gulf gave her a great advantage in the new western trade...she knew how to profit by it'.[5] As early as Homer, Corinth had won the description of being wealthy.[6]

Destroyed in 146 BCE by the Romans, the city was rebuilt just over a century later by Julius Caesar. Within a short period of time Corinth was again a commercial centre. It was the capital of Achaia and its geographical location remained an essential asset for growth. Strabo observed that 'Corinth is called wealthy because of its commerce, since it lies at the Isthmus and controls two harbors, one of which is near Asia, the other near Italy, and it makes reciprocal exchange of cargoes easy...'[7] Corinth became the administrative and economic focal point in Greece. Consequently, there was 'money to be made in Corinth, and there were opportunities for the ambitious'.[8]

---

1. See Chapter 6.
2. Downey, 'Who is my Neighbor?', p. 13; cf. A.H.M. Jones, *The Greek City* (Oxford: Clarendon Press, 1940), p. 295.
3. *Social Setting*, p. 146.
4. J.E. Stambaugh and D.L. Balch, *The New Testament in its Social Environment* (Philadelphia: Westminster Press, 1986), p. 157.
5. T. Frank, *An Economic History of Rome* (Baltimore: The Johns Hopkins University Press, 1927), p. 20.
6. *Iliad* 2.570; cf. 13.664.
7. W.A. Meeks, *The First Urban Christians* (New Haven: Yale University Press, 1983), p. 47; Strabo, *Geography* 8.6.20.
8. Stambaugh and Balch, *Social Environment*, pp. 157-59.

Evidence of the city's wealth can be found in the extensive building projects that took place particularly during the reigns of Tiberius, Gaius and Claudius: 'by the time of Nero the public center of the city was one of the largest and handsomest of Greece'.[1] Also, that Corinth hosted the Isthmian games, sponsoring the contests at her own expense, indicates the prosperity of the city.[2] Certainly some, perhaps many, of the residents were wealthy.[3]

Little is known of the pre-Christian Roman city, yet certainly there was social stratification in Corinth and indications of tension and conflict between the rich and the poor have been recognized in Paul's first extant letter[4] to the Corinthians. The apostle gives specific attention to a problem in the Christian community that is more generally stated in the judgment of a late second-century author: 'I did not enter Corinth after all; for I learned in a short time of the sordidness of the rich there and the misery of the poor'.[5]

The Apostle Paul refers to the Corinthian Christians' status in society, in the world, and maintains that God has reversed the priority of men.

> For consider your call, brethren; not many of you were wise according to worldly standards, not many were powerful, not many were of noble birth; but God chose what is foolish in the world to shame the wise, God chose what is weak in the world to shame the strong, God chose what is low and despised in the world, even things that are not, to bring to nothing things that are, so that no human being might boast in the presence of God (1 Cor. 1.26-29).

This description surely refers to the social and economic class of the majority of Corinthian Christians. Paul intentionally distinguishes between the wise and the foolish, the powerful and the weak, the noble

---

1. Meeks, *Urban Christians*, p. 47.

2. See J.M. O'Connor, *St Paul's Corinth* (Wilmington, DE: Michael Glazier, 1983), pp. 14-15. Cf. Plutarch, *On Exile* 604C.

3. Two names of rich benefactors have come down to us: Cn. Babbius Philinus and Erastus (who may have been a Christian, see Rom. 16.23), Meeks, *Urban Christians*, p. 48.

4. For a thorough study of the apparent first letter to the community, see J. Hurd, *The Origin of 1 Corinthians* (New York: Seabury, 1965).

5. Alciphron (*Letters of Parasites* 24.3.16, translated by A.R. Benner and F.H. Fobes); cited by O'Connor, *Corinth*, p. 120 and by Stambaugh and Balch, *Social Environment*, p. 159.

born and the low. Most members of the community were poor. Indeed there were a few (ὀλίγος?) who were affluent and enjoyed prestige, but the majority, who represented the lower classes, stood in sharp contrast to 'a few influential members' who were wealthy.[1]

The conflict between the rich and the poor Christians in Corinth is addressed by the apostle in 1 Cor. 11.17-22.

> The source of the problem is stated clearly... the contempt of the rich for the poor, an attitude typically exhibited by wealthy Romans toward the lower classes. Those who have houses and plenty to eat despise and humiliate those who are hungry and have nothing.[2]

As the *whole* church celebrated the Lord's Supper, in the midst of a community meal largely provided by the wealthy, the more affluent members 'formed self-serving cliques', eating and drinking far more than their equal share.[3]

The apostle is outraged by the wealthy who have humiliated their poorer brethren. He later emphasizes that in the body members ought to have care for one another (12.25) and this theme is present in his instructions to the Romans (12.4-5, 8, 13, 16).[4] Paul insists that if the wealthy are intent on eating and drinking separately, enjoying an abundance of food, they should do so at home:

> if they cannot wait for others (v. 33), if they must indulge to excess, they can at least keep the church's common meal free from practices that can only bring discredit upon it. Their behaviour shows contempt of the community as a whole.[5]

---

1. Theissen, *Social Setting*, pp. 36, 39; L.L. Welborn, 'On the Discord in Corinth', *JBL* 106/1 (1987), pp. 96-97; Meeks, *Urban Christians*, pp. 69-70.

2. Welborn, 'Discord', p. 93. For further support that the tensions in the Corinthian church as they 'celebrated' the Lord's supper were rooted in social divisions within the community, see Meeks, *Urban Christians*, p. 159; cf. Stambaugh and Balch's endorsement of Theissen's views, *Social Environment*, p. 114; M.E. Thrall, *1 and 2 Corinthians* (Cambridge: Cambridge University Press, 1966), p. 83; C.K. Barrett, *The First Epistle to the Corinthians* (New York: Harper & Row, 1968), pp. 262-64.

3. Theissen, *Social Setting*, p. 151; Countryman, *Rich Christian*, p. 149; O'Connor, *Corinth*, pp. 158-60.

4. 1 Corinthians, like Romans, has a strong love ethic (13.1–14.1; cf. 8.1).

5. Barrett, *The First Epistle to the Corinthians*, p. 263.

Lucian's *Saturnalia* provides a striking parallel. Its significance warrants an extensive quotation.

> Cronus to the Rich—Greetings.
>
> The poor have recently written me complaining that you do not let them share what you have, and, to be brief, they asked me to make the good things common to all and let everyone have his bit. It was right, they said, for there to be equality and not for one man to have too much of what is pleasing while another goes without altogether... Now these requests seem to me to be reasonable. 'How', they say, 'can we, shivering in this extreme cold and in the grip of famine, keep festival as well?' So if I wanted them too to share in the festival, they bade me compel you to give them a share of any clothing you have above your needs or any too coarse for you, and to sprinkle on them a little of your gold... These things are not at all difficult for you to grant out of all that you are rightly blessed with.
>
> Oh yes, the dinners and their dining with you—they asked me to add this to my letter, that at present you gorge alone behind locked doors, and, if ever at long intervals you are willing to entertain any of them, there is more annoyance than good cheer in the dinner, and most of what happens is done to hurt them—that business of not drinking the same wine as you, for instance—goodness! how ungenerous that is! They themselves might well be condemned for not getting up and going during the proceedings and leaving the banquet entirely up to you... The rest is so disgraceful that I hesitate to mention their complaints of the way the meat is apportioned and how the servants stand beside you until you are full to bursting, but run past them...[1]

Cronus counsels the wealthy to provide for the poor: 'the expense is nothing to you, but they will never forget that you gave in time of need... Who would not pray for him [i.e. a benefactor] to live as long as possible in the enjoyment of his blessings?'[2]

One final aspect of the Corinthian community may bear on the issue of social stratification in that congregation. With reference to the Corinthian congregation, Paul twice speaks of the whole church (Rom. 16.23; 1 Cor. 14.23) and the same concern may be implied in

---

1. Lucian, *Saturnalia* 31–32. Translated by A.M. Harmon.

2. Lucian, *Saturnalia* 33. This reciprocity of the poor interceding for the (generous) wealthy, and the rich giving alms to the poor is a definite feature of early Christianity's emerging doctrine of redemptive almsgiving. Its appearance in a non-Christian text is striking.

1 Cor. 11.17-18. The adjective ὅλος is unnecessary if it were the regular practice of the Corinthian Christians to meet as one congregation. A gathering of the *whole* church as a single body appears to have been exceptional, presumably because of the difficulty in housing fifty or more people. If, then, the Corinthian community sometimes divided into smaller groups,[1] it is reasonable to assume that this separation was reinforced by the social stratification within the church. This possibility is important for understanding the schism that prompted the writing of *1 Clement* and it will be central to our interpretation of *2 Clement*.

The disparity between the rich and the poor and the consequent, perhaps inevitable, conflict between the classes is a vital aspect of the Graeco-Roman setting for Christian communities, particularly in Rome and Corinth. Social stratification is evident in both congregations. The doctrine of redemptive almsgiving in early Christianity was largely shaped by this feature. This will be pursued more explicitly in a later section, 'The Social Problems', a sociological analysis of texts from the Apostolic Fathers.

1. R. Banks, *Paul's Idea of Community* (Grand Rapids: Eerdmans, 1980), p. 38; O'Connor, *Corinth*, p. 168. Cf. B. Bowe, *A Church in Crisis* (Minneapolis: Fortress Press, 1988), pp. 14-15.

Chapter 2

THE GRAECO-ROMAN BACKGROUND OF REDEMPTIVE ALMSGIVING

It is commonplace to regard early Christianity as a deviation from, if not simply a sect of, Judaism in the first two centuries of the Common Era. The Hebrew Bible, as well as the Apocrypha and Pseudepigrapha, are often the primary focus of most 'Backgrounds of the New Testament'. This is, to a large degree, justified inasmuch as Jesus was in fact a Jew and his earliest followers regarded him as the Messiah, the one who had fulfilled the scriptures. Certainly the Christian community traces its origin to Judaism and to Palestine.

There remain, nevertheless, compelling reasons to seek the significant cultural, linguistic, philosophical and social influences on early Christianity which are found in the Graeco-Roman environment that surrounded and permeated the primitive church, even in Palestine.[1] There is a growing recognition of the need 'to bring the world of ancient Rome into closer conjunction with that of early Christianity...to locate the Christian movement within the world in which it arose'.[2]

In surveying the background of redemptive almsgiving in early Christianity, it is vital to give attention to the views of wealth and charity in the Graeco-Roman (as well as the Jewish) tradition.

Classical Greek did not have a specific term which meant 'alms' or 'a gift to the poor'. The word ἐλεημοσύνη came to carry the definition of almsgiving only in the 'Greek-speaking orient', that is, in the literature of so-called Hellenistic Judaism. This more precise, and

1. See M. Hengel, *Judaism and Hellenism*, I, II (Philadelphia: Fortress Press, 1974).

2. R.L. Wilken, *The Christians as the Romans Saw them* (New Haven: Yale University Press, 1984), p. xv; cf. R.M. Grant, 'Introduction: Christian and Roman History', in S. Benko and J.J. O'Rourke (eds.), *The Catacombs and the Colosseum* (Valley Forge, PA: Judson, 1971), p. 24.

perhaps 'un-Greek', meaning of the term is found within extant literature for the first time among pagan writers in Diogenes Laertius.[1] The
lack of terminology in the Greek tradition (and the Roman as well)
for the concept of almsgiving proves to be symptomatic of a certain
disinterest in the plight of the impoverished.[2]

The roots of this attitude can be traced back at least as far as the
fourth century BCE. Plato held that 'if a man is superlatively good, it
is impossible that he should also be superlatively rich'.[3] His reasoning
is based on the assumption, and the working definition, that the good
man will only spend his money on 'honourable objects' and that his
income will be derived from 'honest sources'. With this restriction
and balance, Plato concludes that the truly good man 'will not find it
easy to become either remarkably wealthy *or remarkably poor*'.[4]

This implicit ethic of moderation underlies much of the general
Graeco-Roman tradition concerning wealth. While property and
money are taken for granted as being appropriate to the status of a
good man, greed and unlawful gain are both considered unworthy of
the wise man. Poverty is generally regarded as a condition to be
avoided. It is only with the Cynic movement that the prevailing attitude towards wealth is seriously challenged and another put into practice. Significantly, the Cynics preceded Christian writers not only in
'urging the total renunciation of material possessions by the wealthy'
but also 'in advancing as a prime motive for doing so the opportunity
which it provided for the contemplation of real and lasting values'.[5]

As Plato had maintained that the good man would direct his wealth
toward 'honourable objects', it was widely held that money should be

1. 5.1.17 (third century CE). H. Bolkestein, 'Almosen', *RAC*, I, p. 302. Also,
H. Bolkestein, *Wohltätigkeit und Armenpflege im vorchristlichen Altertum* (Utrecht:
A. Oosthoek, 1939), p. 429.

2. Cf. J.E. Stambaugh and D.L. Balch, *The New Testament in its Social
Environment* (Philadelphia: Westminster Press, 1986), p. 64.

3. *Laws* 5.742E–743A. Translation by A.E. Taylor.

4. *Laws* 5.743B, C; italics mine. We find here the common belief (among the
intellectual element) that the destitute, the πτωχός, cannot be a good man.

5. A.R. Hands, *Charities and Social Aid in Greece and Rome* (London: Thames
& Hudson, 1968), p. 76. Hands adds this important comment, '...the few who
applied this ethic did not anticipate the Christian insistence that the possessions so
renounced should go to those most in need'. This will be seen in the discussion of
the Cynics below.

used, not hoarded. The desire and lust for wealth was repudiated, but a 'moderate enjoyment' of possessions was considered healthy. So Isocrates counselled, 'Try to make of money a thing to use as well as to possess'.[1]

Liberality (ἐλευθεριότης) was considered a virtue appropriate and necessary to the character of the good man. Only the liberal man could practise the proper use of wealth.[2] The exercise of liberality was not, however, to be motivated by compassion for an individual in need; rather, the purpose was to promote one's own developing good character. Thus, for Aristotle, 'acts of virtue are noble and are performed for the sake of their nobility'. More specifically, the reason that the liberal man will give is precisely because of 'the nobility of giving'. This is preserved by the restrictive conditions placed on liberality; a man must 'give rightly', that is, 'he will give to the right people', providing 'the right amount... at the right time'.[3]

Although Graeco-Roman philanthropy is commonly perceived as having been prompted by a desire for 'the praise of men',[4] it should be stressed here that Aristotle (and others) advocated liberality principally because it is a virtue. The good man will be generous. It is, nevertheless, striking that the ambition for praise and recognition emerges as a principal motive for liberality in later Graeco-Roman practice so much so that one can speak of 'the classical preoccupation with φιλοτιμία [which] left little room for any mention of pity—or of "the poor" as peculiarly deserving of such pity'.[5]

Interestingly, both Plato and Aristotle regarded the love of honour to be as reprehensible as the lust for gain.[6] And both philosophers considered the love of money to be unworthy of the good man. Indeed, φιλαργυρία came to be treated as one of the 'classic vices of Hellenistic moral philosophy'.[7] Love of money continued to be

---

1. Isocrates 1.27. Translation by George Norlin.
2. Aristotle, *Nichomachean Ethics* 4.1.6.
3. *Nichomachean Ethics* 4.1.12. Translation by H. Rackman.
4. W.S. Davis, *The Influence of Wealth in Imperial Rome* (New York: Macmillan, 1913), p. 251.
5. Hands, *Charities*, p. 61; cf. Countryman, *Rich Christian*, p. 106.
6. Plato, *Republic* 347B; Aristotle, *Politics* 2.6.20.
7. L.T. Johnson, *Sharing Possessions* (Philadelphia: Fortress Press, 1980), p. 119.

condemned as a principal source of multiple evils.[1] In the first century BCE, Cicero claimed that the most obvious and notorious characteristic of a selfish person was a passion for wealth. 'There is nothing more honourable and noble than to be indifferent to money if one does not possess it and to devote it to beneficence and liberality if one does possess it.'[2]

This liberality, however, was to be discriminating and selective. Just as Aristotle had maintained that the virtuous liberal man would only give to the 'right people',[3] the prevailing Graeco-Roman attitude was that benefits should be given exclusively to those who were regarded as worthy. Plato had mandated severe guidelines: 'The true object of pity is not the man who is hungry or in some similar needy case, but the man who has sobriety of soul or some other virtue, or share in such virtue, and misfortune to boot'.[4] In general, those who were considered deserving of benevolence were one's social peers, fellow-citizens, family members and friends. This standard is heartily endorsed by Cicero,[5] and is echoed by Pliny the Younger. For the latter, the ethic of friendship required that a generous man provide for his peers who were in need. Again, however, liberality was directed primarily towards 'country, neighbours, relatives, and friends'.[6] Countryman observes, 'The claim on the giver consisted not in need, but in some pre-existing personal relationship'.[7] Significantly, within the broadly classified popular morality of the Graeco-Roman tradition, we find no specific exhortations to the rich that they should give to the poor.[8]

Poverty by itself was not regarded as a condition meriting liberality.[9]

---

1. Cf. Diogenes Laertius 6.50.

2. Cicero, *On Duty* 1.20.68, translation by Walter Miller. Plutarch describes φιλαργυρία as a 'disease of the soul', *Concerning Talkativeness* 502E.

3. *Nichomachean Ethics* 4.1.12.

4. Plato, *Laws* 11.936B, translation by A.E. Taylor.

5. *On Duty* 1.42-50.

6. Pliny, *Epistles* 9.30, translation by William Melmoth.

7. Countryman, *Rich Christian*, p. 105; cf. Bolkestein, *Wohltätigkeit*, pp. 95-100, 114-15; W.D. Boer, *Private Morality in Greece and Rome* (Leiden: Brill, 1979), p. 178.

8. Bolkestein, *Wohltätigkeit*, p. 114; Boer, *Private Morality*, p. 172.

9. Countryman, *Rich Christian*, pp. 105-106; Hands, *Charities*, p. 61; Stambaugh and Balch, *Social Environment*, p. 64.

Evidence exists, however, that two prominent philosophers practised almsgiving (at least once each) without concern for determining the 'worthiness' of the recipient. Diogenes Laertius reports of Aristotle that he was once 'reproached for giving alms to a bad man'. According to this account, Aristotle replied, 'It was the man and not his character I pitied'.[1]

According to Herodes Atticus, Musonius Rufus provided a thousand sesterces for a beggar posing as a philosopher. A number of people objected that the man was 'a bad and vicious fellow, deserving of nothing good'. Musonius's reply was, 'Well, then, he deserves money'.[2]

Neither of these incidents, whether or not they are apocryphal, illustrates the principle that the virtuous man must give wisely, knowing that his beneficiaries are deserving of his generosity. Aristotle specifically identifies pity as his motivation. The popular morality is reflected, nevertheless, in the witness's clear disapproval of both Aristotle's and Musonius's liberality. The crowds assume that alms ought to be given only to good men. Inasmuch as the impoverished were not considered a virtuous group,[3] they would not be regarded as worthy of benevolence.

Plato's ideal republic has no room for the destitute, the πτωχοί, although the working 'poor', namely, those who had to labour for a living, would of course be necessary to the existence of the state.[4] Beggars are a symptom of crime, 'a defective culture and bad breeding and a wrong constitution of the state'.[5] Plato's insistence that compassion should be shown not to every man who may be hungry or needy, but only to the virtuous who have experienced misfortune, virtually takes the form of law.

> Whence in a state where constitution and citizens alike are even middling good, it will be strange to find any such man, slave or free, so wholly neglected that he comes to utter beggary. Such men will be in no danger if

1. Diogenes Laertius 5.1.17, translation by R.D. Hicks.
2. Cited by Lutz ('Musonius', pp. 144-45. Aulus Gellius, *Noctes Atticae* 9.2.8).
3. Quite in contrast to the Hebrew concept of the 'pious poor'.
4. Hands, *Charities*, pp. 63-64. The distinction between the working poor (πένης) and the destitute (πτωχός) is important. The πένης 'earned a living by their hands'; the πτωχός had nothing. Boer, *Private Morality*, pp. 151, 162-65; Countryman, *Rich Christian*, pp. 24-25.
5. *Republic* 552D, E; translation by Paul Shorey.

the legislator enact the following statute: There shall be no beggar (πτωχός) in the state. If anyone attempt it and seek to scrape up a living by his incessant entreaties, he shall be expelled from the marketplace by the commissioners of the market and from the city by the urban commission and escorted over the borders by the rural police that our land may be entirely cleaned of such creatures.[1]

At points in the Graeco-Roman tradition, the attitude expressed toward the helpless poor is almost hostile. Plautus remarks cold-heartedly, 'He does the beggar but a bad service who gives him meat and drink, for what he gives is lost, and the life of the poor is but prolonged to their own misery...'[2] This contempt for the πτωχός characterizes popular morality.[3]

Despite its repudiation of wealth and comfort, even the Cynic movement displays no compassion for the needy; on the contrary, poverty is praised. Thus, the model Cynic, Diogenes, begged only for enough to meet his most basic needs. Apparently he offered justification for his own begging: 'All things belong to the gods. The wise are friends of the gods, and friends hold things in common. Therefore all things belong to the wise.'[4] The primitive Cynic attitude towards 'almsgiving' was that people ought to sustain the Cynic, but there is no cry for sympathy toward the poor. Indeed, there is no cry for sympathy toward the Cynic.

While he was dependent on the generosity of others, Diogenes still consistently expressed contempt for wealth and for those who sought riches. He spoke of love of money as the homeland of all evils.[5] It was said that the Cynic preferred the simple life, considering it the happiest, and that he would not have traded his own poverty for the throne of Alexander the Great or the treasure of the Medes and Persians.[6] Because he chose to abandon his own property and beg from others, Diogenes was scorned as a πτωχός.[7] Ironically, his contempt for wealth

1. *Laws* 11.936B, C; translation by A.E. Taylor.
2. *Trinummus* 339; translation by Paul Nixon.
3. See G. de Ste Croix, 'Early Christian Attitudes to Property and Slavery', in D. Baker (ed.), *Church, Society and Politics* (Oxford: Basil Blackwell, 1975), p. 11; F. Hauck, 'πτωχός', *TDNT*, VI, p. 887.
4. Diogenes Laertius 6.37.
5. Diogenes Laertius 6.40.
6. Dio Chrysostom 4.10.
7. Dio Chrysostom 9.8-9.

was paralleled by the disgust others felt towards his own poverty.

The tradition about Diogenes, whether it be historical or apocryphal, suggests that his apparent concern for charity was in many respects self-centered. The Cynic argued that he had a right to what he needs from other men's riches. For Diogenes, almsgiving was not an act of mercy; indeed, *where he was the recipient* it was an obligation. Furthermore, there is reason to doubt whether Diogenes would approve of any almsgiving to the poor beyond providing them money for a necessary meal. Certainly the Cynic would repudiate the idea of redistributed wealth. Poverty is the ideal; it requires the wise men to lead a self-sufficient life. Too generous almsgiving would only burden, even choke, the beneficiary.

Finally, we have no explicit instructions from Diogenes as to what a wealthy man should do with his property in order to dispose of it and become a philosopher. Perhaps where Jesus of Nazareth would say, 'Sell what you have and *give to the poor*, and you will have treasure in heaven; and come follow me' (Mk 10.21), Diogenes' counsel would be, 'Give up your fields for sheep pasture and throw your money into the sea, and come follow me'.[1]

Given this analysis, it is necessary to reject Dudley's claim for the Cynics that 'their invective against wealth was as much for the spiritual benefit of the rich *as for the material betterment of the poor*'.[2] There is little, if any, evidence that the Cynics sought to improve the material conditions of the poor.[3] Poverty was a blessing!

The observation of Samuel Dill, made a half century ago, is indeed accurate: the 'self-centered isolation of the Cynic', condemning wealth but unconcerned with the plight of the impoverished is in stark contrast to the Stoic belief in the brotherhood of men which promoted compassion for the poor.[4] Here, Stoicism clearly differentiates itself from Cynicism.

Musonius Rufus is the most significant model of the Stoic-Cynic. He has been classified as both. This first-century CE teacher not only

1. Cf. Diogenes Laertius 6.87; also Lucian, *Philosophies for Sale* 9.
2. D.R. Dudley, *A History of Cynicism* (London: Methuen, 1937), p. xi; italics mine.
3. Again, Hands, *Charities*, p. 76; M. Rostovtzeff, *The Social and Economic History of the Hellenistic World* (Oxford: Clarendon Press, 1941), II, pp. 1129-30.
4. S. Dill, *Roman Society from Nero to Marcus Aurelius* (London: Macmillan, 1937), pp. 190, 323.

preached the theoretical virtues and joys of poverty—the simple life—
he himself adopted a 'rigorous austerity which seems closer to the
Cynic than to the Stoic ideal'.[1] Yet, while the Cynic philosophy
generally manifested a self-interested concern, Musonius exhibited a
genuine sympathy for other men and women. This compassion is
'completely opposed' to the Cynics' contempt for society.[2] According
to Lutz, Musonius was 'one of the first to advocate contributing to the
common good by devoting one's resources to charity'.[3]

Musonius Rufus, the 'Roman Socrates', the Cynic-Stoic, advocated
the distribution of charity to those in need although his teachings also
demonstrate a traditional concern for friends, peers, and fellow-
citizens.[4] He himself was known to give alms but his primary motivation in benevolence was not an interest in reciprocity nor in the
necessity of forsaking wealth. Instead, he stressed that unselfish giving
imitates God's own generosity.[5] As such, it is an obligation and privilege. Just as Musonius cared nothing for the return favour that might
be 'owed' to him as a benefactor, he made no reference to any theological principle that charity earned merit before God (or the gods).

In general, the Graeco-Roman background for the emergence and
development of the doctrine of redemptive almsgiving in early
Christianity does not, in many respects, appear to be significant.[6] It is
perhaps chiefly the motive of self-interest that came to influence the
Christian attitude towards a reward for almsgiving.[7] The idea of
redemption for sin is not a major theme in Graeco-Roman tradition
and it is not mentioned as a motive for almsgiving. Within early
Christianity, the evolution of the doctrine of redemptive almsgiving
cannot be attributed to the influence of the popular morality of the
Graeco-Roman world.

1. Lutz, 'Musonius', p. 28.
2. Lutz, 'Musonius', p. 29.
3. Lutz, 'Musonius', p. 30.
4. Lutz, 'Musonius', 'On Clothing and Shelter', pp. 121-23.
5. Lutz, 'Musonius', 'On Clothing and Shelter', pp. 121-23; also, 'Must One
Obey One's Parents under All Circumstances', p. 107; 'That Kings Should Also
Study Philosophy', pp. 65, 67; 'Should Every Child That Is Born Be Raised?',
p. 97; 'What is the Best Viaticum for Old Age?', p. 109; cf. Lk. 6.35.
6. Note should be made of the theological importance given to hospitality: Homer,
Odyssey 14.56-58; 17.457-87; Ovid, *Metamorphoses* 8.626-91.
7. Cf. Hands, *Charities*, p. 60; also, Countryman, *Rich Christian*, pp. 108-109.

Chapter 3

THE JEWISH BACKGROUND OF REDEMPTIVE ALMSGIVING

a. *The Hebrew Scriptures*

When compared to the attitude towards the poor found in the aristocratic Graeco-Roman literature, the view of the impoverished reflected in the Hebrew scriptures is striking. The Hebrew Bible consistently describes the poor as pious, innocent and specially protected by the Lord. Only Proverbs records a harsh judgment of the destitute and even this is more an indictment of foolishness and laziness: 'Poverty and disgrace come to him who ignores instruction' (13.18; see also 6.10-11 = 24.33-34; cf. Jer. 5.4).

On the whole, however, the poor are identified as God's people. This view originates in the self-understanding of Israel, interpreting her own pilgrimage as that of an orphan, a slave, whom the Lord rescued from Egypt (Deut. 24.17-18; Ezek. 16.3-5). Yahweh is spoken of as the God of the poor (Pss. 68.5, 10; 109.21-22, 31; 140.12; Isa. 41.17).[1] This provides the primary theological foundation for Jewish charity. Less explicit than the Stoic tradition,[2] the theme is similar: benevolence to the needy imitates the character of God. While this ethical standard was sufficient motive for Musonius's liberality, the Hebrew scriptures go beyond encouraging charity as the imitation of God. Further impetus comes from both the promise of divine reward and the threat of judgment for those who do not help the poor, the slave, the sojourner. These themes are found together in Torah where Israel is called to remember the compassion of Yahweh and warned that disobedience will be severely punished.

---

1. This designation is rare in the Graeco-Roman tradition, though Hands (*Charities*, p. 78) exaggerates in saying that Zeus is *never* referred to as the god of beggars. See Homer, *Odyssey* 6.207-8; 14.56-58; Epictetus, *Discourses* 3.11.4.

2. Cf. Seneca, *Benefits* 4.3.1-3; 4.25.1-3; 1.1.9; Epictetus, *Discourses* 2.14.13.

You shall not wrong a stranger or oppress him, for you were strangers in
the land of Egypt. You shall not afflict any widow or orphan. If you do
afflict them, and they cry out to me, I will surely hear their cry; and my
wrath will burn, and I will kill you with the sword, and your wives shall
become widows and your children fatherless. (Exod. 22.21-24)

The prospect of judgment for mistreating the poor was grounded in
Yahweh's previous mercy to Israel and his expectation that his people
would be charitable and hospitable (Exod. 22.25-27). At the same time,
the promise of material blessing for those who showed compassion to
the poor further promoted obedience (Deut. 14.28-29; 15.7-15).

Nothing in Torah, however, suggests that charity is redemptive in
the sense of having the power or merit to gain the forgiveness of sin.
Perhaps the only reference even to imply that acts of mercy can
redeem the individual would be the report concerning the hospitality
of Lot (Gen. 19.1-23) where, it was later interpreted, his kindness
rescued him from death.[1]

Clearly, however, within Torah it is the cultic sacrificial system
which provides the means of atonement. And this fundamental belief
gave prominence to the Temple and its worship.[2] It is ironic, then,
that the money collected for the service of the Temple was itself
regarded as redemptive, making atonement for the people. However,
this was by no means a charitable donation offered voluntarily. On the
contrary, the so-called Temple tax was legislated and obligatory for
both the rich and poor (Exod. 30.11-16).

Outside Torah, the significance of the sacrificial cult diminishes
dramatically. New priorities emerge in the religion and ethics of
Israel. Sacrifice becomes secondary, even unnecessary (1 Sam. 15.22;
Ps. 50.12-15; Prov. 21.3; Isa. 1.10-17; Hos. 6.6; Mic. 6.6-8). Speaking
in the name of the Lord, Jeremiah repudiates the cult: 'In the day that
I brought them out of the land of Egypt, I did not speak to your
fathers or command them concerning burnt offerings and sacrifices.
But this command I gave them, "Obey my voice..."' (7.21-23).

The voice of the Lord in the Prophets and Writings calls for
compassion to the needy. This commandment is surely rooted in

1. See T.D. Alexander, 'Lot's Hospitality: A Clue to his Righteousness', *JBL*
104 (1985), pp. 289-91; H. Chadwick, 'Justification by Faith and Hospitality', in
Studia Patristica 4 (Berlin: Akademie Verlag, 1961), pp. 281-85.
2. G. von Rad, *Old Testament Theology* (New York: Harper & Row, 1965), II,
p. 281.

Torah even while the sacrificial system, also based on Torah, is largely rejected. The significance of stressing the obligation to the poor lies in the fact that the social responsibilities of justice for the oppressed receive far greater attention than the responsibility to maintain the Temple cult.

Within the Prophets, three themes reflect the general attitude toward wealth and charity: (1) even more than sacrifices and offerings, Yahweh desires that the poor be comforted; (2) the rich and powerful who abuse the needy are denounced; (3) the eschatological vision of the future depicts a time when the rights of the poor will be respected.

For Isaiah, an abundance of sacrifices meant nothing to the Lord. True repentance was shown and redemption was made through doing good works. '... Seek justice, correct oppression; defend the fatherless, plead for the widow' (1.10-17). The prophet later describes genuine fasting:

> Is it not to share your bread with the hungry, and bring the homeless poor into your house; when you see the naked to cover him... If you pour yourself out for the hungry and satisfy the desire of the afflicted, then shall your light rise in the darkness and your gloom be as the noonday (58.6-10).

By contrast, the Lord is furious with those who mistreat the impoverished; their judgment will be harsh. 'What do you mean by crushing my people, by grinding the face of the poor?' (3.13-15; cf. 1.23; 10.1-3). Isaiah looks to the hope of an eschatological reversal that will bring justice for the needy (11.1-4; 26.1-6; cf. 61.1 with Lk. 4.18).

Each of these themes is found in the Prophets but the greatest stress is on the wickedness of powerful (and wealthy) men who exploit the poor. Their neglect of the widow, the orphan and the destitute is not only reprehensible but unforgivable. Atonement cannot be made; the punishment will not be set aside (Jer. 5.26-29; Ezek. 22.29; Amos 2.6-7; 4.1; 5.11-15; 6.4; 8.4-6; Mic. 2.1-2; 7.11).

The Prophets lay much of the theological groundwork for the doctrine of redemptive almsgiving. Good works, notably charity, demonstrate the individual's personal righteousness and these determine whether he is 'acceptable' to the Lord. A failure to uphold the rights of the poor and to meet their needs is a sin provoking the severe wrath of Yahweh.

In the Writings of the Hebrew scripture, several texts virtually endorse the belief that almsgiving earns divine protection or a heavenly reward. The term $ṣ^e dāqâ$, 'righteousness', begins to function in a way that permits later Judaism to identify almsgiving with righteousness. Again the redemption available through the Temple cult is largely ignored; it is the individual's character and actions that win God's favour, even meriting redemption from sin.

Job is portrayed as a blameless and wealthy man who, for no apparent reason, suffers at the hands of Satan. It is certainly clear that Job's anguish is not a punishment from the Lord; there is nothing to indicate that his ordeal is due to his failure to be charitable.[1] He is an innocent man and objects that his suffering is unjust because he has been abundantly generous to the needy, and he readily concedes that if he had in any way neglected the poor he would deserve to be punished (29.12-16; 31.16-23).

Eliphaz accounts for Job's suffering as retribution for his not being compassionate towards the needy (22.6-13). While Eliphaz and Job clearly disagree as to how charitable the latter was, they are nevertheless united in the belief that the generous man ought to be protected by God and the man who abuses the poor ought to suffer. This is the principle they both endorse and yet the author of Job apparently challenges its truth. Still, he represents a minority opinion in the Writings of the Hebrew Scripture.

Passages in the Psalms clearly indicate that the man who provides for the needy will be rewarded, protected and enriched. While almsgiving is not explicitly described as earning the forgiveness of sin, it is considered a good deed which merits the Lord's blessing (41.1-3). Psalm 112 promises wealth to the man who 'delights in the commandments', and the character of this individual is shown in his treatment of the needy. 'It is well with the man who deals generously and lends, who conducts his affairs with justice... He has distributed freely, he has given to the poor; his righteousness endures forever' (vv. 5, 9). The idea of an abiding righteousness which is virtually

---

1. The rabbinic tradition, however, found it necessary to justify Job's suffering as punishment for his unwillingness to be as hospitable and as charitable as Abraham, *ARN* (version 1), 7, 17a, b.

identified with almsgiving becomes significant within later Judaism.

Psalm 82—regardless of some features of interpretation—is an indictment of those who oppress the poor: 'How long will you judge unjustly and show partiality to the wicked? Give justice to the weak and the fatherless; maintain the right of the afflicted and the destitute. Rescue the weak and the needy; deliver them from the hand of the wicked' (vv. 2-4). To neglect or to abuse the impoverished carries the sentence of death (v. 7).

The book of Psalms maintains the developing emphasis on the obligatory nature of almsgiving and its abundant reward as well as stressing the punishment that will result for those who do not care for the poor. In the same way even Proverbs with its highly favourable view of wealth strongly defends the rights of the needy and warns of the judgment that awaits the uncharitable. The LXX translators of Proverbs make several significant interpretations which serve to increase the 'theological value' of almsgiving, yet within the Hebrew text, the theme of helping the poor is still important. Three categories define the relevant texts: (1) the command to give or the assumption that the righteous will be generous; (2) the promise of reward for those who give; and (3) the warning that failure to provide for the poor will be punished.

Prov. 3.27-28 is, in the Hebrew, somewhat ambiguous: 'Do not withhold good from those to whom it is due, when it is in your power to do it. Do not say to your neighbour, "Go and come again, tomorrow I will give it"—when you have it with you.' The passage may advocate honesty as well as benevolence, but the LXX stresses that one is to assist the poor promptly. Yet it is clear from Prov. 21.26 and 31.8-9 that the righteous man must 'give and not hold back', defending the rights of the poor. Furthermore, the good wife is praised for her compassion to the impoverished (31.20).

Like the other sections of the Hebrew Scripture, Proverbs promises a reward for those who show kindness to the needy. Charity to the destitute is reckoned as if it were done for the Lord himself (11.25; 14.21b, 31b; 19.17; 22.9; 28.27a).[1] Conversely, those who abuse the needy mock their maker and bring judgment upon themselves (14.31a; 17.5; 28.27b). Proverbs is the source of two of the most significant rabbinic proof-texts for redemptive almsgiving (10.2; 11.4). In both,

---

1. Cf. Mt. 25.34-40.

ṣᵉdāqâ, 'righteousness', is said to rescue from death. The crucial feature of the rabbinic interpretation is the identification of ṣᵉdāqâ with almsgiving.[1] While this linguistic development probably dates from as early as the second century BCE,[2] the Hebrew text of Proverbs gives no clear indication that 'righteousness' *is* almsgiving. This vital stage in the evolution of doctrine is found within later Judaism, in the period 200 BCE to 150 CE.

Among the books included in the Hebrew canon, Daniel is almost certainly a writing from this era, specifically from the time of the Maccabaean revolt.[3] Daniel contains one of the earliest uses of 'righteousness' to refer to charity, and the clearest passage to support redemptive almsgiving in the Hebrew Scripture. In Daniel 4, Nebuchadnezzar is warned that he will be punished for his sins. Daniel hoping that the monarch might escape judgment if he repents, offers advice:

> O King, let my counsel be acceptable to you; break off your sins by practising righteousness, and your iniquities by showing mercy to the oppressed, that there may perhaps be a lengthening of your tranquility.

The parallelism indicates that 'practising righteousness' is synonymous with 'showing mercy to the oppressed'. The LXX introduces the term ἐλεημοσύνη to interpret the act of righteousness. It is likely, however, that such an interpretation is already implicit in the Aramaic.[4]

Within the Hebrew Scripture there is a remarkably consistent interest in the needs and the rights of the poor. Charity is grounded in the character of Yahweh revealed through the Exodus; it is firmly rooted in the Torah. Compassion towards the impoverished is promised a reward; neglect of the poor will be severely punished. This is reinforced by the Prophets to the neglect of the sacrificial cult. In the Writings almsgiving begins to function as a virtual proof of

---

1. See below, pp. 56-59.

2. F. Rosenthal, 'Sedaka, Charity', *HUCA* 23 (1950–51), Part 1, p. 411.

3. For a study on the dating of Daniel, see L.F. Hartman and A.A. DiLella, *The Book of Daniel* (Garden City, NY: Doubleday, 1989), pp. 29-42.

4. Von Rad, *Old Testament Theology*, I, p. 383; JPSV: '... break off thy sins by almsgiving... by showing mercy to the poor; if there be a lengthening of thy prosperity'; cf. NEB.

righteousness that is expected to protect the individual from judgment. It is with the LXX that a more calculating doctrine of redemptive almsgiving emerges.

b. *The Septuagint and the Apocrypha*

The translation of the Hebrew Scripture into Greek, the so-called Septuagint (LXX) version, was carried out during the third and second centuries BCE.[1] More precise dates are not known. Particularly because of the widespread effects of Hellenism, the influence of the Septuagint was enormous. To a large degree it was the Septuagint which was to become the version of the scriptures preferred in the early church. Thus any developments of the doctrine of redemptive almsgiving in the Greek Bible would have had a clear impact on early Christianity.

The translation of Dan. 4.27 (MT, 4.24) is of considerable significance. The LXX version reads,

> O king, let my counsel please you. Redeem your sins by 'almsgiving' (τῶν ἁμαρτιῶν σου…ἐν ἐλεημοσύναις λύτρωσαι) and your iniquities by compassion on the poor. It may be that God will be long-suffering of your trespasses.

The Greek translation of Daniel renders the original reference to 'righteousness' as ἐλεημοσύνη. This identification is found elsewhere in the LXX (and underlies rabbinic thought). Such word association may be present in early Christianity. The Daniel passage can be taken to mean that the form of righteousness that will provide a ransom (λύτρον) for sins is almsgiving, the financial outpouring of compassion on the poor.

The Greek translation of Proverbs perhaps reveals further development of the doctrine of redemptive ἐλεημοσύνη. While the Hebrew form of 16.6 reads, 'By loyalty and faithfulness iniquity is atoned for', the LXX (= 15.27a) states, 'By ἐλεημοσύνη and faithfulness sins are purged away'. Similarly, Prov. 20.28 in the Hebrew claims, 'Loyalty and faithfulness preserve the king and his throne is upheld by loyalty', yet the LXX translates the verse, 'ἐλεημοσύνη and

---

1. The tradition preserved by Philo, *Vit. Mos.* 2.26-42 and the *Epistle of Aristeas* 301-16 is largely legendary. Nevertheless, the process of translation may well have been initiated during the era they report.

truth are a guard to the king and will surround his throne with *righteousness*'. It is possible that Prov. 15.27a and 20.28 in the LXX could largely explain the Greek translation (and interpretation) of Dan. 4.24/27. These passages from Proverbs clearly teach that ἐλεημοσύνη serves to redeem sin and to preserve a king's dominion. For the Greek editor of Daniel, Nebuchadnezzar would provide the specific example in which to promote the emerging doctrine. Even if it were to be argued that Prov. 15.27a and 20.28 (again, LXX) had no influence on the Greek version of Dan. 4.24/27, it is undeniable that the term *ṣᵉdāqâ*, 'righteousness', has been rendered by ἐλεημοσύνη. Righteousness is identified with the term that comes to mean almsgiving, and this theme certainly emerges in Proverbs (LXX).

Ch. 21 of Proverbs (LXX) introduces some significant ideas that shape the developing doctrine of redemptive almsgiving. Verses 3 and 21 read, 'To do justly and truthfully is more pleasing to God than the blood of sacrifices... The way of righteousness and ἐλεημοσύνης will find life and glory'. These two verses, in their Hebrew form, are both cited in rabbinic discussions of redemptive almsgiving where *ṣᵉdāqâ* ('righteousness') is interpreted as the giving of alms.[1]

It is striking that here in the LXX translation, ἐλεημοσύνη is used to render not *ṣᵉdāqâ* but *ḥesed*. Throughout the Greek Old Testament, ἐλεημοσύνη and δικαιοσύνη both are used to translate the two Hebrew terms.[2] This 'overlapping is indeed a curious linguistic phenomenon'.[3] It may well point to the evolution of the belief that almsgiving is both an act of kindness and mercy, and that it is a righteousness that redeems from sin and death, a righteousness more acceptable to the Lord than sacrifice. Sirach and Tobit provide considerable evidence of this stage of the doctrine.

The pseudonymous author of Tobit claims to have lived with many of his fellow Jews in Nineveh before its destruction. He boasts of his goodness, insisting that he 'walked in the ways of truth and righteousness (δικαιοσύνης)' his whole life and frequently practised ἐλεημοσύνας among his countrymen (1.3). Tobit's charity included

---

1. See *b. Suk.* 49b; *b. B. Bat.* 9b.

2. B. Przybylski, *Righteousness in Matthew and his World of Thought* (Cambridge: Cambridge University Press, 1980), p. 99.

3. C.H. Dodd, *The Bible and the Greeks* (London: Hodder & Stoughton, 1964), p. 65.

feeding the hungry, clothing the naked, and providing for the burial of the dead (1.16-17; cf. 4.16). The author clearly advocates a belief in redemptive ἐλεημοσύνη.

> Give alms (ἐλεημοσύνην) from your possessions to all who live uprightly, and do not let your eye begrudge the gift when you make it. Do not turn your face away from any poor man, and the face of God will not be turned away from you. If you have many possessions, make your gift from them in proportion; if few, do not be afraid to give according to the little you have. So you will be laying up a good treasure for yourself against the day of necessity. For almsgiving rescues from death (ἐλεημοσύνη ἐκ θανάτου ῥύεται) and keeps you from entering the darkness; and for all who practice it almsgiving (ἐλεημοσύνη) is an excellent offering in the presence of the Most High (4.7-11).

> Prayer is good when accompanied by fasting, almsgiving and righteousness. A little with righteousness is better than much with wrongdoing. It is better to give alms (ποιῆσαι ἐλεημοσύνην) than to treasure up gold. For almsgiving rescues from death and it will purge away every sin (ἀποκαθαριεῖ πᾶσαν ἁμαρτιαν). Those who give alms and do righteousness will have fulness of life... (12.8-9).

Tobit virtually identifies 'almsgiving' with 'righteousness' and apparently interpreted Prov. 10.2 and 11.4 in light of his belief in the redemptive power of almsgiving. The passages from Proverbs claim that 'righteousness' rescues from death'.[1] Tobit has made the significant step of regarding almsgiving as the manifestation of righteousness.[2] This is also borne out in the parallelism: 'A little with righteousness is better than much with wrongdoing [cf. Prov. 16.8]. It is better to give alms than to treasure up gold'. Finally, Tobit agrees with Proverbs (LXX) that ἐλεημοσύνη purges sin.[3]

Sirach, which strongly denounces greed and a perverse interest in wealth,[4] advances the doctrine of redemptive almsgiving. While it is certainly possible for a rich man to be righteous (cf. 31.8), the wealthy must consistently give alms (31.11). The Greek translator of Sirach clearly treated 'almsgiving' as an appropriate meaning for the

---

1. Prov. 11.4 is not found in the LXX.
2. Cf. A. Cronbach, 'The Social Ideals of the Apocrypha and the Pseudepigrapha', *HUCA* 18 (1944), pp. 132-33.
3. Prov. 15.27a.
4. A. Buchler, 'Ben Sira's Conception of Sin and Atonement', *JQR* 13 (1923), p. 461.

Hebrew *ṣᵉdāqâ*. He has made this translation/interpretation in at least six passages (3.14, 30; 7.10; 12.3; 40.17, 24).

Sirach's understanding of the power of almsgiving is stated succinctly in 3.30, 'Water extinguishes a blazing fire: so almsgiving atones for sin'. Thus the author admonishes his reader to assist the needy, to provide for the poor, to care for orphans and widows. The reward is tremendous: 'You will then be like a son of the Most High and he will love you more than does your mother' (4.1-10).[1]

Dishonest wealth cannot protect a man from trouble (5.8), but compassion to the poor will earn a blessing (7.32; cf. 7.10). The uncharitable will not be blessed but the man who wisely gives alms will be repaid by the Lord himself (12.2-7). A man's almsgiving is like a signet with the Most High (17.22).

> Lay up your treasure according to the commandments of the Most High, and it will profit you more than gold. Store up almsgiving in your treasury and it will rescue you from all affliction; more than a mighty shield and more than a heavy spear, it will fight on your behalf against your enemy (29.11-13; cf. 40.24).

Sirach implies that providing for the poor is more important than ritual sacrifices or sin offerings. In any event, the offerings of those who abuse the needy are meaningless (34.18-22). Almsgiving, by contrast, is a sacrifice of praise (35.2). Finally, the Hebrew phrase, 'righteousness endures forever', is rendered in the Greek Sirach as '*almsgiving* endures forever' (40.17). This may well have been an interpretation of the description of the generous man in Ps. 112.1-9.[2]

The Greek Scriptures, particularly Daniel, Proverbs, Tobit and Sirach, move beyond the Hebrew Old Testament in specifically identifying righteousness and almsgiving[3] and in explicitly claiming that ἐλεημοσύνη has the power to purge sin, to atone for and redeem iniquities. Almsgiving rescues from death.

---

1. It is worth noting the striking parallel in Lk. 6.30-35, the only sayings of Jesus which use the term, 'Most High'.
2. Cronbach, 'Social Ideals', pp. 131-33.
3. Cf. Bolkestein, *Wohltätigkeit*, p. 430.

c. *Early Rabbinic Literature*

As a doctrine, redemptive almsgiving is strongly advocated in the Talmud. There the identification of 'righteousness' with 'almsgiving' is taken for granted; no justification is thought to be necessary.[1] Much of the talmudic evidence, however, comes from a period well after 150 CE, and the question must be raised whether earlier rabbinic sources indicate that redemptive almsgiving was being endorsed in Judaism contemporary with the Apostolic Fathers. Recovering these traditions is a complicated procedure, but there is strong reason to believe the talmudic doctrine has its roots in the teachings of the tannaitic rabbis in the late first and early second centuries CE.

The destruction of the Temple in 70 CE certainly precipitated a crisis within Judaism. While other causes are recognized,[2] the devastation of the cultic sanctuary by the Romans must be regarded as the chief reason for the termination of the sacrificial system. The loss of the Temple was mourned.[3] Perhaps in the ashes of Herod's Temple, R. Johanan ben Zakkai became one of the principle architects of the doctrine of redemptive almsgiving, building anew on the foundation of the Prophets.

> It happened that R. Johanan b. Zakkai went out from Jerusalem and R. Joshua followed him and he saw the burnt ruins of the Temple. And he said, 'Woe is it that the place where the sins of Israel found is laid waste'. Then said R. Johanan, 'Grieve not, we have an atonement equal to the Temple, the doing of loving deeds, as it is said, "I desire love and not sacrifice"'.[4]

To establish the degree of historical reliability of this tradition would be very difficult and largely conjectural. Furthermore, there is evidence that R. Johanan ben Zakkai regarded almsgiving as redemptive for *Gentiles*, not for the Jews: 'Just as the sin offering makes

---

1. See *b. B. Bat.* 9b; 10a-b; 11a; *b. Šab.* 156b; *b. Roš. Haš.* 16b; *b. Suk.* 49b.

2. A. Guttmann, 'The End of the Jewish Sacrificial Cult', *HUCA* 38 (1967), p. 148.

3. See *m. Soṭ* 9.12, 15. For reflections on the first destruction, see Lam. 2.

4. *ARN* (version 1) 4, 11a, translation by Judah Goldin; cf. Mt. 12.1-7. Also, J. Neusner, *Judaism in the Beginning of Christianity* (Philadelphia: Fortress Press, 1984), pp. 96-97.

atonement for Israel, so charity makes atonement for the heathen'.[1]

This distinction is significant. Perhaps certain 'signs of repentance' were required of Gentile converts to Judaism.[2] If so, the theme of redemptive almsgiving for Gentiles is central to the story of the king of Adiabene. Both the Talmud and Tosefta report the king's lavish almsgiving which he justified as an investment which would bear a heavenly profit: 'My fathers stored up below and I am storing above... My fathers gathered for this world, but I have gathered for the future world...'[3]

There is evidence that several prominent rabbis during the period 120–160 CE were strong advocates of the redemptive power of almsgiving for Jews and Gentiles. R. Ishmael, R. Akiba, R. Eleazar and R. Meir are all cited as proponents of the doctrine.[4] It is further significant that R. Judah, the editor of the Mishnah, is represented as teaching redemptive almsgiving:

> It has been taught: R. Judah says, Great is almsgiving ($s^e d \bar{a} q \hat{a}$), in that it brings the redemption nearer... Death is stronger than all, and almsgiving ($s^e d \bar{a} q \hat{a}$) saves from death, as it is written, Righteousness ($s^e d \bar{a} q \hat{a}$) delivers from death.[5]

Given the various traditions of Tannaim who supported the belief that almsgiving would earn a heavenly reward, it is striking that the Mishnah contains virtually no mention of the doctrine. Indeed, it is unusual that the Mishnah uses the term 'righteousness' in only seven passages.[6] Even so, there are indications that the Mishnah has preserved early interpretations of 'righteousness' as almsgiving and the view that charitable giving earns a reward.

In *m. Abot* it is claimed that Simeon the Just (c. 200 BCE) held that the Law, the Temple service and deeds of loving-kindness sustained the world.[7] The deeds of loving-kindness were often associated with,

1. See *b. B. Bat.* 10b, translation by Rabbi Dr I. Epstein.
2. Cf. *Jos. Asen.* 10.11-13; cf. Berger, 'Almosen', pp. 188-90.
3. See *b. B. Bat.* 11a; *t. Pe'ah* 4.18, translation by Rabbi Dr I. Epstein. Cf. Mt. 6.19-21; Lk. 12.33-34.
4. *Mek. Nez.* 10 (on Exod. 21.30) quotes Dan. 4.24 as a prooftext for redemptive almsgiving; *b. Git.* 7a; *b. Šab.* 156b. *t. Pe'ah* 4.21; *b. Suk.* 49b; *b. B. Bat.* 10a.
5. See *b. B. Bat.* 10a, translation by Rabbi Dr I. Epstein.
6. Przybylski, *Righteousness in Matthew*, p. 66.
7. See *m. Ab.* 1.2.

yet distinguished from, strict almsgiving. Loving-kindness was regarded as compassion superior to that of the simple act of giving alms.[1] Acts of loving-kindness would, however, include almsgiving.

In order to be able to practice charity for the needy, it is always implicit that the individual must have some property or income. It is of particular interest that *m. Abot* strongly encourages manual labour because work provides the opportunity to secure a righteousness which both endures forever and which shall be rewarded.

> Rabban Gamaliel the son of R. Judah the Patriarch said: Excellent is study of the Law together with worldly occupation, for toil in them both puts sin out of the mind. But all study of the Law without [worldly] labour comes to naught at the last and brings sin in its train. And let all them that labour with the congregation labour with them for the sake of Heaven, for the merit of their fathers supports them and their righteousness endures forever. And as for you, [will God say,] I count you worthy of great reward as though ye [yourselves] had wrought.[2]

> R. Eleazar said: Be alert to study the Law and know how to make answer to an Epicurean, and know before whom thou toilest and who is thy taskmaster who shall pay thee the reward of thy labour.[3]

Inasmuch as the 'primary meaning' of $s^e d\bar{a}q\hat{a}$ in the tannaitic tradition 'is without doubt that of almsgiving',[4] it is worth considering the interpretation of those texts as they relate to redemptive almsgiving. *M. Ab.* 2.2 and 2.14 could well imply that those who labour and share their wages with the poor of their congregation gain a righteousness that endures forever.[5] The passages would indicate that God himself will reward labour done for the purpose of earning money in order to give alms. Work would be valued as the means for one's own redemption from sin through the use of wages in charity. If such an interpretation is reasonable, a startling parallel is found in the Apostolic Fathers:

> You shall remember the day of judgment day and night and you shall seek daily the society of the saints, either labouring by speech and going out to exhort, and striving to save souls by the word, or working with your

1. See *t. Pe'ah* 4.19, 21; *b. B. Bat* 10a; *b. Suk.* 49b.
2. *M. Ab.* 2.2, translation by Herbert Danby.
3. *M. Ab.* 2.14, translation by Herbert Danby, see also *m. Ab.* 2.16.
4. Przybylski, *Righteousness in Matthew*, p. 66.
5. Cf. Ps. 112.9; 2 Cor. 9.6-12; *b. B. Bat* 10b.

hands for the ransom of your sins. You shall not hesitate to give, and
when you give you shall not grumble but you shall know who is the good
paymaster of the reward.[1]

Finally, there is a saying attributed to Hillel: '...the more
righteousness, the more peace'.[2] This is an apparent allusion to Isa.
32.17 which is cited in the Talmud with reference to redemptive
almsgiving.[3] While 'righteousness' in the Hillel saying may refer to
almsgiving, the logion is without context and we are wisely cautioned,
'No definite conclusions as to its meaning can be reached...'[4]

It is indisputable that talmudic Judaism regards almsgiving as
redemptive, literally identifying it with righteousness, but it is far
more difficult to establish that such a doctrine existed in rabbinic
thought during the tannaitic period. Yet there is evidence that rabbis
from that era advocated a belief in redemptive almsgiving. The traditions, however, are historically elusive; the authenticity of material
attributed to R. Johanan ben Zakkai, R. Akiba or others is perhaps
impossible to establish.

It is not my task to seek causes for the evolution of the doctrine in
rabbinic Judaism. Undoubtedly the authority of the Hebrew Scripture
sanctioned the idea, and the end of the sacrificial cult necessitated an
alternative means of atonement. The development of the doctrine was
apparently accelerated by the destruction of the Temple. Its earlier
stages may well reflect a discontent with the sacrificial system; this
tension is already evident in the Prophets.

Early Christianity has its own crisis that stimulates the growth of
the doctrine of redemptive almsgiving. And the church also looked to
her Scripture to 'authenticate' the emerging tradition. The Jewish
background of this doctrine offers a fascinating parallel to its
emergence in early Christianity.

1. *Barn.* 19.10-11. See Appendix A.
2. See *m. Ab.* 2.7.
3. See *b. B. Bat.* 9a.
4. Przybylski, *Righteousness in Matthew*, p. 68.

Chapter 4

THE BACKGROUND IN EARLY CHRISTIAN TRADITION

The doctrine of redemptive almsgiving in early Christianity emerges distinctively in the Apostolic Fathers. It is my contention that certain sociological factors were responsible for that development but at the same time the idea of *redemptive* almsgiving is clearly a theological concept. It has roots in the Apocrypha,[1] and for the early church willingly to compromise the view that after the death of Jesus there is no longer any offering for sin, suggests that the earliest Christian tradition implicitly supported the doctrine.

Any reconstruction of the beliefs of early Christianity must depend heavily on the New Testament. There are also important sources outside the canon; these significant traditions are 'voices in the wilderness', outside the so-called orthodoxy of the early church. It is difficult, however, to assess the prominence and influence of such material. Still, we seek the background of the doctrine of redemptive almsgiving in the primitive Christian tradition.

a. *The Sayings of Jesus*

The reported teaching of Jesus is quite negative in its attitude towards wealth. Riches are regarded as not only a possible danger (as a temptation), but as an inevitable obstacle both to faith and the love of God. Consistent with this, some passages advocate the complete renunciation of property as a condition of discipleship. There are, however, other logia which prescribe responsible stewardship, a prudent use of property, and a practice of charity that would require some wealth. These latter traditions imply that followers of Jesus would retain some of their possessions.

1. See Chapter 3, Section b.

1. *Harsh Words about Wealth*

My primary concern is with the reported sayings of Jesus. While redactional questions are indeed significant, early Christian attitudes were based largely on the logia of Jesus, and it is this tradition which must be our primary focus. Luke reveals a keen interest in the topic of wealth, and this may have influenced his use and shaping of the tradition. Luke portrays Jesus as hostile to wealth but this view is consistent with what is found in other sources. It is the tradition, then, not redactional issues, which is of concern.

Luke alone reports the unqualified denunciation, 'Woe to you that are rich for you have received your consolation' (6.24). This is balanced by the beatitude, 'Blessed are you poor, for yours is the kingdom of God' (6.20). It is an important Lukan theme that Jesus announces good news to the poor (4.18; 7.22 // Mt. 11.5) while offering dismal prospects for the rich. The parable of the foolish and wealthy farmer (where Jesus warns against laying up treasure for oneself) is also peculiar to Luke (12.15-21). In the story later called Dives and Lazarus, the rich man is condemned to fiery torment presumably for his neglect of one needy man.[1] By contrast, the poor man, Lazarus, is carried by the angels to Abraham's bosom. His only apparent merit was his poverty (16.19-31).

In reporting the Markan tradition about the rich man who wished to know how to inherit eternal life, Luke preserves his source's words of Jesus: 'How hard it is for those who have riches to enter the kingdom of God! For it is easier for a camel to go through the eye of a needle than for a rich man to enter the kingdom of God' (Lk. 18.24-25 // Mk 10.23, 25 // Mt. 19.23-24). And Luke, like his source, indicates that the disciples have given up their property (ἀφέντες τὰ ἴδια 18.28) in order to follow Jesus. Such is the standard Jesus has established: 'Whoever of you does not renounce all that he has cannot be my disciple' (Lk. 14.33).

The importance of surrendering one's wealth is twofold. On the one hand, riches are described as thorns which can (and will) choke the

---

1. Cf. de Ste Croix, *Class Struggle*, p. 432. But this interpretation is not self-evident. Rather, the rich man is told that he had already received his 'good things' (16.25; cf. 6.24b). See, however, the story of the rich man reported in Origen's *Commentary on Matthew* 16.14, attributed to the Gospel of the Hebrews, where Jesus rebukes the man for failing to help the poor.

word (Mk 4.7, 19 // Lk. 8.7, 14 // Mt. 13.7, 22). On the other hand, a love for money is completely incompatible with a love for God. The two passions (or loyalties) cannot co-exist in one heart (Lk. 16.13 // Mt. 6.24).

2. *Contentment with the Necessities of Life*

The teaching of Jesus insisted that the disciple should not be anxious about clothing or food. God would provide for those whose first priority was the kingdom of God. There ought to be no worries about tomorrow (Mt. 5.25-34 // Lk. 12.22-31). It was sufficient to pray for 'daily' bread (Mt. 6.11 // Lk. 11.3).[1]

There are various traditions which claim that Jesus himself generally adopted a simple lifestyle consistent with the demands he made of his followers. And yet, ironically, because Jesus was willing to enjoy the festive company of certain hosts (Mk 2.13-17 // Mt. 9.9-13 // Lk. 5.27-32), he was labelled a glutton and a drunkard (Mt. 11.19 // Lk. 7.34). As a rule, however, he was dependent on the hospitality of others, the generosity of contributors, and often had 'nowhere to lay his head' (cf. Lk. 8.1-3; 19.5; Mt. 8.20 // Lk. 9.58).

Sending the disciples out, the tradition reports that Jesus fully expected that they too would have to rely on the compassion of strangers (Mk 6.7-11 // Lk. 9.1-6 // Mt. 10.5-15). Significantly, rewards are promised to the hospitable (Mk 9.41; Mt. 10.40-42).[2]

3. *Give without Expecting a Return*

It might be expected that the follower of Jesus would have no property, no possessions, possibly no income. The comparison between the early Christian missionaries and the wandering Cynics is striking.[3] Yet the traditions of Jesus' teaching provide numerous examples of instruction to the disciples to *give* without expecting a

---

1. See W. Foerster, 'ἐπιούσιος', *TDNT*, II, pp. 590-99.

2. Note the remarks of Gerd Theissen, 'To put it plainly: to begin with, support was no more than bread cast on the waters. Only in the future judgment would its usefulness be shown. At that time a welcome to apostles and prophets would provide magical protection and rejection of them would exact its revenge' (*Sociology*, p. 14).

3. For a recent study, see F.G. Downing, 'Cynics and Christians', *NTS* 30 (1984), pp. 584-93. See also, J. Corbett, 'The Pharisaic Revolution and Jesus as Embodied Torah', *SR* 15/3 (1986), pp. 390-91.

return. This certainly suggests that the followers of Jesus must have retained sufficient material resources to enable them to give.

The synoptic tradition reports that Jesus taught the disciples to give indiscriminately to all who asked (but cf. *Did.* 1.6) and to provide for them generously (Mt. 5.42 // Lk. 6.30; Lk. 6.32-35). There is an implicit injunction to give to the poor (Mk 14.7) and a clear command to practise almsgiving (Mt. 6.1-4). The *Gospel of Thomas*, which repudiates almsgiving (logion 14), nevertheless includes the saying, 'If you have money, do not lend it at interest, but give to one from whom you will not get it back' (logion 95).

The teachings of Jesus further promise a heavenly reward for those who are charitable and that almsgiving earns a lasting treasure. Perhaps this is implied in the saying, 'It is more blessed to give than to receive' (Acts 20.35).

4. *Charity as a Heavenly Investment*

Luke's Gospel incorporates the Q logion that warns that people will be judged, condemned or forgiven by God in the same way that they treat others (6.37 // Mt. 7.1-2). Within this context Luke promises, through the words of Jesus, that giving will also earn a reciprocal reward from God: 'Give and it will be given to you; measure, pressed down, shaken together, running over, it will be put into your lap. For the measure you give will be the measure you get back' (6.38). Such a saying counsels readers to make intelligent use of their earthly treasure, to 'invest' in the poor.

Two of the agrapha, the unwritten (i.e., non-canonical) words of Jesus, may bear on this. Both recommend a prudent exercise in economics. The first of these logia is the often quoted, 'Become reliable money changers'.[1] Certainly the proper interpretation of this proverb is a remote possibility apart from knowing its original context, yet it is at least plausible that the saying was meant to encourage the exchange of earthly for heavenly 'coin'. Assuming its authenticity, Jesus could have intended this logion to motivate his followers to give to the poor because God would reward them; they would show themselves to be wise money changers. The second saying is reported

---

1. Resch lists sixty-nine citations of the saying; see A. Resch, *Agrapha* (Leipzig: Hinrichs, 1906), pp. 116, 233.

by Ephraem in the late fourth century;[1] it is unlikely to be a genuine word of Jesus. It may, however, be related to earlier traditions: 'Buy for yourselves, O children of Adam, through these transitory things which are not yours, that which is yours and which cannot pass away'. This passage seems to echo a saying in Luke's parable of the unjust steward: 'I tell you, make friends for yourselves by means of unrighteous mammon, so that when it fails they may receive you into the eternal habitations' (Lk. 16.9).

This logion, found at the end of the parable, is the focus of considerable controversy regarding both its (presumed) original context and meaning as well as the Lukan purpose in its present setting. Several scholars have cautiously suggested that the 'prudent use of "mammon of dishonesty"' refers to almsgiving.[2] Indeed, early Christian writers cite Lk. 16.9 as a proof-text supporting the doctrine of redemptive almsgiving.[3] Ephraem's logion surely advocates the use of transitory wealth to purchase heavenly treasure and may be included among sayings which teach that charity is an investment.

The most detailed description of charity which earns a reward is found in Mt. 25.31-46. The ones who inherit the kingdom of God are those who feed the hungry, give drink to the thirsty, welcome the stranger, clothe the naked, and visit the sick and those in prison.[4] By contrast, the uncharitable—those who did not perform such works—shall be condemned. Charity merits heavenly treasure. We must assume that the righteous had the financial resources (however limited) to provide for the needy. Perhaps it was necessary to deprive oneself of certain necessities in order to be able to give to the poor. Such sacrifice would presumably earn even greater rewards. In this connection it is noteworthy that Origen refers to an unknown saying

---

1. Ephraem Syrus, *Evang. Conc. Expositio*. See J.D. Donehoo, *The Apocryphal and Legendary Life of Christ* (New York: Macmillan, 1903), p. 249.

2. J. Fitzmyer, *The Gospel according to Luke X–XXIV* (Garden City, NY: Doubleday, 1985), pp. 1106-1107; F.E. Williams, 'Is Almsgiving the Point of the "Unjust Steward?"', *JBL* 83 (1964), pp. 293-97; I.H. Marshall, *The Gospel of Luke* (Grand Rapids: Eerdmans, 1978), pp. 621-22; W. Stegemann, *The Gospel and the Poor* (Philadelphia: Fortress Press, 1984), pp. 62-63.

3. E.g. Clement of Alexandria, *Rich Man* 31-32.

4. See also Lk. 14.12-14; for Matthew's phrase, 'You have done it for me', cf. Prov. 19.17. For the relationship deeds of loving-kindness and almsgiving, see J. Jeremias, 'Die Salbungsgeschichte Mc 14, 3–9', *ZNW* 35 (1936), pp. 75-82.

of Jesus: 'Blessed is he who fasts for this, that he might feed the poor'.[1]

The explicit instruction to invest wisely is found in Mt. 6.19-21:

> Do not lay up for yourselves treasures on earth, where moth and rust consume and where thieves break in and steal, but lay up for yourselves treasures in heaven [cf. Sir. 29.11-12], where neither moth nor rust consumes and where thieves do not break in and steal. For where your treasure is, there will your heart be also.

Luke applies this tradition to the renunciation of property and to almsgiving:

> Sell your possessions and give alms; provide yourselves with purses that do not grow old, with a treasure in the heavens that does not fail, where no thief approaches and no moth destroys. For where your treasure is, there will your heart be also (12.32-34).

Significantly, Luke sets this passage in the context of the parable of the rich and foolish farmer and the sayings to the disciples to have no anxiety about food or clothing (Lk. 12.15-31).

For Matthew, charity—deeds of loving-kindness—earns a reward. Mammon invested in the needs of the poor will be rewarded. For Luke, almsgiving emerges as the most important act of charity that earns heavenly treasure. The Markan tradition of the rich man who comes to Jesus supports Luke's interest.

> And as he was setting out on his journey, a man ran up and knelt before him, and asked him, 'Good Teacher, what must I do to inherit eternal life?' And Jesus said to him, 'Why do you call me good? No one is good but God alone. You know the commandments...'
>
> And he said to him, 'Teacher, all these I have observed from my youth'. And Jesus looking upon him loved him and said to him, 'You lack one thing; go, sell what you have,[2] and give to the poor, and you will have treasure in heaven; and come follow me'. At that saying his countenance fell, and he went away sorrowful, for he had great possessions (Mk 10.17-22; cf. Lk. 18.8-23 // Mt. 19.16-22).[3]

---

1. Origen, *Homily on Leviticus* 10.2; cf. Aristides, *Apology* 15 on early Christian practice; Hermas, *Similitude* 5.3.7-8.

2. Here Luke (18.22) adds πάντα; it 'intensifies the demand and recalls the frequent occasions' where wealth is discussed by Luke (S.G. Wilson, *Luke and the Law* [Cambridge: Cambridge University Press, 1983], p. 27).

3. A version of this story is found in Origen's *Commentary on Matthew* where Jesus says to the man, 'How can you say, "I have fulfilled the law and the

Fulfilling the requirements of discipleship by renouncing one's possessions and giving to the poor merits heavenly bounty.[1] The story serves Luke's purposes well.

Finally, Luke alone reports that Jesus said, 'Give for alms those things which are within; and behold, everything is clean for you' (11.41; cf. Mt. 23.26). Scholars have generally regarded the Matthaean version of the logion as 'more original' (i.e. closer to the ultimate source of the tradition) than is the Lukan version. Some appeal has been made to a misunderstanding of an underlying Aramaic term but the significance of the difference between the two accounts is probably to be found in Luke's great interest in almsgiving.

In any event, while this logion ought to be traced to the sayings source (Q) common to Matthew and Luke, it is only the Lukan form of the saying which has importance for the topic of redemptive almsgiving. Luke portrays Jesus as advocating almsgiving as a means to cleanse (from sin?). Origen, Cyprian and Chrysostom all cite Lk. 11.41 as a proof-text to support the doctrine that almsgiving redeems sin.[2] Even Augustine referred to this passage to justify his belief that almsgiving was redemptive.[3]

b. *Acts*

In the Third Gospel, Luke gives particular attention to the demand for 'radical divestment of wealth' as a condition of discipleship, indeed as a prerequisite for those who would gain eternal life.[4] This theme appears in Acts as well. According to Luke's account of the early history of the church, Tabitha, a woman well-known for her good works and almsgiving, was raised from the dead (Acts 9.36-42). While the story has been cited as New Testament evidence for the stress on almsgiving and deeds of loving-kindness within pre-70

---

prophets"? For it is written in the law, "Love your neighbour as yourself", and yet many of your brothers, sons of Abraham, are filthy and dying of hunger while your house is full of many good things and nothing at all comes forth from it to them!'

1. Cf. Zacchaeus, Lk. 19.1-9.

2. Cyprian, *On Works and Almsgiving* 2; Chrysostom, *Homilies on St John*, Homily 81; Origen, *Homily on Leviticus* 2.4.

3. Augustine, *Enchiridion*, ch. 19 (72-73); cf. Jerome, *Letter 108: to Eustochium* 16.

4. Wilson, *Luke and the Law*, p. 28.

Palestinian Judaism,[1] this tradition may provide implicit support for the view that redemptive almsgiving is advocated in early Christian literature prior to the Apostolic Fathers. In light of passages such as Tob. 4.10 and 12.8-9 and Luke's concern for the duty of helping the poor, it is arguable that Luke reports the story of Tabitha to indicate that she was raised from the dead *because of* her almsgiving. Life was her reward. Such was Cyprian's interpretation.[2]

Luke makes another allusion to the rewards earned by almsgiving (and piety) with regard to the inclusion of the Gentiles in the outreach of the church:

> At Caesarea there was a man named Cornelius, a centurion of what was known as the Italian Cohort, a devout man who feared God with all his household, gave alms liberally to the people and prayed constantly to God. About the ninth hour of the day he saw clearly in a vision an angel of God coming in and saying to him, 'Cornelius'. And he said to him, 'Your prayers and your alms have ascended as a memorial before God[3] (...αἵ ἐλεημοσύναι σου ἀνέβησαν εἰς μνημόσυνον ἔμπροσθεν τοῦ θεοῦ...). Cornelius, your prayer has been heard and your alms have been remembered before God' (10.1-4, 31).

It is striking that in this passage almsgiving is virtually identified with the 'doing of righteousness' (10.35). Berger observes that Luke regards the benevolence of Cornelius towards the Jews as a work meriting his inclusion among the people of God.[4]

In Acts Luke portrays Paul as interpreting the 'collection for the saints' as a type of alms (24.17) but the apostle does not use such terminology in his own letters.[5] The term ἐλεημοσύνη is not found in the Pauline corpus. For Luke, however, the collection for the needy in the Jerusalem church was genuine almsgiving and, like Paul, Luke felt that everyone should give as he was able (Acts 11.29; 1 Cor. 16.2). Yet the author of Acts does not suggest that this particular act of benevolence was redemptive; it was simply a duty for every

1. Jeremias, 'Salbungsgeschichte', pp. 77-79.

2. Cyprian, *On Works and Almsgiving* 6; cf. *Phil.* 10.2.

3. See also W. Stegemann, *The Gospel and the Poor* (Philadelphia: Fortress Press, 1984), p. 48.

4. The description of Cornelius's prayers and almsgiving as 'ascending' likens his conduct to the smoke of a sacrifice or burnt offering. See F.F. Bruce, *The Acts of the Apostles* (London: Tyndale Press, 1964), p. 216; cf. *Phil.* 4.18; Heb. 13.16.

5. Bolkestein, 'Almosen', pp. 180-81.

committed disciple (cf. Lk. 14.33). Ironically, it is Paul, not Luke, who seems to exalt the collection as a means of achieving an enduring righteousness for the Gentiles, justifying their inclusion among God's people. Luke's portrayal of Cornelius thus offers an intriguing parallel to the apostle's view of the Gentiles who participate in the collection.[1]

c. *The Letters of Paul*

For Paul, the unity of the church, the body of Christ, obliterates any spiritual distinction between Jews and Gentiles (Gal. 3.28; 1 Cor. 12.12-13; cf. Eph. 2.11-19). Within the 'body' individual members ought to promote the well-being of the community, and in turn each member's contribution is to be honoured.

> Having gifts that differ according to the grace given to us, let us use them... he who contributes, in liberality[2]... Let love be genuine... love one another with brotherly affection... Contribute to the needs of the saints; practise hospitality (Rom. 12.4-10, 13).

As Paul seeks to build up the church, particularly in his own mission to the Gentiles, he is anxious—and prompted by those who were sent to the Jews—to remember the poor (τῶν πτωχῶν, Gal. 2.7-10). 'The Jerusalem leaders requested that Paul continue to stimulate charitable concern among the Gentile Christians with whom he was to work, in view of the dire economic situation existing in Jerusalem.'[3]

The collection for the Jerusalem Christians is regarded as central and vital to the interests of a growing, healthy and united church. Generosity is a gift to be exercised. Along with hospitality, benevolence to the needy is a work of genuine love. The concern for the unity of the church prompts the apostle to find added significance in the collection as a demonstration of the solidarity between Gentile and Jewish believers.[4] He argues that as Gentiles have come to receive

---

1. N.A. Dahl, *Studies in Paul* (Minneapolis: Augsburg, 1977), pp. 32-34; K. Nickle, *The Collection* (London: SCM Press, 1966), p. 70.
2. Bolkestein, 'Almosen', pp. 195-204. For an interesting connection to the idea of ṣᵉdāqâ, see Clement of Alexandria, *Paedagogus* 7.12: 'the habit of liberality which prevails among us is called "righteousness" (δικαιοσύνη)'.
3. Nickle, *The Collection*, p. 114.
4. Nickle, *The Collection*, pp. 59, 114, 119, 129.

the spiritual benefits of inclusion in the olive tree (cf. Rom. 11.13-24), a place intended for the Jews, so it is now the duty of Gentiles in turn to provide financial assistance for the Jewish Christians: 'Indeed they are in debt to them, for if the Gentiles have come to share in their spiritual blessings, they ought to be of service to them in material blessings' (Rom 15.25-27).

Again, Paul's desire for the unity and health of the body motivates him. Gentiles have an obligation to give of their material resources to those who have shared their spiritual treasure, namely the promise to Abraham. The collection demonstrates the gratitude of the Gentiles and the legitimacy of their participation among God's people.

In 2 Corinthians 8 and 9 Paul appeals on behalf of the collection:

> See that you excel in this gracious work also. I say this not as a command, but to prove by the earnestness of others that your love is also genuine... as a matter of equality your abundance at the present time should supply their want, so that their abundance may supply your want, that there may be equality...
>
> So give proof, before the churches, of your love and of our boasting about you to these men...
>
> The point is this: he who sows sparingly will also reap sparingly and he who sows bountifully will also reap bountifully... And God is able to provide you with every blessing in abundance, so that you may always have enough of everything and may provide in abundance for every good work. As it is written, 'He scatters abroad, he gives to the poor; his righteousness endures for ever'. He who supplies seed to the sower and bread for food will supply and multiply your resources and increase the harvest of your righteousness. You will be enriched in every way for great generosity...
>
> You will glorify God by your obedience in aknowledging the gospel of Christ, and by your generosity of your contribution for them and for all others while they long for you and pray for you... (2 Cor. 8.8, 14, 24; 9.6, 8-11, 13-14)

Paul maintains here, as in Romans 12, yet with greater emphasis, that generosity to the needy is a demonstration of genuine love. Since love must motivate giving or else the benefactor gains nothing (1 Cor. 13.3),[1] presumably the one who gives out of love may expect to gain *something*. Paul promises, however ambiguously, a spiritual reward,

---

1. See L.W. Countryman, 'Welfare in the Churches of Asia Minor under the Early Roman Empire', *SBL Seminar Papers, 1979*, I (Missoula, MT: Scholars Press, 1979), p. 132.

an increased 'harvest of righteousness' for those who provide for the poor. The giver will be enriched in every way, not least of which will be through the prayers of those who are helped, through the 'abundance' that they possess. The unity of the body is promoted through the rich helping the poor and the poor interceding with God on behalf of the rich.[1]

Paul's use of Ps. 112.9 (2 Cor. 9.9) may refer to the enduring value of almsgiving, identifying almsgiving with 'righteousness'. If so, the apostle is a vital link in the chain of development in the doctrine of redemptive almsgiving. This text would indicate that Paul shared the belief of early rabbinic Judaism that almsgiving and $s^e d\bar{a}q\hat{a}$ were virtually equivalent terms.[2]

d. *Other New Testament Passages*

There are two New Testament texts which encourage the view that labour should be seen as a means to earn wages which may be used (or ought to be used) to help the needy. This implicit work ethic with a goal of almsgiving is apparently part of the foundation of the injunction, 'Of whatever you gain by your hands, give a ransom for your sins' (*Didache* 4.6; cf. *Barn.* 19.10). Indeed, allowing that the *Didache* passage may be earlier than Acts 20.33-35 and Eph. 4.28, it is possible that these New Testament texts assume that almsgiving is redemptive.[3] It must be recognized, however, that neither explicitly endorses such a belief.

In light of the harsh words directed towards the wealthy that are

---

1. Hermas, *Similitude* 2.5-9 (cf. 1.8-9); Clement of Alexandria, *Rich Man* 33–35. For a more thorough sociological analysis, see Chapter 6, Section a.

2. For the Talmudic interpretation of Ps. 112.9, see *b. B. Bat.* 10b. On 2 Cor. 9.9, see R. Bultmann, 'ἔλεος', *TDNT*, II, p. 486 n. 3; J. Reumann, *Righteousness in the New Testament* (Philadelphia: Fortress Press, 1982), pp. 52-53. It may be noted that in Phil. 4.17-18 Paul regards the gift from the Philippians as 'a spiritual *investment* entered as a *credit* to the *account* of the Philippians, an investment which will *increasingly* pay them rich dividends' (G. Hawthorne, *Philippians* [Waco, TX: Word Books, 1983], p. 206). Hawthorne notes the parallel with 2 Cor. 9.8-11 but Paul surely did not regard the Philippians' gift as almsgiving. His attitude is more closely connected to the thought in Mt. 10.41-42.

3. Cf. A.T. Geoghegan, *The Attitude towards Labor in Early Christianity* (Washington: Catholic University of America, 1945), pp. 115-16.

reported in the synoptic tradition, it is striking to find an accommodation of the rich within the New Testament. This is found in 1 Tim.
6.17-19 where giving to the poor justifies the possession of wealth.

> As for the rich in this world, charge them not to be haughty, nor to set
> their hopes on uncertain riches but on God who richly furnishes us with
> everything to enjoy. They are to do good, to be rich in good deeds, liberal
> and generous, thus laying up for themselves a good foundation for the
> future, so that they may take hold of the life which is life indeed.

The phrase, 'a good foundation', could be rendered 'good treasure'
based on Tob. 4.9-10.[1] The idea of treasure is certainly implicit in the
verb ἀποθησαυρίζοντας. The heavenly fund is built up through
liberality. The passage clearly indicates that benevolence by the rich
will be advantageous for them in the future where they may 'take hold
of the life which is life indeed'. While this still falls short of an
unequivocal endorsement of redemptive almsgiving, the text is clearly
consistent with such a doctrine.

The epistle to the Hebrews places considerable emphasis on the
unique atoning power of the death (or blood) of the Son of God (e.g.
9.12, 28; 10.10). The author warns that any neglect of this sacrifice or
any return to sin will be severely punished (2.3; 6.1-8; 10.26-31). Yet
the epistle offers hope that Christians can somehow achieve merit and
even offer sacrifices which God will acknowledge and honour. As in
Paul's letters, there is a strong love ethic and again love shows itself in
hospitality, almsgiving and contributing to the needs of the saints
(Heb. 6.9-10, a significant assurance in light of the author's warning;
13.1-3, 5, 16). Buchanan comments,

> In addition to caring for the sick and elderly and providing hospitality for
> traveling sectarians, a third way of ministering to the saints involved
> providing financial support to those in Jerusalem who were dependent
> upon contributions from the diaspora for their livelihood (Rom. 15.25, 2
> Cor. 8.4; 9.1). The readers to whom the author of Hebrews wrote were
> meritorious in one or more of these respects. *Therefore they were assured
> that the better things of the salvation that was coming would be theirs*
> (6.9).[2]

---

1. J. Moffatt, *The Bible, a New Translation* (New York: Harper & Brothers,
1935), p. 266 of the New Testament.
2. G.W. Buchanan, *To the Hebrews* (Garden City, NY: Doubleday, 1972),
p. 113; italics mine. For the importance of the love ethic in charity and for the
assurance of pleasing God, see also 1 Jn 3.17-19.

The letter of James exhibits a hostility to wealth that is paralleled in the synoptic Gospels. James, too, pronounces woes on the rich (5.1-6). For James, a concern for the poor is the priority of all who claim to have faith (2.14-17). True religion is demonstrated in compassion for the widow and the orphan (1.27). Bolkestein maintains that for the author, almsgiving is thus equated with 'sacrifice and the worship of God'.[1]

To this point the New Testament and extra-canonical sayings of Jesus only implicitly endorse a doctrine of redemptive almsgiving. The term ἐλεημοσύνη is not specifically identified as a work meriting the forgiveness of sins. Rather, emphasis is placed on the importance of love, genuine love, a work more efficacious than sacrifice and burnt offerings.[2] While ἀγάπη is stressed as the redeeming virtue, almsgiving, charity and hospitality are consistently promoted as the practical expression of love.

The significant context for early Christian instruction concerning love and charity is one of eschatological urgency: the day of the Lord is imminent.[3] With a clear warning of that danger, 1 Peter recommends love as able to 'compensate' for sin. 'The end of all things is at hand; therefore keep sane and sober for your prayers. Above all hold unfailing your love for one another, since love covers a multitude of sins. Practise hospitality ungrudgingly to one another.' (1 Pet. 4.7-9). Here the expected parousia makes wise conduct imperative. And love is recommended as both a fulfilment of the Christian ethic (cf. 1.22; 3.8) and as a means to redeem those sins that may stain one's character at the return of Christ. The author is concerned that his readers may fall into the sin that characterized their earlier lives, the sin that baptism had washed clean (3.21–4.5). Due to the nearness of the end,[4] the letter strongly encourages the virtue of love because ἀγάπη 'covers' a multitude of sins (καλύπτει πλῆθος ἁμαρτιῶν). This may be an allusion to Prov. 10.12 but in its Hebrew, not Septuagintal, form: 'Love covers all offenses'.[5]

---

1. Bolkestein, 'Almosen', p. 304. A helpful survey of the letter is found in P.U. Maynard-Reid, *Poverty and Wealth in James* (Maryknoll, NY: Orbis Books, 1987).

2. See Mk 12.33. Matthew and Luke, however, omit this passage.

3. See Mt. 25.31-46; Rom. 13.8-13 (cf. 1 Thess. 5.1-11); Jas. 5.1-9; Heb. 10.32-37; 1 Jn 4.16-17 (2.18); etc.

4. τὸ τέλος ἤγγικεν; cf. Mk 1.15 (where repentance is called for).

5. See B. Reicke, *The Epistles of James, Peter, and Jude* (Garden City, NY:

1 Pet. 4.8 may be citing a popular proverb rather than quoting the Hebrew scripture; still the term 'cover' almost certainly represents the Hebrew concept of 'covering sin' (cf. Ps. 32.1; LXX Ps. 84.2). Certainly the passage is consistent with the doctrine of redemptive almsgiving, that love 'has effects like those of propitiatory sacrifices in reconciling men to God'.[1]

The epistle does not explain the concept of the redemptive power of love; indeed, love itself is hardly defined by any specific actions, with the exception of hospitality. While it is uncertain whether the author himself would have sanctioned the idea that *almsgiving* (as an expression of love) could redeem sin, early Christian writers did cite 1 Pet. 4.8 as a proof-text to support the belief that almsgiving (again as a deed of love) was redemptive.[2]

The eschatological pressure that motivated a concern for redemption is highly significant. For the author of the epistle, because the end is near readers ought to be conscientious in their piety and alert to behaviour which will 'cover' their sins. As will be seen below, the prospect of judgment leads the writer of *2 Clement* to warn his readers of the means to redeem their sins. This sense of need to redeem sins prior to the imminent end of the world, when there will no longer be opportunity for repentance (*2 Clem.* 8.1-3), is central to the early Christian doctrine of redemptive almsgiving. This eschatological expectation is rooted in the New Testament although other traditions are found there as well.

Doubleday, 1964), p. 122; however, cf. C.E.B. Cranfield, *The First Epistle of Peter* (London: SCM Press, 1950), p. 95; F.W. Beare, *The First Epistle of Peter* (Oxford: Basil Blackwell, 1947), pp. 184-85.

1. E.G. Selwyn, *The First Epistle of Peter* (London: Macmillan, 1964), p. 217; E. Best, *1 Peter* (Grand Rapids: Eerdmans, 1971), p. 159. See *Diogn.* 9.2-3 where λύτρον and καλύψαι (with reference to sin) are in striking juxtaposition. See also *1 Clem.* 50.5-6.

2. Especially *2 Clem.* 16.4; Clement of Alexandria, *Rich Man* 38-40; *Stromata 2*, chs. 9, 13 and 15. Perhaps *1 Clem.* 49.5 and 50.5 ought to be mentioned. The redemptive power of love was also supported by Lk. 7.47.

e. *Doctrina*[1]

The ancient Latin document known as *De Doctrina* is almost certainly a translation of the Two Ways tradition that is more primitive than the forms found in the *Didache* or *Barnabas-Doctrina* in its original Greek source pre-dates the Apostolic Fathers. Here we have an early glimpse of the developing doctrine of redemptive almsgiving in the first generations of Christianity.

The social tensions within his community apparently provoked the editor of the Greek *Doctrina* to rebuke the wealthy and arrogant and to insist on compassion for the needy. It will be seen that similar concerns motivate the author of *2 Clement*.[2] And for both, almsgiving is made more attractive because of its redemptive power.

Doctrina forbids the love of money or any anxiety about social prestige and status: 'You shall not exalt yourself or honour yourself among men, or admit arrogance to your soul. You shall not join yourself in soul with higher men, but you shall associate with upright and humble men' (= the pious poor? 3.5-9; cf. Rom. 12.16).[3] The warning is given that the way of death is walked by those 'without pity for the poor...neglecting the appeals of the upright' (5.2).

Those who are able to help the needy must do so and they shall be rewarded.

> You shall not discourage anyone in his misfortune, nor shall you doubt whether it will be true or not. Do not keep stretching out your hands to receive, and drawing them back when it comes to returning. If through your hands you have earned a ransom for your sins, you shall not hesitate to give it or grumble when you give, for you know who is the good payer of such wages. You shall not turn away from the needy, but shall share everything with your brethren, and you shall not say it is your own. For if we are partners in what is immortal, how much more ought we to consecrate from it! For the Lord wishes to give of his gifts to all. (4.4-8)

The social issues in early Christian communities which shaped the doctrine of redemptive almsgiving emerge more clearly in *Doctrina*. In much the same way, the *Shepherd of Hermas* provides evidence at a

---

1. For a fuller consideration of *Doctrina* in relation to the *Didache* and *Barnabas*, see Appendix A.
2. See Chapter 5, Section c.
3. Translation by E.J. Goodspeed.

later date of the conflict between rich and poor Christians.[1] This social framework for the doctrine establishes certain features of the context (and interpretation) of *1* and *2 Clement* and the developing doctrine of redemptive almsgiving.

f. *Summary*

The early Christian tradition, from New Testament writings and from the *Doctrina* and the agrapha, allows for, and even encourages, a doctrine of redemptive almsgiving. This implicit attitude towards the salvific power of charity is in conflict with the view of Jesus' death as the unique and sufficient means of atonement. This tension characterizes the early tradition but there is no attempt to resolve it.[2]

The eventual unhesitating endorsement of a doctrine which seems utterly inconsistent with the belief that Jesus died for sins once for all must be seen as more than an uncritical development of the idea of penance. The doctrine is a dramatic attempt to resolve a severe crisis in the faith and practice of early Christian communities.

My thesis is that a theological and a sociological analysis of certain significant passages in the Apostolic Fathers will provide valuable insights into the needs that prompted the doctrine. Attention is drawn to an issue raised by Maynard-Reid:

> With the delay of the Parousia, the church had to deal with the reality of the social and economic structure of the overall societies in which it found itself and with the relationship between those societies and the individual Christian communities.[3]

The parousia's 'postponement' also caused significant theological problems; one of the more significant is the crisis provoked by post-baptismal sins: how were Christians to find atonement for sins they had committed after their redemption in Christ? These two concerns, social and theological, were central in shaping the doctrine of redemptive almsgiving in early Christianity.

1. See Chapter 5, Section b.
2. Cf. Bolkestein, 'Almosen', pp. 185-86.
3. *Poverty and Wealth*, p. 37.

Chapter 5

THE APOSTOLIC FATHERS

The early Christian communities were zealous to alleviate the suffering of poor brothers or sisters. Almsgiving and charity characterize the church of the first two centuries. This was claimed by Christian and non-Christian witnesses.[1]

While almsgiving often was a genuine and altruistic expression of compassion and love, among the sources are 'a number of passages in which the undisguised desire of being rewarded for benevolence stands out in bold relief'.[2] It is with the Apostolic Fathers that the idea of redemptive almsgiving clearly begins to emerge as a doctrine.

Sifting the evidence from the Apostolic Fathers with a primary interest in the social implications of the material, I will attempt to reconstruct the conflicts within the Christian community that served to promote the doctrine of redemptive almsgiving. Consequently the exegetical features of certain passages will be a secondary concern. My objective is to gain a broad understanding of part of the social structure of early Christianity. Within this context individual texts are considered.

Methodologically, *1 Clement* is a reasonable starting point as a late first-century Christian document whose origins are fairly certain: it was written from Rome about 96CE.[3] The *Shepherd of Hermas* introduces later Roman tradition and provides specific evidence of the social and theological tensions in that community which shaped

---

1. Justin, *Apology* 14; 67; Aristides, *Apology* 15; Lucian, *Peregrinus* 11, 12; cf. Julian, *Epistle* 49.
2. A. Harnack, *The Mission and Expansion of Christianity* (London: Williams & Norgate, 1904), I, p. 186.
3. The date, however, is controversial. See below.

the Christian view of almsgiving as redemptive. *Hermas*, for our purposes, supplements *1 Clement*.

Both Ignatius and Polycarp offer information regarding developments and concerns in the churches in the eastern part of the empire during the first third of the second century CE. The Two Ways tradition of *Barnabas*, *Didache* and *Doctrina* draws attention to a Jewish source for the idea of redemptive almsgiving.[1] Polycarp's citation of Tobit 4.10 (or 12.9) as a proof-text for the doctrine and the Two Ways paraenesis indicate that the vital roots of the belief in redemptive almsgiving are to be found in Judaism.

Again, however, it is the *why* of early Christianity's adaptation of the doctrine that provokes interest. It is the 'Roman connection' that more fully explains how and why such a belief was taken up by the church. Here *2 Clement* is the most intriguing and, I shall argue, the most revealing piece of the puzzle. After considering the primary texts, sociological and theological analyses will be made of the material.

a. *1 Clement*

The work known as the *First Epistle of Clement* is often regarded as significant because it is 'the earliest Christian document that has come down to us outside the New Testament'.[2] Although 'common opinion' has placed the date of this epistle to about 95 or 96 CE, at the close of the reign of Domitian,[3] it is a position that has been questioned.

In the twentieth century, the most forceful attack on the traditional dating of *1 Clement* has been led by George Edmundson in his *The Church in Rome in the First Century*.[4] His thesis, that the epistle was composed much earlier, perhaps even in 'the early months of 70', has been defended by J.A.T. Robinson in his *Redating the New Testament*.

---

1. See Appendix A on the *Didache*, *Barnabas*, and *Doctrina*.

2. E.J. Goodspeed, *The Apostolic Fathers* (New York: Harper & Brothers, 1950), p. 47; M. Staniforth (trans.), *Early Christian Writers* (Harmondsworth: Penguin, 1968), p. 17.

3. J.B. Lightfoot, *The Apostolic Fathers* (New York: Macmillan, 1889), I.1, p. 346. Cf. D.A. Hagner, *The Use of the Old and New Testaments in Clement of Rome* (Leiden: Brill, 1973), pp. 4-5.

4. London: Longmans, Green & Co. 1913.

While accepting the view that the epistle was indeed written by Clement who was the bishop of the Roman church during the 90s of the first century, Edmundson and Robinson object to the assumption that the document must be dated in that decade. 'The sole question is whether he wrote it when he was bishop or at an earlier stage.'[1]

While it is surely conceded that the epistle makes no reference or appeal to episcopal authority (or jurisdiction) and that the office of bishop seems, as in much of the New Testament, to be equivalent to that of elder (42.4-5; 44.4-5; 54.2; 57.1),[2] still there is both external and internal evidence that *1 Clement* was written while Clement was bishop during the period at the end of the persecution of Roman Christians by Domitian.

Irenaeus (200 CE) maintains that this 'most powerful letter' was composed in the time of Clement's episcopate, following the service of Linus and Anacletus who were bishops before him.[3] Hegesippus and Eusebius suggest that while Clement was bishop in the midst of Domitian's persecution of Christians, he wrote to the Corinthian church.[4]

Early Christian authors consistently refer to two persecutions of the church in the first century: one during the reign of Nero, the other while Domitian was emperor.[5] It seems clear that *1 Clement* was written shortly after one of these persecutions. Edmundson argues that Nero's campaign is the context for the epistle: 'there does not exist any definite evidence, internal or external, that the epistle was written during or immediately after the persecution of Domitian'.[6]

Others, however, maintain that *1 Clement* distinguishes between the Neronian hostilities against the church and the terror the Roman community had recently endured.[7] Clement refers to the martyrs who suffered 'in our generation'. He includes Peter and Paul and a 'multitude of the elect' who suffered apparently under Nero (5.1–6.1). In 1.1 Clement indicates that the church of Rome has just been

---

1. *Redating*, p. 328; G. Edmundson, *Church in Rome*, pp. 188-89; cf. L.L. Welborn, 'On the Date of *First Clement*', *BR* 29 (1984), pp. 35-54.
2. Robinson, *Redating*, p. 328.
3. Iraenaeus, *Adv. haer.* 3.3.3.
4. Eusebius, *Ecclesiastical History* 3.13-17.
5. Lightfoot, *Apostolic Fathers*, I.1, p. 350.
6. Edmunson, *Church in Rome* 189.
7. Lightfoot, *Apostolic Fathers*, I.1, pp. 350-51.

through a period of turmoil and many scholars regard this as a reference to the persecution under Domitian.[1] The issue then focuses on the question whether Clement reveals a significant separation in time from the martyrdom of Peter and Paul to the time of his writing.

Clement maintains that as the apostles were commissioned by Christ, they in turn appointed bishops and deacons and made the provision that, as these officers died, other 'approved' men should continue in their place (42.4; 44.2). Thus the author is indignant that the Corinthians have unjustly removed certain presbyters from their office who have served with the approval of the whole church for a long time (πολλοῖς χρόνοις, 44.3-6). A date of 70 CE does not seem appropriate to this context. Clement is aware that the apostolic foundation of the Corinthian community now has a second generation built on it and these men have served *many* years. A setting in the mid-90s is perfectly consistent with this.[2]

In this connection Clement describes the Corinthian church as 'ancient' (ἀρχαίαν, 47.6). The adjective hardly seems appropriate for a date for the epistle shortly after Nero's reign: 'I can scarcely believe that a community not yet twenty years old would be so designated'.[3] It is more reasonable to regard the term 'ancient' as a description compatible with a later date for *1 Clement*.

The letter itself was delivered to the Corinthian community by trusted messengers: 'We have sent faithful and prudent men who have lived among us without blame from youth to old age...' (63.3). These men must have been known to the Roman church for a period of some thirty or forty years. Again this evidence contradicts the view of an early date for the epistle; on the other hand it is consistent with the traditional view.[4]

Mention should also be made of Clement's use of Hebrews, 1 Peter and even 1 Corinthians. The author's knowledge of these other documents is not impossible if he wrote in 70 CE, providing that Hebrews and 1 Peter were composed before then; but it is far more reasonable to believe that a body of early Christian literature had not been

---

1. Note Robinson's comment, *Redating*, p. 329.
2. Lightfoot, *Apostolic Fathers*, I.1, p. 349.
3. Lightfoot, *Apostolic Fathers*, I.1, pp. 349-50.
4. See the cumulative argument in R.M. Grant and H.H. Graham, *The Apostolic Fathers* (New York: Thomas Nelson & Sons, 1965), II, p. 16, note on 1.1.

collected and circulated before 90 CE.[1] On the whole, then, it is reasonable to conclude (and in turn to assume) that *1 Clement* was written around 95 or 96 CE.

While it is certainly clear that Clement seeks to restore the unity of the church by returning authority to the presbyters who had been (from Clement's perspective) wrongfully treated, it is equally true that his objective in writing was to reconcile the divided Christians in the Corinthian congregation and so bring to an end any partisanship that threatened to destroy the body.[2] The apostle Paul had similar (though not identical) concerns in 1 Corinthians. It may be assumed that several of the tensions that had existed in the Corinthian church of Paul's day continued to divide the congregation close to forty years later.[3] We will find reason to believe that one conflict Clement, like Paul, sought to resolve was between the rich and the poor members of that community.

In *1 Clement*, as in the Corinthian letters (and much of the New Testament), love is the supreme virtue that must characterize the life of the believer:

> Without love nothing is well-pleasing to God... how great and wonderful is love, of its perfection there is no expression... Let us then beg and pray of his mercy that we may be found in love, without human partisanship, free from blame... Blessed are we, beloved, if we perform the commandments of God in the concord of love, that through love our sins may be forgiven (49.5–50.5).

Within the epistle, hospitality is regarded as one of the most important expressions of love. Indeed, for Clement hospitality is *the* good work which along with faith justifies the believer. J.B. Lightfoot complained that this emphasis on works, however vital they may

---

1. Cf. 'Publication and Early Christian Literature', in E.J. Goodspeed, *New Chapters in New Testament Study* (New York: Macmillan, 1937), pp. 1-21.

2. I am following the lead of Barbara Bowe:

> Far from being exclusively dominated by a concern for undergirding the hierarchical order in the Church, *1 Clem.* contains a strong and urgent appeal for unity and solidarity based not on hierarchical agendas but on the conviction that Christians form a common ἀδελφότης which must be preserved (*A Church in Crisis* [Minneapolis: Fortress Press, 1988], p. 4, cf. pp. 5, 17, 123, 153).

3. Hagner, *Use*, p. 6; Bowe, *Church in Crisis*, p. 11.

be, was un-Pauline.[1] Yet Lightfoot's objections, like those of
T.F. Torrance,[2] do not offer constructive suggestions for understanding *1 Clement*. They are simply theological criticisms from an
evangelical Protestant perspective and in fact they are challenged by a
'catholic counterpart', namely, 'that Clement provides primitive
evidence for the continuity of the church's understanding of justifying
faith as *fides caritate formata*'.[3]

Given Clement's knowledge and use of the New Testament writings
(e.g. Romans, Hebrews and 1 Peter), it is by no means unexpected that
hospitality would be important to him and all the more because of the
ever-growing need to provide for travelling Christians.[4] The New
Testament strongly encourages hospitality as an expression of
Christian love.[5] Again, love is a central theme in *1 Clement*.

Clement praises the Corinthians for their 'magnificent' reputation
for hospitality. All who had visited the Christian community in
Corinth were impressed by the kindness, virtue and faith of their hosts
(*1 Clem.* 1.2-3a). In his catalogue of evils, those sins which are
particularly 'hateful to God', Clement lists inhospitality at the end
(35.5-6) suggesting that being inhospitable is somehow the
'culminating vice'.[6]

Clement indicates that hospitality was rewarded—was virtually
redemptive—for three Old Testament figures.

> Abraham believed God and it was counted unto him for righteousness.
> Because of his faith and hospitality a son was given him in his old age...
> For his hospitality and piety Lot was saved out of Sodom... For her faith
> and hospitality Rahab the harlot was saved (10.6-7; 11.1; 12.1).[7]

For Clement, then, hospitality is one of the most significant demon-
strations of love. It is probable that he regarded hospitality as the
ministry of the rich who were most able to offer food and shelter

1. Lightfoot, *Apostolic Fathers*, I.1, p. 397.
2. See above, pp. 20-22.
3. Chadwick, 'Justification by Faith and Hospitality', pp. 281-82.
4. Meeks, *Urban Christians*, pp. 16-23, 109.
5. E.g. Rom. 12.9-13; Heb. 13.1-2; 1 Pet. 4.8-9.
6. Chadwick, 'Justification', p. 281.
7. Cf. 2 Pet. 2.7-8; T.D. Alexander, 'Lot's Hospitality: A Clue to his
Righteousness', *JBL* 104 (1985), pp. 289-91.

freely for strangers as well as for fellow members. The strong, the wise and the rich (cf. 1 Cor. 1.26) are instructed to 'do righteousness' (ποιεῖν δικαιοσύνην);[1] they must be kind and merciful, and they must give. These virtues will be rewarded. 'Be merciful *in order that* (ἵνα) you may obtain mercy... As you give so shall it be given to you... As you are kind, so shall kindness be shown to you' (13.1-2).

Hospitality (φιλοξενία) is indeed the expression of love for a stranger. It is, for Clement, the supreme act of kindness within the body of Christ. The unknown visitor is embraced in love solely because he bears the name of Christ. Where the heart is hospitable, there can be no thought of schism (cf. Rom. 14.1). Such is the interpretation of Clement's high regard for hospitality, a virtue that together with faith can justify the individual before God.

Clement later instructs the rich to 'bestow help on the poor' and, in turn, he reminds the poor to thank God that 'he gave him one to supply his needs' (38.2). In light of our knowledge of the social stratification in Corinth and the tensions between rich and poor Christians in the Corinthian congregation earlier in the first century,[2] it is reasonable to assume that one of the volatile divisions Clement hoped to reconcile was between wealthy and less affluent believers. Clement encourages mutual appreciation and support (cf. 37.4), that the rich would provide for the poor and that those who benefited would be grateful to God for those who gave. In later authors this developed into the expected reciprocity that the poor should pray for the rich, interceding on their behalf, fulfilling the role of friends made by means of unrighteous mammon.[3]

Clearly, however, Clement does not explicitly endorse a doctrine of redemptive almsgiving. In fact, while he does encourage wealthy members of the community to provide for their poor brothers, Clement does not use the usual term for almsgiving, ἐλεημοσύνη. Surely from his knowledge of the Gospel tradition alone he was familiar with the word, but undue stress ought not to be placed on this omission. The epistle's purpose is to restore and to preserve and then

---

1. It is certainly possible that Clement interpreted this to mean 'give alms'.
2. Lampe, *Die stadtrömischen Christen*, p. 69.
3. (Cf. 2 Cor. 8.14; 9.13-14) *Herm. Sim.* 2.5-9 (cf. 1.8-9); Clement of Alexandria, *Rich Man* 33-35; see also Grant and Graham, *Apostolic Fathers*, II, p. 66.

to strengthen the unity of the Corinthian Christian community. Clement's chief concern is to end the rebellion within that church, to return the 'legitimate' elders to their office, and to heal the divisions that remain. Clement's appeal is that 'love admits no schism, love makes no sedition, love does all things in concord' (49.5). Just as the sharing of material blessings promotes the fellowship of rich and poor believers, so obedience to authority is meant to end the dissension among certain factions. Clement later comments,

> We have now written to you, brethren, sufficiently touching the things which befit our worship, and are most helpful for a virtuous life to those who wish to guide their steps in piety and righteousness. For we have touched on every aspect of faith and repentance and *true love* and self-control and sobriety and patience, and reminded you that you are bound to please almighty God with holiness in righteousness and truth and long-suffering, and to live in concord, bearing no malice, in *love* and in peace with eager gentleness. (62.1-2)

The lack of specific reference to almsgiving is not surprising, given Clement's broader concerns. Significantly, he insists that rich Christians give to their poor brothers both to show (prove) their love and to nurture the unity of the body. This act of compassion to the needy is a demonstration of redemptive *love*. In this connection it is striking that Clement quotes 1 Pet. 4.8—'Love covers a multitude of sins' (49.5). Evidently, the passage is taken to mean that redemption is achieved by means of acts of love. 'Blessed are we, beloved, if we perform the commandments of God in the concord of love, that through love our sins may be forgiven' (50.5).[1] Clement is anxious that the community restore its practice of *brotherly love* (48.1).

A conflict between the wealthy and the less affluent members of the Corinthian congregation (indicative of the lack of brotherly love) was one critical source of tension in the Pauline community.[2] Apparently, this crisis continued and Clement, like the apostle, was aware of the mistrust and contempt that characterized the relationship between the rich, established and influential members of the congregation and the poorer Christians who sought acceptance and recognition within the body of Christ. Whether the schism that became the occasion for

1. Grant and Graham, *Apostolic Fathers*, II, p. 82; cf. Bowe, *Church in Crisis*, pp. 156, 186-87.
2. Theissen, *Social Setting*, pp. 96, 151.

writing the epistle had its roots in this division appears likely but cannot be proven from our sources.

There is evidence, however, to suggest that Clement believed that it was the discontented among the neglected poor who attempted to remove the wealthy elders/presbyters from office permanently.[1] In praying for unity, Clement says, 'Thou makest rich and makest poor' (59.3). He goes on to ask of God, 'Save those of us who are in affliction, have mercy on the lowly, raise the fallen, show thyself to those in need, heal the sick, turn again the wanderers of thy people, feed the hungry, ransom our prisoners, raise up the weak, comfort the faint-hearted' (59.4). Just as Clement admonished the rebellious faction for abusing the authority of the elders/presbyters, so he reprimands the wealthy for failing to meet the needs of the poor in the community. The epistle is intended to reconcile the two groups by calling each of them to correct their errors and to seek the unity of the body.[2]

Eusebius may provide further evidence that the cause of the trouble which Clement confronts was that the rich members of the church had neglected the poorer members, thus provoking their defiance of authority. In his *Ecclesiastical History*, Eusebius refers to Dionysius who was bishop of Corinth in 170 CE.

> There is, moreover, extant a letter of Dionysius to the Romans addressed to Soter who was then bishop, and there is nothing better than to quote the words in which he welcomes the custom of the Romans, which was observed down to the persecution in our own times: 'This has been your custom from the beginning, to do good in manifold ways to all Christians, and to send contributions to the many churches in every city, in some places relieving the poverty of the needy, and ministering to the Christians in the mines, by the contribution which you have sent from the beginning, preserving the ancestral custom of the Romans, true Romans as you are. Your blessed bishop Soter has not only carried on this habit but has even increased it, by administering the bounty distributed to the saints and by exhorting with his blessed words the brethren who come to Rome, as a loving father would his children'.

1. Countryman notes that *1 Clement* may imply that 'the insurgents really belong to the lower orders of society, *Rich Christian*, p. 156.
2. Cf. Bowe, *Church in Crisis*, pp. 107-21 on Clement's use of ταπεινοφροσύνη. Also, R.M. Grant, *Early Christianity and Society* (New York: Harper & Row, 1977), p. 130. In attempting to promote harmony and peace in the Corinthian congregation, Clement virtually assumes the role of the statesman calling upon the πόλις to restore order.

In this same letter he also quotes the letter of Clement to the Corinthians, showing that from the beginning it had been the custom to read it in the church (*Ecclesiastical History* 4.23.9-11).

The bishop of the Corinthian community in 170 CE speaks of a long tradition in the Roman church of helping the poor. Dionysius applauds Soter's continued diligence in this area. On the occasion of his writing, the Corinthian bishop has reason to cite *1 Clement*, the epistle of about 96 CE from Rome to Corinth. It was Dionysius's belief that Clement's letter was inspired by the Roman concern for the poor and, we may assume, the awareness that the needy Christians in Corinth had been provoked to schism because they had been neglected by the elders. Presumably because of its impact, the epistle was cherished by the Corinthian church and Dionysius makes reference to its abiding influence as he congratulates the Roman Christians for their commitment to aiding the poor. We have seen that the epistle provides strong evidence to corroborate Dionysius's view of Clement's objectives.

Both Roman charity and the Corinthian reading of *1 Clement* are said to be 'customs' dating back to 'the beginning'. The close connection between the two bears witness that Clement was not solely concerned (as he is often portrayed) with restoring legitimate authority but that he was also anxious that hospitality, love and charity be shown to impoverished members of the body of Christ. The eventual effectiveness of his appeals may be inferred from both Corinth's preservation of the letter and from Dionysius's knowledge and admiration for the Roman community's program of assistance for the needy.

The *First Epistle of Clement* does not explicitly advocate the doctrine of redemptive almsgiving. There are, nevertheless, significant indications in the letter that social tensions within the Christian community are directing attention to the responsibility of rich Christians toward their poor brethren. Theologically, the ethics of love are prescribed within a framework of divine reciprocity: hospitality justifies the individual; love covers a multitude of sins; be merciful in order that mercy will be shown to you. This is the theological context that *permits* early Christianity to adopt a belief in the redemptive power of almsgiving. The *necessity* of that belief is not yet evident.

Finally, *1 Clement* focuses our attention on the significance of Rome, the Roman practice, the Roman teaching, as the leading authority within the church advocating the doctrine of redemptive almsgiving. This question also needs a more complete analysis. How important was the Roman church in the influence and wide acceptance of the view that giving alms merits the forgiveness of sins?

b. *The Shepherd of Hermas*

The *Shepherd of Hermas*, an early Christian apocalypse, is definitely of Roman origin. There is virtually no reason to seek a different geographical location for it.[1] Dating this source is much more problematic. Scholars have generally argued that the *Shepherd* was composed over several decades, being unified by the mid second century.[2] Yet there is evidence to suggest that much of the material may come from the late first century or in the first decade of Trajan's reign.[3]

First, in the *Shepherd of Hermas*, as in *1 Clement*, there is 'no sign yet of a monarchical episcopate, even in Rome'.[4] Indeed, there is no clear distinction for Hermas between bishops and elders; ἐπίσκοποι is roughly equivalent to πρεσβύτεροι.[5] This would suggest that at least in part the *Shepherd* was composed before the time of Pius, bishop of Rome in 140–155 CE. Yet the Muratorian canon (c. 200 CE) claims that Hermas wrote his work while his brother Pius was 'on the throne of the Roman church'.[6] This claim seems mistaken:

> It is on the face of it highly unlikely that one who tells us he was a foster child sold into slavery in Rome (*Herm. Vis.* 1.1.1)... should have had a brother in Rome called Pius who was head of the church there at the time but whom he never mentions, despite several references to his family.[7]

1. G.F. Snyder, *The Apostolic Fathers* (London: Nelson, 1968), VI, p. 19; Osiek, *Rich and Poor*, p. 13.

2. Snyder, *Apostolic Fathers*, VI, p. 24; L.W. Barnard, 'The Early Roman Church', *ATR* 49 (1967), pp. 378-79.

3. Snyder, *Apostolic Fathers*, VI, p. 24; Barnard, 'Early Roman Church'; *idem* 'Hermas and Judaism', in *Studia Patristica 8* (Berlin: Akademie Verlag, 1966), p. 7; E.J. Goodspeed, *A History of Early Christian Literature* (rev. R.M. Grant; Chicago: University of Chicago Press, 1966), pp. 30-31.

4. Robinson, *Redating*, p. 322, citing *Herm. Vis.* 2.4.3; cf. Snyder, *Apostolic Fathers*, VI, p. 24.

5. *Similitude* 9.27.2; *Vision* 3.5.1; Snyder, *Apostolic Fathers*, VI, pp. 46-47, note on 13.1.

6. Cited in W. Schneemelcher and E. Hennecke (eds.), *New Testament Apocrypha* (London: SCM Press, 1973), I, pp. 42-45.

7. Robinson, *Redating*, p. 320.

As to the origins of the *Shepherd of Hermas*, we can confidently assert little more than that the apocalypse comes from the Roman church in the late first or early decades of the second century CE: 'Certainty about the dating of Hermas is impossible'.[1]

The *Shepherd of Hermas*, though not a letter, has many features in common with *1 Clement*. First, Hermas greatly values hospitality. Among the Apostolic Fathers, only *1 Clement* and Hermas employ the term φιλοξενία.[2] Secondly, Hermas, like Clement is clearly anxious to motivate rich Christians to provide for their poor brethren. For Hermas, such generosity is not simply in the interests of the church as a body. He maintains that the rich will reap spiritual benefits for their acts of charity. Here, Hermas confronts the problem of how the rich man may enter the kingdom of God (*Herm. Sim.* 9.20.1-4). Thirdly, it is significant that both *1 Clement* and the *Shepherd of Hermas* originate from the Roman community.

Hermas claims that 'bishops and hospitable men' who welcome the servants of God into their homes, and especially those bishops who have 'ceaselessly sheltered the destitute and the widows' shall themselves 'always be sheltered by the Lord'. Hospitality earns a place 'with the angels' (*Herm. Sim.* 9.27.2-3). Compassion for widows was a concern in the church from an early period.[3] This passage, however, regards such charity as a virtual sacrifice before God.[4] In this connection, it is striking to find Polycarp referring to widows as an *altar* of God (θυσιαστήριον θεοῦ, *Phil.* 4.3).[5] The practical application of this teaching can be seen from Eusebius's report that by 250 CE the

1. Osiek, *Rich and Poor*, p. 11.
2. For the idea of hospitality, however, see also *Did.* 12, *Diogn.* 5.7, and *Ign. Smyrn.* 9.2; 10.1.
3. E.g. Acts 6.1; 1 Tim. 5.3-5.
4. Cf. Bolkestein's view of Jas 1.27; see above, p. 106.
5. For the theological development of this theme in early Christianity, see *Apostolic Constitutions* 3.3.2; 12.1.2; 14.1; cf. *Didascalia* 2.1-3, 26; 3.6:

> O bishop, be mindful of the needy, both reaching out your helping hand and making provision for them as the steward of God, distributing seasonably the oblations (προσφορά) to every one of them, to the widows, the orphans, the friendless, and those tried with affliction . . . It is your duty to oversee all people and to take care of them all . . . Let the widow therefore own herself to be the altar of God . . . Let the widow who has received the alms join with the other in praying for him who ministered to her . . . Let the widow pray for him that gave her alms, whosoever he be, as being the holy altar of Christ.

church in Rome was supporting 1500 widows and poor people.[1]

While it undoubtedly became the bishop's responsibility to manage the distribution of alms and to provide lodging for visiting Christians, Hermas apparently wrote when this duty was not the exclusive or principal duty of the office. He speaks not only of the bishop but of hospitable men (*Herm. Sim.* 9.27.2). Furthermore, Hermas lists the works that *everyone* must do in order to be saved: 'To minister to widows, to look after (ἐπισκέπτεσθαι!) orphans and the destitute, to redeem from distress the servants of God, to be hospitable for in hospitality may be found the practice of good' (*Herm. Man.* 8.7-10). Hospitality and kindness to the needy are obligatory virtues to be shown by Christians. Obedience will guarantee that the believer will 'live to God' (*Herm. Man.* 8.12); he will be sheltered by the Lord, earning a place with the angels (*Herm. Sim.* 9.27.3). It is evident that Hermas and Clement agree that a believer is justified (or saved) by faith and hospitality. This, however, does not decisively show that Hermas regarded hospitality as redemptive (i.e. having the power to redeem sin). It will be seen though that the author is concerned to find a 'remedy' for sins committed after baptism, and hospitality is an essential feature of that meritorious labour.

Hermas insists that wealthy Christians are obligated to help the needy. Riches are a danger to faith, even where repentance is possible (*Herm. Vis.* 1.1.8-9). Repentance by the rich must be 'speedy' if they are to enter the kingdom of God, and that repentance must be shown in 'doing good'[2] (*Herm. Sim.* 9.20.1-4). The danger is that there is no repentance—and thus no forgiveness of sins—for the greedy, for those who 'lust for gain' (*Herm. Sim.* 9.19.3). Even a preoccupation with business will lead to blasphemy (*Herm. Sim.* 8.8.2).

While it might be expected that Hermas would condemn wealth itself as an evil—and he does write, 'They who have riches in this world cannot be useful to the Lord unless their wealth be cut away from them' (*Herm. Vis.* 3.6.6)—nevertheless, he allows that money and property do have a purpose and a value within the Christian community (*Herm. Sim.* 9.30.4-5). Thus, while Hermas cautions his readers, 'Follow not after the wealth of the heathen' (*Herm. Sim.*

1. Eusebius, *Ecclesiastical History* 6.43.11.
2. What Hermas means by 'doing good' is considered below, see pp. 91-92, 124. Also, see again, *Herm. Man.* 8.10.

1.10) and 'Refrain from...the extravagance of wealth' (*Herm. Man.* 8.3; cf. *Herm. Man.* 12.2.1), still he counsels:

> Instead of lands, purchase afflicted souls, as each is able, and look after widows and orphans, and do not despise them. And spend your wealth and all your establishments for such fields and houses as you have received from God. For this reason, did the Master make you rich, that you should fulfil these ministries for him. It is far better to purchase such lands and houses, as you will find in your own city, when you go to it. This wealth is beautiful and joyful, and has neither grief nor fear, but has joy (*Herm. Sim.* 1.8-10).

It is not riches themselves which are evil, it is a 'lack of sharing' (ἀσυνκρανία) that is harmful to the wealthy. They are warned to 'consider the judgment which is coming' (thus the eschatological urgency). In light of the approaching end, the rich are admonished to 'seek out those who are hungry'. If they do not, they risk that the poor will groan, that the Lord will hear their complaint and the rich with their goods will be shut out of the kingdom of God (*Herm. Vis.* 3.9.4-6).

Just as the groaning of the poor who have been neglected is sufficient to exclude the rich from the presence of God,[1] so the prayers of the poor on behalf of their benefactor are efficacious. As we have seen, Hermas recommends, in effect, that the wealthy 'make friends by means of unrighteous mammon' (Lk. 16.9), purchasing (ἀγοράζετε) widows and orphans (*Herm. Sim.* 1.8). Hermas further instructs his readers to fast for the sake of the poor, reckoning the price of what would have been eaten and giving that amount in charity.[2] As a result, 'he who receives it may fill his own soul and pray to the Lord for you'. Hermas assures his readers that in this, 'your sacrifice[3] shall be acceptable to God and this fast shall be written down to your credit' (*Herm. Sim.* 5.3.7-8).

For Hermas, then, almsgiving has the potential to be redemptive because of the prayers of the poor who intercede for the rich.

---

1. Cf. Deut. 15.9.
2. Cf. Aristides, *Apology* 15. Here even the poor are able to be charitable. Cf. *1 Clem.* 55.2; Origen, *Homily on Leviticus* 10.2; and Mk 12.41-44. Still, however, it is assumed that the poor, by virtue of being poor, will inherit the kingdom of God (Lk. 6.20; Jas 2.5; cf. Lk. 16.22-23).
3. ἡ θυσία.

The rich man has much wealth, but he is poor as touching the Lord, being busied about his riches, and his intercession and confession towards the Lord is very small, and that which he has is weak and small and has no other power. But when the rich man rests upon the poor, and gives him what he needs, he believes that what he does to the poor man can find a reward with God, because the poor man is rich in intercession and confession, and his intercession has great power with God. The rich man, therefore, helps the poor in all things without doubting. But the poor man, being helped by the rich, makes intercession to God, giving him thanks, for him who gave to him,[1] and the rich man is still zealous for the poor man, that he fail not in his life, for he knows that the intercession of the poor is acceptable and rich toward the Lord. Therefore the two together complete the work, for the poor works in the intercession in which he is rich, which he received from the Lord: this he pays to the Lord who helps him. And the rich man likewise provides the poor, without hesitating, with the wealth which he received from the Lord; and this work is great and acceptable with God, because he has understanding in his wealth, and has wrought for the poor man from the gifts of the Lord, and fulfilled his ministry rightly...

So also the poor, interceding with the Lord for the rich, complement [fulfil?] their wealth, and again, the rich helping the poor with their necessities complement their prayers. Both, therefore, share in the righteous work (*Herm. Sim.* 2.5-9).

This theological principle (namely, that the poor, who are closer to God, intercede for the rich while the rich, who are weak in prayer, provide for the material needs of the poor) seems to be sociologically grounded and may have its Christian origin in 2 Cor. 8.14; 9.13-14 and is found more fully developed in Clement of Alexandria (c. 215 CE).[2] Perhaps the roots of this idea could be traced to the word of Jesus, 'Make friends by means of unrighteous mammon' (Lk. 16.9).

The belief that charity was a means of gaining redemption for sin certainly fills a critical need for Hermas. It is clear that he was anxious to secure and to provide a second 'repentance' for those who were guilty of post-baptismal sin. In a study of the history of penance, the *Shepherd of Hermas* is the 'most important of the non-canonical writings of the sub-apostolic period'.[3] Hermas's apprehension may be summed up in one passage: 'If this sin is recorded against me, how

1. Cf. *1 Clem.* 38.2; Osiek, *Rich and Poor*, pp. 79-82.
2. *Rich Man* 33-35.
3. O.D. Watkins, *A History of Penance* (New York: Longmans, Green & Co., 1920), I, p. 47.

shall I be saved? Or how shall I propitiate God for my completed sins?' (*Herm. Vis.* 1.2.1).

The 'Angel of Repentance'[1] reveals to Hermas that one opportunity of a second repentance will be given to those who have sinned after baptism. The form of that μετάνοια in Hermas is a subject of some dispute. It has been common to regard Hermas as an early advocate of the later practice of penance and indeed the classic doctrine finds support.

> 'But see sir,' said I, 'they have repented with all their heart'. 'I know', he said, 'that they have repented with all their heart. But do you think that the sins of those who repent are immediately forgiven? By no means; but he who repents must torture his own soul, and be humble in all his deeds and be afflicted with many divers afflictions' (*Herm. Sim.* 7.4).

Furthermore, martyrdom and suffering for the faith apparently guarantee salvation (*Herm. Vis.* 3.1.9–2.2; *Herm. Sim.* 8.3.6-7; 9.28.1-8).[2] There is, nevertheless, in the *Shepherd of Hermas* a consistent emphasis that obedience to the commandments and good works are the truly redeeming form of repentance (*Herm. Sim.* 10.2.4; 8.11.3-4). And it is understood that this second repentance must lead to a sinless life (*Herm. Man.* 4.3.1-7). This obedience is characterized as the 'doing of righteousness' (*Herm. Vis.* 2.2.7; 2.3.3). 'Righteousness', in all probability, does not carry the specific, contemporary meaning of the Hebrew term ṣ⁽ᵉ⁾dāqâ, 'almsgiving'. Yet Hermas does in fact regard hospitality, compassion for the poor and charity as essential works meriting a reward worthy of a second repentance. The book closes with the admonition to 'do right';[3] the practice of good is profitable.

> Every man ought to be taken out of distress, for he who is destitute and suffers distress in his daily life is in great anguish and necessity. Whoever therefore rescues the life of such a man from necessity gains great joy for himself. For he who is vexed by such distress is tortured with such anguish as he suffers who is in chains. For many bring death on

1. ὁ ἄγγελος τῆς μετανοίας, *Herm. Vis.* 5.7; often translated (anachronistically) 'angel of penitence'.
2. And even warning others of the dangers of sin is regarded as redemptive (*Herm. Vis.* 3.8.11; cf. Jas 5.20; Origen, *Homily on Leviticus* 2.4).
3. K. Lake interprets this to mean, 'to do good in the sense of charity', *Apostolic Fathers* (London: Heinemann, 1976), II, p. 305 n. 1.

themselves by reason of such calamities when they cannot bear them.
Whoever therefore knows the distress of such a man and does not rescue
him incurs great sin and becomes guilty of his blood. Therefore do good
deeds, all you who have learnt of the Lord, lest the building of the tower
be finished while you delay to do them. For the work of the building has
been broken off for your sake. Unless therefore you hasten to do right the
tower will be finished and you will be shut out[1] (*Herm. Sim.* 10.4.2-4).

Hermas does not employ the term ἐλεημοσύνη. In this respect
alone he does not explicitly promote redemptive almsgiving. It is clear
nonetheless that Hermas was anxious that wealthy Christians provide
for their needy brethren. If the rich refused, they risked that God
would hear the 'groans' of the poor and the rich would certainly incur
judgment. On the other hand, if the wealthy assisted the needy, they in
turn would be strengthened (and protected) by the intercession of the
poor on their behalf. In this way the rich would offer an acceptable
sacrifice to God. This feature of Hermas's attitude towards charity is
all the more significant because of his passionate concern to secure a
second repentance that would gain remission for post-baptismal sin. It
is compassion for the needy which is central to the good works, the
obedience, of that second repentance. Here Hermas discovers the way
to propitiate God.[2] Hermas, even more than Clement, endorses the
emerging doctrine of redemptive almsgiving. While Clement was
primarily concerned with social stratification in the Corinthian
community, Hermas was motivated by circumstances within his own,
the Roman, community and by a pressing theological issue: how are
sins committed after baptism to be redeemed? Both for Clement and
Hermas almsgiving—sharing with the needy—was a central part of
the solutions they proposed.

The *Shepherd of Hermas* is motivated by an expectation that the end
of the world is near, that repentance and forgiveness are vital for post-
baptismal sins. This theological context not only permits, but to a degree
makes necessary, the doctrine of redemptive almsgiving. It will be
seen that *2 Clement* exhibits several thematic similarities to Hermas.
For now, however, it is clear that during the period of the Apostolic
Fathers (roughly 70–135 CE), social and theological pressures were at
work in early Christianity's attitude towards wealth and charity.

1. For the image of being shut out of the tower, cf. *Herm. Vis.* 3.9.4-6; for the
mandate to 'do good', cf. *Herm. Man.* 2.4-7 (cf. *Did.* 1.5).
2. See *Herm. Vis.* 1.2.1 (cf. Sir. 3.30).

The significance of Rome as the origin or setting for *1 Clement* (address) and for the *Shepherd of Hermas* (*Herm. Vis.* 1.1.1; 2.1.1; 4.2.1) is intriguing. Could Rome have been the authority behind the church's widespread acceptance of the idea that almsgiving redeems sin? Do we find that the influence of Rome accounts, in some way, for the development of the doctrine of redemptive almsgiving?

Unfortunately, we lack 'direct evidence' for the formative years of Christianity in Rome.[1] Our conjectured pictures of the primitive Roman community are largely based on what can be drawn from Paul's and Ignatius's letters to the Romans, 1 Peter, perhaps Hebrews, Mark and the *Shepherd of Hermas*. Along with these sources, *1 Clement* provides us with some valuable information.[2] An attempted reconstruction of the role of the Roman church in the development of the doctrine of redemptive almsgiving will be made following the analysis of the Apostolic Fathers. At this point, however, certain suggestions can be made.

Within the 'Roman tradition', there is a clear sense of responsibility for rich and poor Christians to share work together, preserving the unity of the body. That the later church in Rome was actively involved in charity and renowned for its work with the needy is attested by Dionysius[3] and Cornelius.[4] Undoubtedly the earlier tradition shaped, and *was shaped by*, the Roman community which sought harmony between rich and poor members. It is striking to find Paul had encouraged these virtues in his letter to the Romans (12.4-13; cf. 15.25-27) and that 1 Peter and Hebrews both call on their readers to continue the practice of hospitality and to show love for the brotherhood (e.g. 1 Pet. 4.8-9; Heb. 13.1-3; also cf. Heb. 13.16 with *Herm. Sim.* 5.3.7-8). It is self-evident even from this scattered evidence that the early Christian community in Rome was made up of both wealthy and poor believers. The rich realized[5] their duty to provide for the needs of their impoverished brothers. This charity was manifested not only in almsgiving but also in hospitality and was regarded as a work

1. R.E. Brown and J.P. Meier, *Antioch and Rome* (New York: Paulist Press, 1983), p. 92.

2. Brown and Meier, *Antioch and Rome*, pp. 105-204.

3. Eusebius, *Ecclesiastical History* 4.23.9-11. Hengel believes that the Roman church enjoyed this reputation far earlier. See *Property and Riches*, p. 44.

4. Eusebius, *Ecclesiastical History* 6.43.11.

5. This process of 'realization' will be discussed more fully below.

of genuine love. Initially, this love itself was regarded as redemptive, able to cover a multitude of sins.

In a parallel development, the poorer members of the early Roman church realized their obligation to thank God for those who became their benefactors and, eventually, to intercede on behalf of the *charitable* rich. Their prayers were to benefit the wealthy (who had assisted them) and so enhance the unity of the body. With this community ethic, Rome, among the churches, became famous for its charity. In social terms, this eased tensions between two groups who would normally be in conflict.

Theologically, redemptive love and the power of the intercession of the poor reinforced the motivation for carrying out the community principle. When the question of redemption for post-baptismal sin was raised—particularly in a context of eschatological urgency—the doctrine of redemptive almsgiving emerged, both assuring that love would express itself in action and providing quantifiable evidence that merit was earned.

This sketch is meant only as an outline or working model to be filled out and modified in the light of further analysis of the relevant material in the Apostolic Fathers. Much more needs to be said, but at this point we have a more defined focus for this study: what is the role of the church in Rome in the development of the doctrine? What sociological and theological principles shaped its emergence?

c. *2 Clement*

During the period 70–135 CE in early Christianity, the doctrine of redemptive almsgiving is most emphatically endorsed by *2 Clement*. The homilist's interest in a ransom for sin is primarily theological; he seeks the means of securing a (second) repentance that will preserve or restore the 'seal of baptism', thus guaranteeing the salvation of those who heed his warning. In many respects, Hermas and *2 Clement* are motivated by a similar crisis.[1] It will be seen that Hermas and *2 Clement* arrive at much the same conclusions, theologically and ethically, as they respond to their respective communities' concerns.

The setting of *2 Clement* within the context of early Christianity remains a mystery. The author does not identify himself; there is

---

1. See *Herm. Man.* 4.3.1-7.

virtually no external evidence concerning the origin of the homily. Eusebius regarded 2 *Clement* with considerable suspicion[1] and it is doubtful whether the homily was even cited by any early Christian authors.[2] If we had clear knowledge of its background and setting, we would of course be in a far better position to interpret the document and other Christian literature of the period might become more intelligible.[3]

My purpose here is to examine one recent attempt to set the homily in a historical context in early Christianity, to offer some modifications of the hypothesis, and to test these as they bear, directly or indirectly, on the topic of redemptive almsgiving.

While many hold a general attitude of scepticism (or agnosticism) toward the question of the provenance of 2 *Clement*,[4] K.P. Donfried has boldly argued that the homily is rightly associated with the genuine letter of Clement.[5] Donfried maintains that *1 Clement* was written between 96–98 CE from Rome with the purpose of healing the division and schism in the Corinthian church which had resulted from the improper removal of some presbyters from office.

Working from the significant assumption that *1 Clement* was well received and quickly achieved the results desired by its author, namely, that the elders were 'in all probability reinstated', Donfried suggests that 2 *Clement*, written between 98–100 CE, was a 'hortatory discourse' read to the Corinthian church by one of the vindicated presbyters. He concludes that 'both 1 and 2 Clement had together averted a severe crisis in the life of this congregation'.[6]

While Donfried's thesis may seem both plausible and appealing, his reconstruction of the setting of 2 *Clement* is nevertheless problematic. Already the question occurs, if *1 Clement* by itself was able to persuade the Corinthians to restore the elders to office, is it not misleading to claim that 'both 1 and 2 Clement together had averted a severe crisis' in that community? There is no evidence whatsoever that

1. Eusebius, *Ecclesiastical History* 3.37.3–38.4.
2. Lightfoot, *Apostolic Fathers*, I.2, p. 192.
3. Cf. V. Bartlett, 'The Origin and Date of 2 Clement', *ZNW* 7 (1906), p. 123.
4. E.g. Grant, *The Apostolic Fathers*, I, p. 46.
5. The Greek manuscripts of *1 Clement* contain 2 *Clement* as well, immediately following the epistle. This is also the case with the Syriac version of *1 Clement*.
6. K.P. Donfried, *The Setting of Second Clement in Early Christianity* (Leiden: Brill, 1974), p. 1.

2 *Clement* contributed to the restoration of the officers and the end of
the schism; on the contrary, Donfried has maintained that the homily
was composed after, and only because, *1 Clement* had achieved its
purpose!

Far more significant is the actual content of the homily. Even if it is
reasonable to assume that 2 *Clement* is an admonition from a group of
presbyters (cf. 17.3), and even if we grant a Corinthian context, there
is virtually nothing that indicates that the homily was composed in the
context of reconciliation. It is striking that *1 Clement*'s exhortation to
repentance is in many respects directed towards the goal of having the
deposed elders reinstated (cf. 44.3-6; 54.1-2; 57.1-2), while 2 *Clement*
offers no commendation, no blessing for the return of authority and
submission Donfried presupposes. Rather, there is an even harsher, a
more impassioned call for repentance, particularly from worldliness
and disobedience (e.g. 8.12-14; 9.7-11; 13.1-3; 16.1-2). 2 *Clement* is
hardly recognizable as a 'hortatory discourse' delivered 'shortly after'
the restoration to office of the Corinthian elders. There is absolutely
no acknowledgment of the congregation's obedient response to
Clement's epistle. On the contrary, there is a warning of judgment for
those who do not heed the elders (17.5). More than ironic, it is
inconceivable that the reinstated presbyters would utterly fail to make
reference to the theme of reconciliation within the church, especially
as *1 Clement* stresses this (e.g. 16.1; 38.1-2; 48.1-6; 50.1-2).

Donfried presents his case comprehensively, yet his hypothesis
proceeds from three interpreted facts. First, several textual witnesses,
of which Codex Alexandrinus is most notable, place *1* and 2 *Clement*
together. Donfried maintains, 'The most likely explanation of this is
that the two were preserved together precisely in that congregation
which felt they had made a valuable contribution to its internal life—
and that could only be the Corinthians'.[1]

Secondly, following Lightfoot's suggestion, Donfried insists that
καταπλέουσιν in 7.1, without reference to a specific city-port, 'can
only mean that the speaker is himself in that city, specifically, in this
case, Corinth, because of the prominence of the Isthmian games'.[2]

Finally, 2 *Clement* is preached, Donfried observes, in the context of

1. K.P. Donfried, 'The Theology of Second Clement', *HTR* 66 (1973), p. 499.
2. 'Theology of Second Clement', p. 499.

exhortations by presbyters (17.3).[1] These are the 'three external facts' upon which Donfried's hypothesis rests.[2] And the controversial interpretation of those facts is the subject of much discussion. Furthermore, for our purposes it is critical to observe that a Corinthian origin and a presbyter author for the homily, even with some connection to *1 Clement*, do not entail the supposition that *2 Clement* was a 'hortatory discourse' read to the reconciled community following the reinstatement of the elders. Another possibility exists. Before considering an alternative hypothesis, Donfried's facts and their interpretation must be examined.

To suppose that the appearance of *2 Clement* following *1 Clement* in a fifth-century manuscript[3] is evidence, much less proof, that these two documents were preserved together by a particular congregation which had received them some 350 years earlier is to be highly speculative. One might as well assume that 1, 2 and 3 John were similarly found together in several manuscripts because a church or an individual had preserved them together from the time they were first read. Certainly these letters were addressed to different persons. Their New Testament (and manuscript) arrangement is due specifically to their identification as Johannine writings. The fact that *1* and *2 Clement* are found together in some sources can most probably be attributed to the belief that the two documents had a common author. Eusebius testifies to the existence of such a belief in his own day but he knows nothing of the homily being 'preserved' by the Corinthian church. Whether it came to be thought of as a second epistle of Clement because of its Corinthian setting/origin is a separate issue.[4]

In *2 Clem.* 7.1, the verb καταπλέω occurs without reference to a specific port. Lightfoot inferred, 'we are naturally led to suppose that the homily was delivered in the neighbourhood of the place where

---

1. 'Theology of Second Clement', p. 499.
2. 'Theology of Second Clement', p. 499.
3. In my reading I have found virtually no consideration given to the argument that if *1 Clement, Barnabas*, and *Shepherd of Hermas* are regarded as having near canonical status because of their inclusion in some New Testament manuscripts, it is only reasonable to grant that the appearance of *2 Clement* in Codex Alexandrinus implies that the homily also was received alongside and among the New Testament documents by at least some part of the early church.
4. Lightfoot, *The Apostolic Fathers*, I.2, pp. 197-99.

these combatants [in the athletic games] landed'.[1] Donfried agrees and both scholars have concluded that Corinth is the port[2] in which the homily was composed or delivered. Surely, however, other ports in the Roman Empire could be the 'home' of *2 Clement*. Vernon Bartlet has complained that 'undue stress' has been placed on καταπλέω 'as though there were only one place, viz. Corinth, where such a reference would be fully appropriate'.[3] Goodspeed and Grant have suggested that Antioch, Alexandria, Ephesus, Corinth and Rome each could be the 'major Christian center' where the homily was composed.[4]

The question remains, however, whether καταπλέω in 7.1, due to its lack of mention of a specific port, must imply that the author had in mind his own city as the destination of those who 'set sail'. Clearly this is not important evidence for the place of origin of *2 Clement*. The reference in 7.1 is intended to be general; no specific games are mentioned. The author's purpose is to prepare for his metaphor in 7.3: 'Let us run the straight course, the immortal contest, and let many of us sail to it (εἰς αυτοῦ καταπλεύσωμεν) and contend...' Here the city-port is not identified because it is inappropriate to the symbolism. One sets sail for the contest, not for the port. Where 7.3 is meant figuratively, 7.1 is more literal only for the purpose of giving force to, and introducing, the metaphor. The omission of a reference to a port in *2 Clem*. 7.1 is not significant. To find evidence here that the homily was composed in Corinth, only one of several 'appropriate' city-ports, is to appeal to conjecture.

Donfried's claim that the homilist is a representative of the elders in his community is quite reasonable. This is the clear interpretation of 17.3. Much more, however, can be claimed for the author's place in the community. The overwhelming use of the pronoun 'we' indicates that he identifies with those whom he addresses. And significantly, he regards their struggle as his own (cf. 13.1; 18.2). Not only is the homilist the voice of the presbyters, he is a man who fully identifies with the needs and failures of his community. This is a critical observation that Donfried apparently neglects.

1. Lightfoot, *The Apostolic Fathers*, I.2, p. 197.
2. Yet Corinth was not itself a port. Its two ports were Cenchreae and Lechaeum.
3. 'Origin and Date', p. 134 n. 1.
4. Goodspeed and Grant, *History*, p. 90.

What, then, can be drawn from the facts which are used to support Donfried's hypothesis? Perhaps it is reasonable to conclude no more than that *2 Clement* was written by an elder in a Christian community, possibly Corinth, and that the homily at some time came to be closely associated with *1 Clement*. The external facts offer very little. Yet, at the same time, Donfried's treatment of the *internal* evidence leaves many unanswered questions.

While he recognizes the vital concern in *2 Clement* that 'once Christians have left this world they can no longer confess their post-baptismal sins or make repentance for them',[1] Donfried nevertheless does not regard 16.4 as a decisive or significant passage related to that concern. He is even reluctant to grant that *2 Clement* may have been influenced by Tob. 12.8-9. Rather, he suggests that *2 Clem.* 16.4 is a response to Gnostic traditions which would scorn almsgiving, prayer and fasting. In particular, Donfried draws attention to the *Gospel of Thomas*: 'Jesus said to them, If you fast you will beget sin for yourselves, and if you pray, you will be condemned and if you give alms, you will do evil to your spirits' (14).

While Donfried's interpretation is creative, he fails to explain why the homilist would equate almsgiving with repentance. If *2 Clement* 16.4 is only meant to correct certain Gnostic tendencies of the community, why is almsgiving elevated to the status of μετάνοια? Donfried seems unaware of the significance.[2] A central question may be asked: what is the purpose of 16.4 especially in light of the author's anxiety about post-baptismal sin and the imminence of judgment?

We may note that Donfried's interpretation, as it stands, is still confusing. Given the intimate knowledge of the synoptic sayings tradition demonstrated in *2 Clement*, we might expect a reply to the Gnostics to be based on the words of Jesus. Fasting, prayer and almsgiving are all commanded (e.g. Mt. 6.1-18; Mk 2.20). Yet, 16.4 goes beyond the explicit teaching of the New Testament and clearly advocates redemptive almsgiving. The author hopes to accomplish far more than just to reply to critics of fasting, prayer and almsgiving. It is the eschatological urgency, the prospect of judgment, that drives this passage (see 16.1-3). Donfried acknowledges that this concern underlies the quotation, 'Love covers a multitude of sins' (16.4) and

1. Donfried, *Second Clement*, p. 132.
2. Berger, 'Almosen', p. 186.

yet he does not develop this critical point.[1]

While he deserves credit for an adventurous and, to a large degree, attractive thesis about the origin of *2 Clement*, Donfried's conclusions (and assumptions) are not fully persuasive. His framework for understanding the homily is too restrictive and much of the material in *2 Clement* resists the interpretation that it is the product of recently reinstated presbyters of the Corinthian congregation. Furthermore, certain features are lacking in the homily that might be expected in an address from such a group. It is difficult to regard *2 Clement* as bringing to an end or helping to avert 'a severe crisis in the life of this congregation'.[2]

Having rejected Donfried's analysis, an alternative setting for *2 Clement* in early Christianity must be proposed. First, however, it ought to be pointed out that some features of Donfried's hypothesis are quite reasonable. A plausible explanation must be offered for the close association of the homily and *1 Clement* in the manuscript tradition. The supposition that Corinth was the provenance for *2 Clement* is not unreasonable; any other view must show that Corinth was an improbable setting. Finally, the author was a member of the community and a representative of its presbyters. Yet again, there is nothing to indicate that the homilist and his fellow elders had been *reinstated* to office.

The following is my 'working model' for interpreting *2 Clement*. In the tenth decade of the first century CE the Corinthian church was torn by internal strife. Doctrinal matters and issues of Christian practice were subjects of some dispute but the primary and fundamental division was sociological; the rich Christians in the Corinthian church were reluctant to associate with, much less support, their poorer brethren. This stratification had its roots in the Pauline community[3] and it is clear that the apostle was well aware that the Corinthian church would need sharp prodding if it was to support the collection for the saints (cf. 2 Cor. 8.1-7; 9.3-6). Paul promises them spiritual benefits for their contributions, and later readers may have taken this to refer to the redemptive power of almsgiving (2 Cor. 9.9-15).

The hostility between rich and poor Christians in Corinth continued

1. *Second Clement*, pp. 91-92.
2. Donfried, *Second Clement*, p. 1.
3. Theissen, *Social Setting*, pp. 96, 151.

to spark divisions, quarrelling, and even schism. The elders of the community, sensitive to the power and prestige of the wealthy, and because of their own social status, tended to favour the rich even to the point of neglecting the poor (cf. 1 Cor. 11.17-22; Jas. 2.1-4). Late in the first century, the Corinthian church separated into two distinct factions divided by their socio-economic class. The wealthy claimed to support the elders of the congregation. The poorer group denounced and rejected the presbyters of the community and refused to submit to their authority. The elders' ministry was disrupted and their role became uncertain.

The bishop of Rome sought to intervene, to restore unity to the Corinthian church. One of his primary objectives was to have the presbyters' office restored (*1 Clem.* 44.3-6; 54.1-2; 57.1-2). He had the wisdom, however, to recognize the root causes of the turmoil. He asks the piercing question, 'Why do we divide and tear asunder the members of Christ, and raise up strife against our own body, and reach such a pitch of madness as to forget that we are members one of another?' (46.7). Both the rich and the poor factions are indicted in *1 Clement*. The author is concerned with far more than having the Corinthian elders returned to office. His attention is drawn to the animosity between believers that threatens even his own church. 'We are not only writing these things to you, beloved, for your admonition, but also to remind ourselves; for we are in the same arena, and the same struggle is before us' (7.1).

The epistle calls for repentance, a repentance that will show itself in obedience to God (cf. 7.4-7; 8.1-5).[1] Mere lip service is condemned (15.2-5) and in the context of both of these passages *1 Clement* reminds its readers of the responsibility to help the poor, widows and orphans (8.4; 15.6).

Perhaps the virtue most stressed throughout the epistle is humility or being humble-minded. Clement suggests that this quality once characterized the Corinthian community: 'You were all humble-minded, and in no wise arrogant, yielding subjection rather than demanding it, giving more gladly than receiving' (2.1). Yet both the rich and poor factions have lost or forsaken their humility and *1 Clement* calls them to recover this spirit so essential to peace.[2]

---

1. Donfried, *Second Clement*, pp. 12-13.
2. For ταπεινοφροσύνη and related forms in the epistle's admonition see 13.1,

Claiming that Christ is of the humble-minded (16.1), the author raises the question, 'If the Lord was thus humble-minded, what shall we do, who through him have come under the yoke of his grace?' (16.17). The unity of the body depends on the simple and humbling admission that 'the great cannot exist without the small, nor the small without the great' (37.4). The epistle is directed both to restore the authority of the elders—calling on the poor to be humble in obedience—and to motivate the wealthy faction to alleviate the conditions which cause hardship for the needy, thus calling on the rich to exercise humility in their dealings with others (cf. especially 48.6).

> Let therefore our whole body be preserved in Christ Jesus, and let each be subject to his neighbour according to the position granted to him. Let the strong care for the weak and let the weak reverence the strong. Let the rich man bestow help on the poor and let the poor give thanks to God that he gave him one to supply his needs. (38.1-2)

Because the church was divided, it is probable that *1 Clement* was read separately by the wealthy and poor factions of the community.[1] Any genuine reconciliation would have required considerable time; consequently, it is assumed that the first century CE ended with the Corinthian church still divided. During those years of continued mistrust and hostility, services of worship for the entire church had become infrequent and there was a gradual degeneration within the wealthy faction into a worldliness and immorality that further separated them from their poorer brethren. At least this was the perception of the homilist, the author of what is known as *2 Clement*.

If *1 Clement* were received by the separate factions in Corinth, undoubtedly the elders were encouraged by the epistle and sympathetic to—if not enthusiastic for—its goal of reconciling the parties in the church. As the presbyters would be socially allied to the affluent members of the congregation and thus rejected by the poor faction, the influence of *1 Clement* through the instruction and admonition of the elders would more likely be significant among the rich.

It is my hypothesis that one of the presbyters of the Corinthian church, to some degree inspired by the letter from Rome, but more

---

3; 16.1-2, 17; 30.2-3, 8; 31.4; 38.2; 44.3; 48.6; 56.1; 58.2; 59.3-4; 62.2. See Bowe, *Church in Crisis*, pp. 107-21.

1. For the evidence that suggests separate factions met in the Corinthian church of Paul's day, see above, pp. 34-37.

intensely provoked by the spiritual decay he was witnessing, addressed the wealthy faction in a homily during one of their private meetings. He was quite disturbed that this group had grown materialistic and worldly; they loved money and pleasure. They were guilty of sexual misconduct. The homilist was concerned that they had never truly repented from their former lives of sin.

Above all, the elder was horrified that many in this faction had broken the seal of baptism; they had little regard for their salvation and they were at risk of disqualifying themselves from entrance into the kingdom of God. They seemed unaware that their disobedience to the commandments would bring judgment upon them. The warning of *1 Clement* haunted the elder: 'Behold, the Lord comes and his reward is before his face, to pay each according to his work' (34.3; cf. 23.5). The threat was even greater for the wealthy who had known God's material and spiritual blessings: 'Take care, beloved, that his many benefits do not bring judgment upon us if we do not live as his worthy citizens, harmoniously doing what is good and well pleasing before him' (21.1).

The address to the wealthy in *2 Clement* begins sternly:

> Brethren, we must think of Jesus Christ, as we do of God, as the judge of the living and the dead.[1] We must not think lightly of our salvation.[2] For if we think little of him we will hope to receive little. And those who listen as though it were a small matter are sinning and we also sin if we do not know whence and by whom and to what place we were called, and how great sufferings Jesus Christ endured for our sake. What return, then, shall we make to him or what fruit shall we offer worthy of that which he has given us? And how great a debt of holiness do we owe him? (1.1-3)

It is evident that *2 Clement* is foremost a call to repentance. The homily is indeed hortatory, its tone clearly indicates that the author is not speaking in a context of recent reconciliation and restored unity. His community is divided, his faction has fallen into grievous sin. The elder has no cause to commend his audience. Along with the summons to repentance, *2 Clement* forcefully urges that the wealthy forsake

---

1. Cf. 1 Pet. 4.5.

2. The contrast is not always recognized: 'we must think (δεῖ ἡμᾶς φρονεῖν)/we must *not* think (οὐ δεῖ ἡμᾶς φρονεῖν)'. The author's concern is not christological; rather he is insisting that his hearers recognize that they will be judged by the one they call Lord.

their love of money and show compassion for their poor brethren. Sharing the intention of *1 Clement*, the homily hopes to inspire a renewed love in the Corinthian church, reconciling the poor and the rich. The author is horrified at the ridicule of the non-believers who mock the Christians:

> For when they hear from us that God[1] says, 'It is no credit to you if you love them that love you, but it is a credit to you if you love your enemies and those that hate you'—when they hear this they wonder at this extraordinary goodness; but when they see that we not only do not love those that hate us, but not even those who love us, they laugh us to scorn, and the name is blasphemed (13.4).

Redemptive almsgiving serves the needs of the homilist. On the one hand, *redemptive* almsgiving offers a means to redeem post-baptismal sin. It is as effective as repentance itself. On the other hand, redemptive *almsgiving* will be a clear demonstration that the wealthy faction is beginning to minister to the needs of their poor brothers. To so distribute their wealth will show that they have forsaken worldliness and the love of money. Redemptive almsgiving is the single answer to the two problems the elder was confronting—providing a ransom for sin and motivating the rich to provide for the needy. Perhaps the homilist had been influenced by *1 Clement.*'s citation of Isa. 1.16-20:

> 'Wash and make yourselves clean, put away the wickedness of your souls from my eyes; cease from your wickedness. Learn to do good, seek out judgment, rescue the wronged, give judgment for the orphan, do justice to the widow, and come let us reason together, says the Lord. And if your sins be as crimson, I will make them white as snow; if they be as scarlet, I will make them white as wool.' (8.4)

It is my hypothesis, then, that the setting of *2 Clement* is to be found in the homily of a Corinthian elder, early in the second century, addressed specifically to the wealthy faction that was still estranged from the poor members of the church. The influence of *1 Clement* is certainly recognizable[2] but the homilist has concerns beyond those of the epistle.

---

1. The loose attribution to God of this saying of Jesus is justified for the homilist by his concern. Cf. 1.1.

2. Other evidence that *2 Clement*'s author was familiar with *1 Clement*: cf. *1 Clem.* 23.3-5 with *2 Clem.* 11.2-4 (note the theme of the imminent parousia); the resurrection issue (cf. 1 Cor. 15), *1 Clem.* 24–26 with *2 Clem.* 9.1-6; *1 Clem.* 48.1 and 50.3 with *2 Clem.* 13.4; 9.6.

The elder, after his initial warning, reminds the wealthy that they ought not to be proud. Before becoming Christians, they had been 'maimed in understanding'; their lives were nothing but death. They had no reason to boast of their calling into the Christian faith. It was God who pitied them as sinners. He did not save them because they were righteous. *2 Clement* humbles its readers: 'He called us when we were not, and it was his will that out of nothing we should come into being' (chs. 1 and 2). This stern passage was perhaps inspired by *1 Clement*:

> Let us consider, then, brethren, of what matter we were formed, who we are, and with what nature we came into the world, and how he who formed and created us brought us into his world from the darkness of a grave, and prepared his benefits for us before we were born (38.3).

The homilist then insists that his hearers genuinely confess the God who has saved them. Confession, however, is not merely a verbal exercise. 'How do we confess him? By doing what he says and not disregarding his commandments' (3.4). Having laid the foundation for his ethical instruction, the elder addresses the needs of his broken community. 'Let us confess him in our deeds by loving one another...not speaking against one another, nor being jealous...we ought to sympathize with each other and not be lovers of money. By these deeds we confess him' (4.3). The wealthy are rebuked for failing to love their brothers or even to sympathize with them. The love that does characterize their lives is a love of money.

The faction is admonished to forsake the world, to abandon their desire for τὰ κοσμικά.[1] They are promised, 'Our sojourning in this world in the flesh is a little thing and lasts a short time', while the kingdom of God will bring rest and everlasting life (5.5). To escape the sin of worldliness, the rich must overcome their love of money. Again referring to the words of the Lord, the elder warns, 'What is the advantage if a man gains the whole world but loses his soul?' It is far better to love heavenly things than the fading τὰ ἐνθάδε (cf. 10.3-4).[2] Salvation itself is at stake. If the wealthy do not preserve their baptism pure and undefiled they have no hope. There will no longer be an advocate (παράκλητος) for the rich (ch. 6).[3]

---

1. Cf. 17.3.
2. Synonymous with τὰ κοσμικά.
3. For the condemnation of advocates of the rich, see *Did.* 5.2; *Barn.* 20.2.

Post-baptismal sin and how it can be redeemed is one of the primary themes of the homily. Those who have not 'kept the seal' risk judgment; those who keep the seal obtain eternal life (7.6; 8.6). Consequently, repentance is vital.

The elder is all the more anxious because of his conviction that there is little time left before the end of the world (8.1-3; 9.7-8; 16.1-3; 17.4; 18.2).

At the conclusion of *2 Clement*, the elder addresses two concerns: first, that the wealthy would envy the non-believers who enjoy luxury without restraint, dreading the prospect of self-control; and secondly, that these wealthy Christians may simply re-direct their passion for gain into a facade of faith.[1] He admonishes them:

> Do not let it grieve your mind that we see the unrighteous enjoying wealth and the slaves of God restricted...[2] None of the righteous has attained a reward quickly, but waits for it for if God should pay the recompense of the righteous speedily, we would immediately be training ourselves in commerce and not godliness. We would seem to be righteous when we were pursuing not piety but gain (20.1, 3-4).

The elder's hope is that the factions will be reconciled, again belonging to the 'first church', the true body of Christ. In light of their current disobedience, their avarice, their worldliness, the wealthy are indicted as a 'den of thieves (14.1-2). *2 Clement* calls its hearers to repent while there is time, to forsake pleasure and desire, because judgment is at hand. This is the immediate context for the homily's concern with redemptive almsgiving (16.1-3). The elder announces,

> Therefore[3] almsgiving is good as repentance for sin.[4] Fasting is better than prayer but almsgiving is better than both. Love[5] covers a multitude of sins; prayer from a good conscience rescues from death. Blessed is every

---

1. Cf. Grant and Graham, 'The idea that they are pursuing profit is encouraged by five references to compensation (αντιμισθία; only here among the Apostolic Fathers...) and seven to reward (μισθός)', *Apostolic Fathers*, II, p. 110.

2. Interestingly, Donfried nowhere comments on 20.1.

3. The particle οὖν suggests that what follows is the reasoned conclusion to be drawn (cf. 14.1; 17.1, etc.).

4. Again for the significance of this claim, see Berger, 'Almosen', p. 186.

5. On the importance of love in *2 Clement*, see 4.3; 9.6; 12.1.

man who is found full of these things, for almsgiving lightens (the load of)[1] sin.

The homilist then encourages his congregation, 'So let us repent with our whole heart, that none of us perish by the way' (17.1).

In *2 Clement,* redemptive almsgiving serves two vital purposes. First, it provides a means to redeem post-baptismal sin. As an act of repentance it merits forgiveness; as an act of love it covers a multitude of sins. And secondly, the love which inspires almsgiving will promote reconciliation between the rich and poor factions of the Corinthian church. Through the giving of alms the wealthy will show their love for their brothers and will begin to free themselves from the love of money and a desire for the things of the world.

d. *Summary*

The Apostolic Fathers reveal a dramatic development in the doctrine of redemptive almsgiving in early Christianity. Theological and social pressures combined to make this acceptable within a movement that professed a belief that the death of Jesus had uniquely and sufficiently atoned for sin. Yet even the New Testament had allowed for alternative means of redemption. We find in the Apostolic Fathers the clear evolution from 1 Pet. 4.8, 'Love covers a multitude of sins', to the belief in *2 Clem.* 16.4 that giving alms is the act of love that, like repentance, merits forgiveness of sin. In this sense the love-ethic of the New Testament is both retained and even strengthened in the Apostolic Fathers.

Polycarp and Ignatius offer little evidence of the context and setting for the emergence of the doctrine of redemptive almsgiving. Polycarp, however, is the first to prooftext his belief from the LXX. Both men regarded help for the poor as an obligation of the Christian faith, but the social and theological issues that shaped the developing idea are apparently not significant for either author.

The *Doctrina*[2] perhaps offers the closest historical link to the pre-70

---

1. W. Bauer, *A Greek–English Lexicon of the New Testament* (trans. W.F. Arndt and F.W. Gingrich; Chicago: Chicago University Press, 1957), p. 448. Bauer draws attention to 1 Esd. 8.84 (8.86 in most versions) and notes 2 Esd. 9.13.

2. See Appendix A.

Christian tradition. The primitive Two Ways material regarded wages distributed for the needy as a ransom for sin. Certain social tensions between the rich and poor are recognizable in the *Doctrina*'s ethics. This stratification is even more intense in the Two Ways' tradition preserved in *Barnabas* and the *Didache*. Wealthy Christians who ignore their poor brethren are judged to be following a path of death; on the other hand, giving to the needy ransoms sin. The *Didache* also suggests that almsgiving had been abused by those who ask, not from need, but from a desire for money. These are warned that they will face a stern judgment. Presumably, the reluctance of the rich to give alms was partly due to their outrage over fraudulent appeals for charity. Their concern was justified and the Didachist struggles to find a solution. Ultimately, his instructions are contradictory:

> Give to everyone that asks of you; do not refuse, for the Father's will is that we give to all from the gifts we have received... But concerning this it was said, 'Let your alms sweat into your hands until you know to whom you are giving' (1.5-6).

Hermas also indicates that he is aware that some have asked for, and accepted, alms for improper reasons. He, too, warns of the consequences (*Herm. Man.* 2.5). Hermas is at the same time acutely aware that the rich have neglected the poor and, as in *2 Clement*, he is anxious to secure a second repentance, a means to atone for post-baptismal sin. For Hermas, providing for the poor is one of the few virtues with redemptive power.

The epistle, *1 Clement*, offers significant insights into the turmoil of the Corinthian community. Calling for reconciliation, this letter from the Roman church hopes to restore the elders to their authority and to motivate the wealthy faction to provide for the poorer members of the church. *2 Clement* is a homily addressed by one of the Corinthian elders to the rich Christians in Corinth. Again seeking reconciliation, the homilist is also anxious about the worldliness, the love of money, the post-baptismal sin of his party. The social conflicts and theological concerns find a single answer: the rich need to give alms, both to reach out to their poor brethren and to provide a ransom for their own sin.

It remains, then, for a more detailed look at the sociological factors, the theological crisis, and the role of the Roman church in the process of early Christianity's acceptance of redemptive almsgiving.

Chapter 6

ANALYSIS

In the preceding sections, the Christian tradition—principally the New Testament and the Apostolic Fathers—for roughly the first one and a half centuries of the Common Era has been explored for the emerging and developed belief that the giving of alms merits the forgiveness of sins. Having surveyed the significant texts which provide the context and the foundation for the doctrine of redemptive almsgiving in early Christianity, it is necessary to draw some conclusions about the socio-logical and theological issues that have been raised. More specifically, what do the Christian sources reveal concerning the socio-economic and the theological needs or crises that called forth a belief seemingly incompatible with the fundamental soteriology of the community, namely, that Jesus died for our sins once and for all?[1]

Throughout the study of different passages, occasional comments and suggestions have been offered as to the relevance of certain material. This has especially been the case with 2 *Clement*. In the present section a more comprehensive analysis and reconstruction of the developing doctrine will be offered. Several loose ends and lingering questions remain.

The sociological issue that must first be addressed is how (and perhaps when) wealthy adherents came to be accepted into a community whose Lord reportedly said, 'Woe to you that are rich' (Lk. 6.35). What did the (blessed) poor expect from their affluent brothers? What tensions existed between these social classes within the Christian community and how—if ever—were they resolved? What role was played by redemptive almsgiving in the attempt to bring unity to the body of Christ, reconciling the rich and the poor? Here Theissen's

1. Cf. Hengel, *The Atonement*, p. 47.

pioneering research provides an essential foundation upon which to construct a working hypothesis.

Certainly the most critical theological problem underlying the early Christian doctrine of redemptive almsgiving was the anxiety over post-baptismal sin. How was one to find redemption for those sins committed after one had been washed clean?[1] This concern was made more urgent by a renewed expectation (or simply a reissued warning) that the parousia was imminent; Judgment Day was at hand. Post-baptismal sin provoked a crisis especially where there was anxiety about the nearness of the end. In the earliest stages of the development of penance, it is almsgiving (along with martyrdom) that is put forward as redemptive, providing a ransom for sin.

To set these social and theological conflicts within a general framework, an attempt will be made to reconstruct the history of the idea of redemptive almsgiving in early Christianity. A broad hypothesis will be offered as a perspective for understanding early Christian tradition.

a. *The Social Problems*

Early in the second century CE, Pliny observed (and complained) that Christianity was spreading rapidly in the provinces of Bithynia and Pontus (cf. 1 Pet. 1.1). He commented that men and women of every age and station (*omnis ordinis*) had been 'infected' with the superstition.[2] Hengel properly concludes that here is clear evidence that 'there were members of Christian communities in all strata of the populace, from slaves and freedmen to the local aristocracy'.[3] Undoubtedly there were wealthy Christians in the early church.[4] This is somewhat unexpected, however, in light of the harsh attitude towards wealth and the ascetic lifestyle of Jesus and his first followers. The Gospel tradition is clear (and there was no apparent attempt to suppress it) that the Master had said, 'It is easier for a camel to go through the eye of a

---

1. An interesting possibility existed for a word-play between the λουτρόν of baptism and the λύτρον of almsgiving, but I have found no examples in early Christian literature.
2. Pliny the Younger, *Epistles* 10.96.9.
3. Hengel, *Property and Riches*, pp. 36-37.
4. Cf. Justin Martyr, *Apology* 67; Tertullian, *Ad Scapulam*, 4.5-6; Eusebius, *Ecclesiastical History* 5.21.2. See Harnack, *The Mission and Expansion of Christianity*, II, pp. 33-42.

needle than for a rich man to enter the kingdom of God' (Mk 10.25 par.) Surely the presence of wealthy Christians was, if not socially, at least theologically awkward for the earliest Christian communities.

The tension between accommodating the rich and denouncing worldliness is striking in 1 Timothy. After scorning the idea that 'godliness is a means of gain' (6.5; cf. *2 Clem.* 20.4), the author goes on to write,

> There is great gain in godliness with contentment;[1] for we brought nothing into the world and we cannot take anything out of the world. But if we have food and clothing, with these we shall be content. But those who desire to be rich fall into temptation, into a snare, into many sense-less and hurtful desires that plunge men into ruin and destruction. For the love of money is the root of all evils; it is through this craving that some have wandered away from the faith and pierced their hearts with many pangs (6.6-10).

Having strongly warned his readers of the dangers of wealth and its potential to corrupt and destroy faith, the author then outlines the behaviour that is expected on the part of affluent Christians. Far from counselling them to sell their possessions and give to the poor (cf. Mk 10.21), he maintains that within certain guidelines they may retain their wealth.

> As for the rich in this world, charge them not to be haughty, nor to set their hopes on uncertain riches but on God who richly furnishes us with everything to enjoy. They are to do good, to be rich in good deeds, liberal and generous, thus laying up for themselves a good foundation for the future, so that they may take hold of the life which is life indeed (6.17-19).

Clearly 1 Timothy was written during a period when early Christianity was struggling to achieve a balance in its attitude towards wealth.[2] On the one hand, the Christian tradition encouraged a simple lifestyle and retained a hostility towards wealth that characterizes much of the teaching of Jesus. On the other hand, the presence of wealthy members in the community and their dominant influence made it necessary to compromise the demand of renunciation and to promote the virtues of hospitality and charity, the good deeds of the rich. Strikingly, this too is sanctioned in the Jesus tradition (e.g.

1. αὐτάρκεια; cf. Phil. 4.11-12; cf. Osiek, *Rich and Poor*, pp. 53, 56.
2. Cf. Countryman, *Rich Christian*, p. 120: 'This combination of positive and negative attitudes toward wealth demands some explanation'.

Mk 14.7; Mt. 25.31-46). It is significant that a wealthy man is given a prominent role in the Gospels as a secret disciple (Jn 19.38; cf. Mk 15.43 = Mt. 27.57).

Whether these apparently conflicting views of wealth are both to be traced to Jesus cannot be determined here. It is beyond the scope of my research. What is significant for the purpose of this study is that the New Testament provides clear evidence that early Christianity had to confront the issue of how the rich were to be accepted into the community of faith. While there are theological aspects to this, it is fundamentally a social problem. Maynard-Reid has observed, 'as Christianity moved out of its incipiency in the Palestinian milieu and into the Gentile world—where a minority privileged class began dominating the Christian community—the church had to modify its harsh position against the rich and riches but at the same time to promote and aim for egalitarianism among its members'.[1] Theissen's research justifies this claim.

In his *Sociology of Early Palestinian Christianity* and in the articles collectively titled *The Social Setting of Pauline Christianity*, Gerd Theissen has established an impressive (and plausible) outline of the sociological development of Christianity in its first generation. He regards 'earliest Christianity', namely, the mission of Jesus and his first followers, as 'a renewal movement within Judaism brought into being through Jesus'.[2]

It was not the intention of Christianity's founder to establish communities; rather, Theissen argues, he 'called into being a movement of wandering charismatics'.[3] These followers of Jesus abandoned their homes and broke from their families with a 'disregard for the demands of piety'.[4] Significantly, these wandering charismatics were to reject property and wealth; they were allowed no more than one day's provisions as they embarked on their journey. 'This manifest poverty was based on an unconditional trust in the goodness of God, who would not let his missionary come to grief.'[5] Theissen claims that

1. *Poverty and Wealth*, p. 36. See also J.G. Gager, *Kingdom and Community* (Englewood Cliffs, NJ: Prentice-Hall, 1975), p. 106.
2. Theissen, *Sociology*, p. 1.
3. *Sociology*, p. 8.
4. *Sociology*, pp. 10-11. Cf. M. Hengel, *The Charismatic Leader and his Followers* (New York: Crossroad, 1981), pp. 8-15.
5. Theissen, *Sociology*, pp. 12-13.

the Jesus movement approved of begging but there is little direct evidence for this. He is on far more solid ground in maintaining that the charismatics took it for granted that they would enjoy hospitality as the due wages of their ministry.[1] Indeed, these Cynic-like missionaries of Christianity could not have survived apart from the generosity of others who had chosen *not* to forsake their homes and possessions.

> Even the most dedicated ascetic, however, requires subsistence. If he himself does not labor, then he is dependent on others who labour for him. In that way he remains firmly tied to this world however much he may otherwise distance himself from it.[2]

Thus the Gospel tradition honours hospitality, promising a prophet's reward to the one who knowingly receives a prophet. Even a cup of cold water offered to a disciple merits a reward that cannot be lost (Mt. 10.40-42). Here is perhaps the earliest role the wealthy could play within the Christian community, to provide food and lodging to host the wandering charismatics.[3]

Initially the Jesus movement was driven by an eschatological hope/fear that the end of the world was at hand. With this conviction, their attitude towards wealth is to be expected.[4] Two factors, however, largely shaped the growing role of wealthy members in the Christian community: (1) The Jesus movement, branching out from Palestine, became an urban phenomenon in the major cities of the empire. The wandering charismatics recruited few followers to their radical lifestyle and instead became involved with local communities of believers. The rich were able to join these congregations without needing to sever their ties to the world. (2) As time passed and communities became well-established, the prospect of an imminent parousia grew more and more remote and upper-class Christians invested more time and wealth in this life. The rich came to regard Judgment Day as only a distant threat to their enjoyment of present prosperity.[5]

---

1. *Social Setting*, p. 31.
2. Theissen, *Social Setting*, p. 27.
3. Berger, 'Almosen', p. 194.
4. Theissen, *Sociology*, p. 15.
5. Maynard-Reid, *Poverty and Wealth*, pp. 36-37; R.M. Grant, *The Sword and the Cross* (New York: Macmillan, 1955), p. 132; Theissen, *Sociology*, p. 18; cf. L. Goppelt, *Apostolic and Post-Apostolic Times* (New York: Harper Torchbook,

In the transition from the Palestinian Jesus movement to the early Christian mission in the urban centres of the empire, it was the Hellenists who were the bold innovators.[1] Theissen observes that it was here that the sect became 'an independent religion'.[2] The leading representatives of the Hellenistic mission, Paul and Barnabas, deliberately chose to renounce their right to be supported as charismatic prophets/apostles (1 Cor. 9.1-15). Instead, Paul was willing to labour to earn with his own hands the money that was needed to finance his ministry (1 Thess. 2.9; 2 Thess. 3.7-9; cf. Acts 20.34).[3] This work ethic of the apostle—which is similar to the views of Dio Chrysostom and Musonius Rufus[4]—was in part motivated by the intention to distinguish himself from both the teaching-for-profit of philosophers and the support-dependent activity of the wandering charismatics.[5] This conscious, radical shift reflects the changing perspective of the movement:

> Such departure by Paul and Barnabas from the norms of early Christianity's itinerant-charismatic posture is in all likelihood related to the altered socio-economic, socio-ecological, and socio-cultural conditions which the mission encountered in the urban Hellenistic world.[6]

Paul in no way condemns wealth; he neither echoes nor pronounces woes on the rich. Far from advocating an imitation of 'Jesus' life of poverty', the apostle's instructions require the believer to be diligent, hard working, earning the respect of outsiders (1 Thess. 4.11-12): 'We get the impression that he demands solid middle-class respectability'.[7] Rather than calling for individuals to forsake their property, Paul maintains that the labourer 'should strive to earn more than is necessary to provide for his own needs, in order to be able to

1970), pp. 135-39.
   1. M. Hengel, *Between Jesus and Paul* (Philadelphia: Fortress Press, 1983), pp. 54-58.
   2. *Sociology*, pp. 117-18.
   3. R.F. Hock, *The Social Context of Paul's Ministry* (Philadelphia: Fortress Press, 1980), p. 26; W.A. Meeks, *Urban Christians*, p. 27.
   4. Dio Chrysostom 3.15; Hock, *Social Context*, p. 67; Musonius, 'What Means of Livelihood is Appropriate for a Philosopher?'
   5. Theissen, *Social Setting*, pp. 35-39.
   6. Theissen, *Social Setting*, pp. 39-40.
   7. N.A. Dahl, *Studies in Paul* (Minneapolis: Augsburg, 1977), pp. 23-24.

relieve the suffering of those who cannot provide for themselves'.[1] Freed from the renunciation of wealth, the Christian movement became more popular among the affluent. Joining with the wealthy who had provided hospitality for the earliest missionaries, more people from the upper classes were drawn to the new religion. It is in the 'urban stage' of the development of early Christianity that the Church experienced 'the influx of wealthy believers' who established the economic foundation of the community and this required a radical 're-evaluation of the traditional deprecation of wealth'.[2]

Abandoning the extreme eschatological ethic of the wandering charismatics, the Christian communities founded by Paul were instructed to adopt a 'familial love-patriarchalism' which preserves the social order, summoning wives, children and slaves to obedience and placing on the wealthy and powerful the responsibility to provide for the community. More specifically, the rich were to support the poor, and they were to be motivated by love. Theissen observes, 'In this setting charismatic begging was inappropriate'.[3] The work ethic is reinforced by the command to provide for needy brethren; the poor should not have to ask for assistance.

Under the umbrella of love-patriarchalism, wealth and labour were honoured inasmuch as they served to relieve the poverty of fellow believers. The social crisis of the needy made almsgiving a necessity. Theological concerns elevated the status of almsgiving to the place where it was regarded as a redemptive act of love. At some stage in the development of these ideas, the distribution to the poor of one's earned wages was considered a ransom for sin. *Doctrina* and the Two Ways tradition preserved in *Barnabas* stress the importance of labour (cf. also *Herm. Man.* 2.4). The *Didache*, despite its strong work ethic (12.1-5), regarded the act of giving to be more significant.

1. Dahl, *Studies*, pp. 23-24.
2. Gager, *Kingdom and Community*, p. 106; cf. Theissen, *Social Setting*, p. 36; E.A. Judge, *The Social Pattern of the Christian Groups in the First Century* (London: Tyndale Press, 1960), p. 61; S.J. Case, *The Social Origins of Christianity* (Chicago: Chicago University Press, 1923), p. 119.
3. Theissen, *Social Setting*, pp. 37, 73, 107; *idem, Sociology*, p. 115; cf. M.S. Enslin, *The Ethics of Paul* (New York: Abingdon Press, 1957), pp. 73-74, 239, 285-86; Countryman, *Rich Christian*, p. 150.

If through your hands you have earned a ransom for your sins, you shall not hesitate to give it or grumble when you give... You shall not turn away from the needy... (*Doctrina* 4.6-8)	...or working with your hands for the ransom of your sins. You shall not hesitate to give and when you give you shall not grumble (*Barn.* 19.10-11).

Of whatsoever you have gained by your hands, you shall give a ransom for your sins. You shall not hesitate to give, nor shall you grumble when you give... You shall not turn away the needy... (*Did.* 4.6-8).

As we shall see, early Christianity certainly had theological motivation for its advocacy of redemptive almsgiving, yet clearly there were social crises that provoked the need to give the rich added incentive to aid the poor. There is widespread evidence that the wealthy failed to fulfil their obligations in the community. Perhaps this was due in part to the popular Hellenistic morality (which prevailed in the cities) that gifts should only be given to those who could reciprocate.[1] The love-patriarchalism ethic failed where the affluent were insensitive to the needy; and in some situations the abused and neglected poor rebelled against the authority of the rich leaders in the Church. This was almost certainly the case in Corinth.

Paul was aware that the socially powerful in the Corinthian congregation were not acting in love towards their impoverished brethren. The most striking passage in his correspondence about this problem is 1 Cor. 11.17-22.

> But in the following instructions I do not commend you, because when you come together it is not for the better but for the worse. For, in the first place when you assemble as a church, I hear that there are divisions among you and I partly believe it, for there must be factions among you in order that those who are genuine among you may be recognized. When you meet together, it is not the Lord's supper that you eat. For in eating, each one goes ahead with his own meal, and one is hungry and another is drunk. What! Do you not have houses to eat and drink in? Or do you despise the church of God and humiliate those who have nothing? What shall I say to you? Shall I commend you in this? No, I will not.

I have argued that this conflict between the rich and the poor Christians in Corinth continued to be a source of great tension in the

1. For the Hellenistic principle, see Hands, *Charities and Social Aid*, pp. 26, 32. See also Chapter 2, 'The Graeco-Roman Background of Redemptive Almsgiving'.

community throughout the first century CE. At some point the indignant poor broke away from the congregation and repudiated the
authority of the elders. *1 Clement* was written with the dual purpose
of restoring the presbyters to office and of reconciling through love
the divided church. Clement sought to restore the program of love-
patriarchalism: the rich supporting the poor and the poor, in turn,
submitting to authority, honouring the leaders of the community
(cf. 38.1-2).

How the rich and the poor factions responded to *1 Clement* is a
matter of some conjecture. It is my hypothesis, however, that
2 Clement is a homily addressed to the affluent members of the congregation, summoning them to repent of their sins of worldliness,
love of money, and their neglect of the poor. The elder-homilist
promises that almsgiving has great power. Inspired by *1 Clement*, it is
his objective to motivate his faction to begin to fulfil their responsibilities to the weaker members of the body. Almsgiving, as an act of
love, covers a multitude of sins.

The *Shepherd of Hermas* witnesses to a similar conflict in the
Roman church of the early second century CE.[1] As in the church in
Corinth, this tension in Rome may well have had roots in the congregation during the time of Paul.[2] Hermas was concerned to prompt the
wealthy to forsake their preoccupation with business pursuits and
worldly pleasures; he called them to meet the needs of the poor.
Significantly, his appeal and challenge is set in the context of an
anxiety over post-baptismal sin and the necessity of a second
repentance. Hermas would surely endorse the claim of *2 Clem.* 16.4,
'Almsgiving is therefore good as repentance for sin...'

Hermas, like Clement, hopes to (re-)establish the pattern of love-
patriarchalism which will bring unity to the body,[3] strengthening the
bonds between members and overcoming the social tensions that
divide the community. Almsgiving is the essential, practical evidence
of the concern of the wealthy. The benefited poor are obligated to
intercede for the rich—to be, in effect, the friends made by means of

1. See above, pp. 86-94.
2. Cf. Lampe, *Die stadtrömischen Christen*, pp. 71-78.
3. Osiek, *Rich and Poor*, pp. 81-83; *Die stadtrömischen Christen*, pp. 74-78.
For the possible success of his appeal, see Justin Martyr, *Apology* 14: 'we who
valued above all things the acquisition of wealth and possessions now bring into a
common stock and communicate to everyone in need'.

unrighteous mammon (*Herm. Sim.* 2.5-9). Hermas regards the prayers of the poor as ensuring the reward for charity. This is perhaps a development from love-patriarchalism to a belief in 'effective compensation'.[1]

The neglect of the needy was a fairly widespread problem in early Christianity. The Two Ways tradition, adopted and modified by the *Didache* and *Barnabas*, offers a severe rebuke and warning to all who oppress the poor. Ignatius is anxious that love heal all divisions in the community; certainly this includes social conflicts. For Ignatius, the heretic is marked by his lack of love—for the widow, the orphan, the distressed, the afflicted. Love could redeem the heretic. Polycarp, while not specifically addressing the wealthy, is adamant in repudiating the love of money, the 'love of this present world'. Like Ignatius, he is anxious that widows be cared for, and to motivate the rich to be generous Polycarp apparently endorses the doctrine of redemptive almsgiving. The bishop of Smyrna apparently adopts the ethic of love-patriarchalism:

> Follow the example of the Lord... loving the brotherhood, affectionate to one another... giving way to one another in the gentleness of the Lord, despising no man. When you can do good, do not delay, for almsgiving sets free from death. Be subject to one another... (*Phil.* 10.1-2).

There were any number of reasons why affluent Christians failed to meet the needs of the poorer members. The inability of the poor to return a benefit probably made the rich reluctant to give. The literature of early Christianity suggests at least one other cause for the unwillingness to give. Certain persons, not genuinely impoverished, had solicited and accepted alms, taking advantage of the rich. In all likelihood, the wealthy pointed to this abuse of charity as justifying their hesitancy to provide for the needy.[2]

The *Didache* and the *Shepherd of Hermas*, dependent on earlier tradition, both recognize the legitimacy of this complaint by the rich. And both are aware that the issue must be resolved if there is to be any hope of bringing unity to the church and inspiring the affluent to meet their responsibilities within the Christian community. While the

---

1. Theissen, *Sociology*, pp. 116-17; cf. Hengel, *Property and Riches*, pp. 60-73.
2. Cf. Lampe, *Die stadtrömischen Christen*, p. 75.

Didache struggles with the problem and its resolution, Hermas is content to warn the offenders and to encourage the wealthy to fulfil their ministry.[1]

The doctrine of redemptive almsgiving emerges in early Christianity as a result of both social and theological tensions in various communities. Undoubtedly the most significant social factor was the stratification caused by the conflict between rich and poor believers. The predisposition of the wealthy to despise the needy was impossible to overcome completely, even in a fraternity where distinctions were not to be made (cf. 1 Cor. 12.12-13; Gal. 3.28). The natural reluctance of the affluent to provide for those who could not make a reciprocal gift was in some cases reinforced by the knowledge of the abuse of charity on the part of those who were not truly in need of assistance. Inevitably, several Christian communities, the most notable being Corinth and Rome, experienced deep social divisions in their fellowship. Redemptive almsgiving offered incentive to the wealthy to distribute part of their abundance. They would be rewarded. At some point it was claimed that the poor could return a benefit to the one who had supplied their need: the poor could (and should) intercede for the rich. Redemptive almsgiving clearly has roots in the social conflicts within early Christianity. 'The theology of a second repentance has an unmistakable social function.'[2]

b. *The Theological Issues*

In the first and early second centuries CE, wealthy Christians enjoyed places of privilege and authority in most local communities of believers. At the same time they were expected to bear responsibility for the material needs of the congregation, implementing what Theissen calls the love-patriarchalism of Paul's ethics.[3] Clearly the rich did not always fulfil their obligations to the body of Christ—at least not to the satisfaction of the needy. This failure is most evident in the Corinthian and Roman communities.

Undoubtedly, several factors explain how each crisis originated but *theologically* it seems likely that in many cases the wealthy had

---

1. *Did.* 1.5-6; *Herm. Man.* 2.4-6 (cf. *Herm. Sim.* 1.9).
2. Lampe, *Die stadtrömischen Christen*, p. 76.
3. *Social Setting*, p. 107; cf. *Sociology*, p. 115.

abandoned the hope/fear of an imminent parousia. Convinced that the Lord was delayed in his return, these servants who exercised considerable power over his household had begun to misuse their position to the neglect of the poor. Perhaps it was not unusual for the rich to fall into drunkenness and become all the more abusive and rude.[1] If this is an accurate representation of some rich factions within the Christian community of the first and early second centuries CE, then at least one Q passage may warrant serious reconsideration as to its *Sitz im Leben* in early Christian tradition.

> You also must be ready for the Son of man is coming at an hour you do not expect.

> Who then is the faithful and wise servant whom his master set over his household to give them their portion of food at the proper time? Blessed is that servant whom his master when he comes will find so doing.[2] Truly I say to you, he will set him over all his possessions. But if that servant says to himself, 'My master is delayed in coming' and begins to beat the menservants and the maidservants, and to eat and drink and get drunk, the master of that servant will come on a day when he does not expect him and at an hour he does not know, and will cut him in pieces and put him with the unfaithful. (Lk. 12.40, 42-46)

Significantly, Luke appends a concluding warning: 'Every one to whom much is given, of him will much be required, and of him to whom men commit much they will demand the more' (12.48b). In light of Luke's great interest in the theme of wealth, it is reasonable to assume that he has adapted the Q material to admonish rich Christians who were tempted to neglect their community responsibilities because they no longer believed in the imminent end of the world. And like Luke, Matthew and other New Testament authors who find it necessary to warn that the parousia is at hand, many of the Apostolic Fathers seek to encourage the hope/fear of Christ's impending return.

Whether the Q logion originates with an early Christian prophet denouncing (or warning) the wealthy for their lack of faith and consequent disobedience or whether the saying is ultimately derived from a genuine word of Jesus directed against the religious

---

1. Cf. 1 Cor. 11.21-22 and the catalogue of wickedness in *Herm. Man.* 8.3 which indicts the rich: '...the lawlessness of drunkenness, evil luxury, overeating, extravagance of wealth, boastfulness, haughtiness, pride...'

2. For an interesting parallel, see *Herm. Sim.* 5.2.9-10.

authorities[1] cannot be determined here. For our purposes, it is striking that Q, a source more or less contemporary with Paul, may well rebuke the rich for their sins as Paul challenged the wealthy Corinthians. And both Q and Paul's first (extant) letter to the Corinthians stress the nearness of the end of the age.

The apostle's conviction that the end of the age is at hand, within the lifetime of his contemporaries, is critical to his anxiety that the Corinthians reform and live as true Christians, not as outsiders. Given the imminence and unexpectedness of the parousia, it was all the more urgent that his readers be prepared to stand before the Lord. It was Paul's hope that they would be 'guiltless' at the coming of Jesus (1.8-9; cf. 1 Thess. 1.10; 3.13; 5.23-24). The warning of judgment, as the terrible consequence of disobedience, is found often in the letter (e.g. 3.13-15; 4.5; 11.31-32).

Paul fully expects that those of the community who were living at the time of the parousia would be miraculously changed from their corruptible bodies into a 'spiritual body', putting on immortality, fitting them to enter the new age. 'For flesh and blood cannot inherit the kingdom of God, nor does the perishable inherit the imperishable' (15.42-54; cf. 1 Thess. 4.14-17). The apostle is outraged, however, that the behaviour of some of the Corinthians will disqualify them from the privilege of the resurrected/transformed life. He reminds them of their 'knowledge' (cf. 1.5). 'Do you not know that the unrighteous will not inherit the kingdom of God? Do not be deceived; neither the immoral...nor the *greedy*, nor *drunkards*...will inherit the kingdom of God' (6.9-10, italics mine).

As the end of the ages has come upon them (10.11), the Corinthians are warned to live as saints worthy of the kingdom of God. The 'appointed time has grown very short' (7.29) and the believers are encouraged to make full use of the vanishing opportunity to please the Lord in this life. The wealthy are admonished: 'Let those who buy live as though they had no goods (μὴ κατέχοντες; cf. 11.22, μὴ ἔχοντας) and those who deal with the world as though they had no dealings with it. For the form of this world is passing away' (7.30b-31).

Despite the unpreparedness of the Corinthians, most notably the

1. J. Jeremias, *The Parables of Jesus* (New York: Charles Scribner's Sons, 2nd edn, 1972), pp. 58, 166.

wealthy members of that community, Paul entertains no hope for the delay of the end of the world so that they might have more time to repent and to change (contrast 2 Pet. 3.9). His closing prayer is μαράνα θά, 'our Lord come' (16.22). Rather than debate with those who have come to doubt that the parousia is at hand, the apostle challenges and confronts their disbelief with the hope/fear that the end *is* near. Those whose faithfulness and obedience have begun to fail are not reprimanded gently; they are bluntly warned that they risk being disinherited from the kingdom of God. Paul's objective is quite similar to Luke's in the latter's use of the Q logion: to alert the wealthy and prominent servants of God that they are neglecting their community (household) responsibilities[1] because they assume their Master is delayed. Their drunkenness and abuse of the poor, their greed will be punished.

Drunken carousing and gluttonous over-feasting were vices which corrupted several factions within early Christianity. The rich were particularly subject to the temptation because such extravagance was well within their means and it was a common and accepted feature of their luxurious lives.[2] Paul warns, as he previously warned[3] the Galatians, that drunkenness and excessive eating would cause them to be refused entrance to the kingdom of God (5.21). In much the same way, the author of 1 Peter seeks to bolster the commitment and repentance of his readers, appealing to the nearness of the parousia:

> Let the time that is past suffice for doing what the Gentiles like to do, living in debauchery, passions, drunkenness, excessive eating, drinking parties, and wanton idolatry. They are surprised that you do not now join them... but they will give account to him who is ready to judge the living and the dead[4]... The end of all things is at hand; therefore keep sane and sober for prayer[5] (4.3-7).

---

1. Cf. Paul's burning question, 'Do you despise the church of God?' (1 Cor. 11.22).

2. Cf. Epictetus, *Discourses* 3.26.5; Petronius, 'Trimalchio's Dinner', *Satyricon* 31–33, 35–37; Juvenal, *Satires*, 5.76-81, 113-24.

3. Thus, the persistence of the sins.

4. Was the author of *2 Clement* aware of this context for his use of the phrase in 1.1?

5. Interestingly, it is in this context that the author goes on to speak of the need for love in the brotherhood, that love covers a multitude of sins.

Luke, well aware of the sad condition in communities where the rich had neglected their responsibilities and fallen into selfish extravagance, reports that Jesus had even warned the Apostles of the danger of forgetting the imminence of the last day: 'Take heed to yourselves lest your hearts be weighed down with carousing and drunkenness and cares of this life[1] and that day come upon you suddenly like a snare' (21.34).

Hermas knows of similar conduct in his own community, the church in Rome. He warns that the angel of wickedness inspires evil deeds, including 'the luxury of much eating and drinking, and many feasts with various and unnecessary foods...' (*Herm. Man.* 6.2.5). That these were sins committed by the wealthy Christians of Rome is certain. Hermas inquires of the angel of repentance, 'What are the evils from which we must restrain ourselves?' The answer is clear: '...from the lawlessness of drunkenness, from evil luxury, from much eating and extravagance of wealth, from boastfulness, haughtiness, and pride' (*Herm. Man.* 8.3). The punishment for these sins is harsh and the rich are again warned to avoid the

> extravagance of wealth, much needless food and drink, and many other foolish luxuries. For all luxury is foolishness and vain for the servants of God. These desires, then, are wicked, and bring the servants of God to death, for this desire is the wicked daughter of the devil (*Herm. Man.* 12.2.1-2).

To a large degree, then, Hermas directs his message to the affluent and self-indulgent members of his community (*Herm. Vis.* 1.1.8).[2] Those who enjoy over-abundance must share with those who are hungry; and time for 'doing good' is short (*Herm. Vis.* 3.9.5-6). The prospect of judgment looms heavy for the wealthy who have neglected their responsibilities to the poor members of their community.

> Now, therefore, listen to me and be at peace among yourselves; look after[3] one another and help one another. Do not take a superabundant share of God's created things for yourselves, but give also a part to those who lack. For *some are contracting illness in the flesh by too much eating*, and are injuring their flesh, and the flesh of the others who have

---

1. On μερίμναις βιωτικαῖς, see Lk. 8.14; 1 Cor. 6.3-4; Theissen, *Social Setting*, p. 97; *Herm. Vis.* 1.3.1; *Herm. Man.* 5.2.2.

2. Osiek, *Rich and Poor*, p. 91.

3. ἐπισκέπτεσθε; cf. *Herm. Sim.* 1.8; *Herm. Man.* 8.10.

nothing to eat is being injured by their not having sufficient food and their body is being destroyed. So this lack of sharing is harmful to you who are rich and do not share with the poor. *Consider the judgment which is coming (Herm. Vis.* 3.9.2-5a [italics mine]).

The uncertainty of the future, the fact that the Lord might return at any moment, makes Hermas's admonition all the more urgent. The tower imagery of the *Similitudes* is clear: the building is almost complete; little time remains. There is a fear that many will be unrepentant, unsuitable for use in the construction of the tower and the angel warns that the Master may come suddenly (*Herm. Sim.* 8.9.4; 9.5.6-7; 9.7.1-2, 6). Any delay in the project's being finished is for the sake of those who need to repent, and the *Similitudes* close with a warning to the rich: they are to do good deeds, to rescue the destitute and any who suffer distress or who are in need. If the wealthy do not respond to the poor they will be guilty of their blood. Hermas challenges his readers,

Therefore do good deeds, all you who have learnt of the Lord, lest the building of the tower is finished while you delay. For the work of the building has been broken off for your sake. Unless therefore you hasten to do right the tower will be finished and you will be shut out (*Herm. Sim.* 10.2-4).

There is some evidence that this condition of the Roman church, namely that the wealthy were haughty, guilty of drunkenness and gluttony, no longer expecting an imminent parousia, existed in some form in the first century, even as early as Paul's letter to the community. We have seen that Clement recognizes the tensions between the rich and the poor in his own church; jealousy and strife threaten the Roman community: 'We are not only writing these things to you, beloved, for your admonition, but also to remind ourselves; for we are in the same arena, and the same struggle is before us' (7.1). Perhaps Clement alludes to the Corinthian (and Roman) debauchery when he writes, 'My Beloved ate and drank, was enlarged, waxed fat and kicked. From this arose jealousy and envy, strife and sedition...'(3.1-2 quoting Deut. 32.15). Whether the passage is meant to refer to specific sins of drunkenness[1] and over-feasting cannot be determined.

In Paul's letter to the Romans, however, there is more explicit

1. Cf. 30.1.

reference to the sins of κῶμος and μέθη with a stern warning that such behaviour is not appropriate to the time of impending crisis. Perhaps the apostle's concern gives added significance to his claim that 'the kingdom of God is not food and drink but righteousness, peace, and joy in the Holy Spirit' (14.17).[1] Inasmuch as Paul makes very few references to the kingdom of God, despite his conviction that the parousia was near, 1 Cor. 6.9-10 and Rom. 14.17 ought to be taken as representative of his partial acceptance of the ascetic ethics of the eschatologically-driven charismatics.[2] Implicit, then, is a criticism of the wealthy.

In the ethical section of his letter to the Romans, Paul addresses the worldly character of his readers, warning them not to be conformed to this age (12.2); instead they are to be transformed, renewed. This abandonment of worldly standards will have the immediate effect that the individual will not 'think of himself more highly than he ought to think' (12.3). Pride, even arrogance, is confronted explicitly in 12.16—'Live in harmony with one another; do not be haughty, but associate with the lowly; never be conceited'. Assuming that the apostle is aware of tensions between the rich and poor Christians in the Roman community,[3] at the very least he is opposed to any behaviour that stems from 'exalted rank'.[4]

Promoting the unity of the body, the apostle encourages those whose gift is to contribute, that they do so liberally (12.8). He appeals to them to be hospitable and to provide for the needs of the saints, presumably the poor in their *own* community, not for the Jerusalem Christians[5] (12.13). Yet, Paul's understanding of the purpose of this charity is, as in the case of the collection, for the sake of the unity and solidarity of the body.

1. See J.B. Lightfoot, *St Paul's Epistle to the Philippians* (Grand Rapids: Zondervan, 1953), p. 155; W. Sanday and A.C. Headlam, *The Epistle to the Romans* (New York: Charles Scribner's Sons, 1905), pp. 391-92.
2. Cf. Theissen, *Social Setting*, p. 36; *idem*, *Sociology*, p. 117. See also E. Troeltsch, *The Social Teaching of the Christian Churches* (London: George Allen & Unwin, 1949), I, pp. 84-85, on 'the combination of conservative and radical elements' in early Christian thought.
3. Lampe, *Die stadtrömischen Christen*, pp. 63-64.
4. Osiek, *Rich Christian*, p. 150; cf. Lampe, *Die stadtrömischen Christen*, p. 64.
5. Paul regards the collection for the Jerusalem saints as completed (15.25-28) and does not solicit Roman support.

The word κοινωνία, used in Rom. 15.26, 2 Cor. 8.4; 9.13, was well calculated to stress the note of fellowship, as in Rom. 12.13 the word κοινωνοῦντες...rather than the colorless διδόντες, emphasized the bond of fellowship that linked them together.[1]

That the affluent members of the Roman church had grown neglectful of their responsibilities, even falling into an abuse of eating and drinking,[2] because they had lost the hope/fear of an immediate return of Christ is suggested by 13.11-13.

> You know what hour it is, how it is full time now for you to wake from sleep. For salvation is nearer to us now than when we first believed. The night is far gone, the day is at hand. Let us then cast off the works of darkness and put on the armor of light. Let us conduct ourselves becomingly as in the day, not in reveling and drunkenness, not in debauchery and licentiousness, not in quarreling and jealousy (cf. 1 Thess. 5.2-8a).

It is possible to rediscover the tensions, due in part to the delay of the parousia, between rich and poor Christians in the Roman congregation by an analytical process, moving 'backwards' from the *Shepherd of Hermas* to Paul's letter to the Romans. Working in the opposite direction, constructively, 1 Corinthians, which reveals a similar conflict in that community, enables us to recognize the continuing problem as it is addressed by a Corinthian elder in *2 Clement*.

While the homilist does not explicitly condemn the sins of gluttony and drunkenness, he is certainly concerned with the temptations of worldly pleasure that have enticed his congregation. He acknowledges that he too is subject to similar desires (18.2). The elder is clearly upset about the sexual sin that has plagued his community (4.3; cf. 12.5), but he is far more anxious about the broader and more corrupting influence of the love of wealth. It is vital that his hearers become obedient to Christ, leading a 'holy and righteous life' and so learn to disregard τὰ κοσμικά, having no desire for them (5.6). Furthermore, the homily addresses the wealthy's indifference to the coming end.

The pleasures of the present will bring 'great torment' in the judgment to come (10.3-4). Worldly lusts and the 'passions of the soul' must be conquered (17.3, 7).[3]

---

1. Enslin, *Ethics*, p. 286.
2. It is ironic that Jesus was labelled a glutton and a drunkard.
3. This is the meaning of self-control in *2 Clem.* 15.1.

Now the world that is, and the world to come are two enemies. This world speaks of adultery, corruption, the love of money and deceit, but that world bids these things farewell.[1] We cannot then be the friends of both; but we must bid farewell to this world, to consort with that which is to come. We reckon that it is better to hate the things which are here, for they are little, short-lived and corruptible, but to love the things which are there, the good things which are incorruptible (6.3-6).

Immorality and greed both characterize this world, but the context of this passage indicates that it is especially worldliness and love of money that jeopardize the spiritual condition of the community: 'The Lord says, "No servant can serve two masters". If we desire to serve both God and Mammon it is unprofitable to us. *"For what is the advantage if a man gain the whole world but lose his soul?"'* (6.1-2; italics mine). Virtually echoing Paul's warning to the Corinthians, the homilist suggests that those who have fallen into such (post-baptismal) sin may not enter the kingdom of God with confidence (6.9).[2] Strikingly, the homilist asks rhetorically, 'Who shall be our advocate (παράκλητος) if we are not found to have pious and righteous works?' (6.9). It is reasonable to conjecture that the elder is warning the rich that their παράκλητοι will be of no use to them on the day of judgment (cf. *Did.* 5.2; *Barn.* 20.2).

To some degree the sins of the rich have resulted from their conviction that the parousia is only a distant threat. The homilist constantly calls them to repentance in the short time they have available (8.1-3; 9.7-8; 12.1; 17.1-4) and nowhere is his warning stronger than in 16.1-4 where he speaks of redemptive almsgiving.

Seeing, therefore, brethren, that we have received no small opportunity for repentance; let us, now that we have time, turn to the God who calls us, while we still have one who awaits us. For if we bid farewell to these pleasures and conquer our soul, by giving up its evil desires, we shall share in the mercy of Jesus. But you know that the day of judgment is already approaching as a burning oven[3] and some of the heavens shall melt, and the whole earth shall be as lead melting in the fire, and then shall

---

1. ἀποτάσσεται, cf. 16.2.
2. Bauer maintains that here τὸ βασίλειος = ἡ βασιλεία (*Greek–English Lexicon*, p. 135).
3. For the oven imagery, cf. 8.1-7.

be manifest the secret and open deeds of men.[1] Therefore almsgiving is
good as repentance from sin...

Almsgiving would be the immediate, practical demonstration that
the affluent are not consumed with a desire for wealth, a desire to gain
the whole world. To distribute from one's property for the sake of the
poor is to show love and righteousness, the prerequisite virtues for
entrance into the kingdom of God (9.6; 11.7; 12.1). Love for the
brotherhood is a quality sadly lacking in the homilist's community
(4.3; 13.4). Almsgiving, as an act of love, would cover a multitude of
sins (16.4).

Reprimanding the wealthy for their lack of compassion for the
poor, rebuking their love of money and announcing the imminence of
judgment, *2 Clement* echoes several significant themes in early
Christian literature and offers a clear perspective on the social and
theological tensions that first promoted the doctrine of redemptive
almsgiving.

Alongside the renewed hope/fear of the imminence of the parousia
was, of course, the warning of judgment that would come upon those
in the church who were guilty of sin, perhaps especially the rich who
had neglected the poor. There is no consolation and reassurance in the
primitive belief that Jesus died for sins once for all.[2] Post-baptismal
sin is to be punished; and the Apostolic Fathers announce the
terrifying prospect. This, then, is a second theological issue prompting
the emergence of the view that almsgiving provides a ransom for sin.

Within early Christian literature, there is one writing that is
certainly addressed to wealthy members of the church and regards
almsgiving as a means of redemption specifically for post-baptismal
sin. While this document suggests that a long history of reflection has
preceded the author's remarks, the Apostolic Fathers, on the other
hand—principally *2 Clement* and Hermas—reveal one of the earliest
stages in the formation of the doctrine. In these sources, in contrast to
Who is the Rich Man that shall be Saved?, redemptive almsgiving is
advocated for pressing social as well as theological reasons. At the

---

1. The homilist harshly warns that those who have not kept the seal of baptism,
those who have not heeded the elders' warnings, shall surely be punished for their
deeds. See the double citation of Isa. 66.24 in 7.6; 17.5-6.

2. The term ἅπας/ἐφάπαξ with reference to the sacrifice of Christ (cf. Rom.
6.10; Heb. 7.27, 9.12; 1 Pet. 3.18) is not found in the Apostolic Fathers.

same time, the crisis of post-baptismal sin contributes significantly to the needs and objectives of *2 Clement* and the *Shepherd of Hermas* and remained a prominent issue in early Christianity.

For Clement of Alexandria, the possession of property was *necessary* if one were to fulfil the commandments. Far from endorsing the abandonment of worldly goods, Clement advocates wise stewardship of one's wealth: 'How could one give food to the hungry and drink to the thirsty, clothe the naked and shelter the homeless, for not doing which he is threatened with fire and the outer darkness, if each man first divested himself of all these things?' (*Rich Man*, 13). The *Shepherd of Hermas* surely, directly or indirectly, influenced Clement's view.[1]

Clement regarded Christ's death as a sacrifice which 'paid the penalty for *former* sins'. Baptism is the crucial line of demarcation and for those who have fallen after the 'seal' of baptism and repent of their post-baptismal sin, there is the opportunity to redeem themselves by making a second repentance.[2] As in *2 Clement*, 1 Pet. 4.8 becomes a critical proof-text.

> Learn the 'more excellent way' to salvation which Paul shows. Love does not seek its own but is lavished upon the brother. For him love flutters with excitement, for him it is chastely wild. Love covers a multitude of sins...
>
> Even though a man be born in sins, and have done many of the works that are forbidden, if he but implant love in his soul, he is able, by increasing the love and by accepting pure repentance, to retrieve his failures. For if you understand who is the rich man that has no place in heaven, and also in what manner a man may so use his substance as to win his way to life through the censure and difficulties caused by wealth, and to be able to enjoy the eternal things...[3]

For the wealthy, love manifests itself in almsgiving. Through the distribution of their riches to the needy, the affluent purchase friends by means of unrighteous mammon. Clement of Alexandria, apparently inspired by the idea found in Hermas—namely, that the poor intercede

---

1. Cf. *Herm. Sim.* 1.8-9, '...for this reason did the Master make you rich'.

2. *Rich Man* 23 (italics mine), 39-40; *Stromata* 2.13.

3. Clement, *Rich Man* 38-39. Cf. 'Love bursts forth in good works', *Rich Man* 28; 'riches are to be bestowed lovingly', *Paedagogus* 3.6.

for the rich—is a staunch advocate of redemptive almsgiving.[1] The rich man is praised for taking the kingdom of God by force through his own benevolence.[2]

While being alert to the dangers of anachronisms, it seems nevertheless reasonable to argue that *2 Clement* and the *Shepherd of Hermas* offer a view of the early development of the themes in Clement of Alexandria's *Who is the Rich Man that shall be Saved?* Within the context of early Christian beliefs about baptism, this hypothesis is all the more tenable.

Tertullian, a contemporary of Clement of Alexandria, also wrestled with the problem of post-baptismal sin. For Tertullian, the repentance that precedes baptism should lead to 'the abolition of former sins'.[3] That repentance ought never to be 'cancelled by the repetition of sin'.[4] Baptism then brings the remission of sin but the baptized believer is obligated to live a new life. For Tertullian, baptism initiates a new birth and without baptism, salvation is impossible.[5] Still, Tertullian is aware that post-baptismal sin is a sad reality in the church; grudgingly he writes,

> Although the gate of forgiveness has been shut and fastened up with the bar of baptism, [God] has permitted it still to stand somewhat open. In the vestibule he has stationed the second repentance for opening to such as knock; but now once for all because now for the second time.[6]

In the mid-second century, Justin maintained the optimistic doctrine that baptism not only brought the forgiveness of *former* sins but guaranteed the 'regeneration' of those who entered the water; they are born again.[7] Justin's claims reflect the attitude (and hope) of the New Testament. As Clement of Alexandria and Tertullian had believed that baptism brought the remission of sins and was intended to mark the beginning of a new life, Justin and the New Testament provide

1. *Rich Man* 13; 31-32; 33-34 (cf. *Herm. Sim.* 1.8-9; 2.4-10); 35; cf. especially, 'O excellent trading! What divine business! One purchases immortality for money', *Rich Man* 32.

2. *Rich Man* 21; *Paedagogus* 3.7.

3. Tertullian, *On Repentance*, ch. 2.

4. *On Repentance*, ch. 5.

5. See Tertullian, *On Baptism*, chs. 1–2; 6; 12; 18; 20.

6. *On Repentance*, ch. 7; for Tertullian on redemptive almsgiving, see *On Patience*, ch. 7.

7. *Apology*, chs. 61, 66.

indisputable evidence that such a theology of baptism was widespread in early Christianity. On this basis, it is justifiable to regard 2 *Clement* and the *Shepherd of Hermas* as significant points in the growing awareness of—and consequent developments from—the crisis of post-baptismal sin.

When Paul rebukes the Corinthians for their conduct and lifestyle which will keep them from inheriting the kingdom of God, he is horrified that those who have been baptized are falling back into their former sin (1 Cor. 6.9-11). It was the apostle's expectation that those who had been baptized would lead new lives by the power of the Spirit (cf. Rom. 6.1-14).

The author of Colossians closely associates baptism, the forgiveness of sins[1] and the new ('resurrected') life of the believer (Col. 2.12-14). Titus 3.5 indicates a belief in baptismal regeneration and 1 Peter regards baptism as essential to salvation; after baptism one should 'cease from sinning' (3.21–4.4). A long list of Christian virtues is given in 2 Peter with the harsh warning that those who do not show these qualities are blind, having forgotten the cleansing of their former sins. The kingdom is open only to those who keep their baptism pure (1.3-11). One must be fit for the kingdom of God (cf. 1 Cor. 6.9-11).

Initially, early Christianity (or some quarters) held to stern view that post-baptismal sin was unforgivable. Such is the clear position of the epistle to the Hebrews (6.4-6; cf. 10.26-31).[2] The *Shepherd of Hermas*, while intending to modify such a strict attitude, nevertheless endorses its appropriateness.[3]

> 'I have heard, Sir', said I, 'from some teachers that there is no second repentance beyond the one given when we went down into the water and received remission of our former sins'. He said to me, 'You have heard correctly, for that is so. For he who has received remission of sin ought never to sin again, but to live in purity' (*Herm. Man.* 4.3.1-2).

---

1. For the view that baptism brings the remission of sins, see Acts 2.38; 22.16; cf. Eph. 5.26; Heb. 10.22; *Barn.* 11.11; 16.8; *Herm. Man.* 4.3.1; *Herm. Sim.* 9.16.3-4.
2. Cf. K. Lake, 'The Shepherd of Hermas and Christian Life in Rome in the Second Century', *HTR* 4 (1911), pp. 25-46 (29). For Hermas's view of baptism, see pp. 28-30 of Lake's article. See also *Didascalia* 2.7.
3. Lampe, *Die stadtrömischen Christen*, p. 76.

While this stern ethic is re-affirmed, Hermas yet reveals a message of opportunity for those who have fallen.[1] After baptism, if a man is 'tempted by the devil' and sins, he is permitted one repentance. There is, however, a warning: 'If he sin and repent repeatedly, it is unprofitable for such a man, for scarcely shall he live' (*Herm. Man.* 4.3.6).[2]

Clearly, the *Shepherd of Hermas* is directed to those who are guilty of post-baptismal sin, calling them to a second repentance that will bring them remission for their sins. At the same time we have seen that Hermas addresses the wealthy Christians who have neglected, even abused, the poor of his community. Redemptive almsgiving is the vital solution to his dual concerns.

In a strikingly similar fashion, *2 Clement* is a homily from an elder who has authority among the rich Christians in Corinth. He too is distressed that the affluent have shown no love for their needy brethren. He rebukes the wealthy for their obsession with gain, their love of money. Even more the homilist is horrified that they have broken the seal of baptism. Again, redemptive almsgiving provides the elder with a single answer to meet the two crises threatening his community.

The *Shepherd of Hermas* and *2 Clement*, roughly contemporary documents, lay the essential theological groundwork for the position that would later become the sanctioned belief of the church, that almsgiving is as good as repentance from sin.[3] Clement of Alexandria's *Who is the Rich Man that shall be Saved?* represents a more developed, reasoned treatise on the subject; yet his argumentation is rooted in the teaching of Hermas and may have been influenced by *2 Clement* as well. Clement of Alexandria, however, writes with virtually no sense of eschatological urgency. It is not apparent that he responds to a crisis, social or theological. He presents his case as one who has the unhurried luxury of reflection and debate. This is not to fault his position but to contrast his situation with that of Hermas and the elder.

Tensions between wealthy and poor Christians created conflicts in

---

1. Cf. *Did.* 16.2; 4.6. One must be perfect but you can supply your own ransom for sin.
2. Cf. Clement of Alexandria, *Stromata*, 2.13.
3. Cf. Origen, *Homilies on Leviticus*, 2.4; Cyprian, *On Works and Almsgiving* 1–6.

both the Roman and Corinthian communities of the first and early second centuries CE. This social stratification was aggravated by a theological problem: the delay of the parousia led the rich into a deeper involvement with this world and a growing neglect of their responsibilities within the body of Christ. This disobedience was perceived as a tragic, even blasphemous, breaking of the seal of baptism. As early Christianity wrestled with numerous issues, including support for the needy and the crisis of post-baptismal sin, redemptive almsgiving emerged as the critical doctrine that would prompt the rich to provide for the needy and to offer a means of redeeming sins committed after being washed of former sins. While redemptive almsgiving has roots in the Apocrypha, the New Testament and the *Doctrina*, and emerges in Polycarp, the *Didache*, and *Barnabas*, it is with *2 Clement* and the *Shepherd of Hermas* that the doctrine becomes a significant theme, addressing social and theological concerns of the community.

c. *Summary*

The Jesus movement, largely motivated by an expectation of the imminent end of the world, demanded a renunciation of property as a necessary requirement of discipleship. All bonds with this world were to be severed. Material wealth was to be distributed to the poor and this almsgiving would be amply rewarded in the coming kingdom of God.

The wandering charismatics of the Jesus movement were dependent on the charity and hospitality of many who retained the bulk of their riches. Alongside the ethic of renunciation there grew up a second standard, the compassionate use of wealth for the followers of Jesus, meeting their material needs. This too would be rewarded in the kingdom of God.

This latter feature of the Jesus movement was adopted in early Christianity under the ethic of love-patriarchalism. As a community rather than an individual principle, love-patriarchalism required the wealthy to support the needy members of their congregation. Love was regarded as the highest virtue of the faith and came to be seen as redemptive, covering a multitude of sins.

In early Christianity the doctrine of redemptive almsgiving evolved in major communities of believers, shaped by changing social and theological issues. Above all, the tension between rich and poor Christians and the crisis of post-baptismal sin (particularly where there was a fear of imminent judgment) contributed to the formation of the doctrine.

Yet the doctrine was certainly not central to the primitive teaching of the church. Indeed, the idea of redemptive almsgiving is in many respects incompatible with the earliest soteriology of Christianity: that Jesus died for sins once for all. Consequently, the widespread acceptance of the new doctrine and the fact that it is not criticized in any extant sources from the period suggest that among those who first advocated redemptive almsgiving were some who held positions of considerable authority in the church of the early empire.

This leads to a consideration of the role of the church at Rome in the development of the doctrine.

Chapter 7

THE ROMAN CHURCH AND THE DEVELOPING DOCTRINE

'Almsgiving was a classic means of atoning for sin, and the appeal to give alms for this reason is a commonplace in patristic literature of every period.'[1] Even in the first half of the second century CE the doctrine of redemptive almsgiving was gaining broad acceptance within the church. Polycarp, as the bishop of Smyrna, testifies to its presence in Asia Minor and through his letter Philippi was at the very least introduced to the idea. *2 Clement* indicates that the belief was strongly held in Corinth. The *Shepherd of Hermas* demonstrates that the Roman church believed that giving to the poor merited the forgiveness of post-baptismal sin. Finally, the pervasive influence of the Two Ways tradition reveals that redemptive almsgiving was taught in Christian communities from Alexandria to Syria.[2]

It remains to be considered, however, whether there is a specific cause for the extraordinary emergence of this idea throughout early Christianity over a fairly wide geographical area. Is it mere coincidence or was there some source or authority which both sanctioned and legitimated a doctrine which contradicts the central claim of the New Testament, that Jesus died for sins once for all?

The redemptive almsgiving of Polycarp and the Two Ways tradition does not seem to be central to the concerns of the authors and we may trace the roots of the doctrine here to the Septuagint and/or Jewish paraenesis. Its appearance in *Christian* texts, however, warrants some explanation. Still, the almost parenthetical nature of the references

---

1. B. Ramsey, 'Almsgiving in the Latin Church: The Late Fourth and Early Fifth Centuries', *TS* 43 (1982), p. 241.

2. Depending where *Barnabas* and *Didache* were composed and how widespread the influence of *Doctrina* was.

makes such an analysis difficult. Our attention is drawn instead to the explicit and emphatic claims of *2 Clem.* 16.4 which are critical to the homily's purpose. Is the elder an innovator of Christian doctrine, or is he dependent upon an earlier (or contemporary) movement that has in some way been 'approved' by the broader church of the empire? Is the citation of 1 Pet. 4.8—a *Christian* passage which may allude as well to the Hebrew scriptures—significant as a proof-text for the doctrine? If so, what is the history (and justification) for such an interpretation of the phrase, 'love covers a multitude of sins?' Finally, inasmuch as *2 Clement* and the *Shepherd of Hermas* both reveal an anxiety for the repentance (and redemption) of post-baptismal sin and warn against the dangers of love of money, urging almsgiving as a necessary demonstration of good works, what is the relationship between the two documents?

2 Clement and the *Shepherd of Hermas* both lead us to consider the church at Rome. The homily, written for the Corinthian community, was influenced by *1 Clement* (which was written from Rome), and it is to be expected that the author as an elder in his congregation was aware of and attentive to the Roman church.[1] The *Shepherd of Hermas* bears directly on the question because it was composed in Rome (*Herm. Vis.* 1.1.1; 2.1.1; 4.1.2).[2] I will attempt, then, to trace the emergence of the doctrine of redemptive almsgiving in the church at Rome and its parallel development in Corinth leading to *2 Clem.* 16.4.

While it would be of great interest to know how the Roman church was founded (and such information would surely be instructive for this analysis), unfortunately virtually nothing is known about the origins of the Christian community in Rome. We can at best conjecture that the gospel was first taken to the capital of the empire by Jewish Christians.[3] Even this, though plausible, is uncertain.

The apostle Paul's letter to the Romans is our earliest source

---

1. For the influence of the Roman community even in the early second century, see R.A. Aytoun, *City Centres of Early Christianity* (London: Hodder & Stoughton, 1915), pp. 205-21; Brown and Meier, *Antioch and Rome*, pp. 132-33; Goppelt, *Apostolic*, p. 126.

2. Brown and Meier, *Antioch and Rome*, p. 203.

3. Cf. Brown and Meier, *Antioch and Rome*, pp. 92-104; Aytoun, *City Centres*, pp. 207-10; L.W. Barnard, 'The Early Roman Church, *ATR* 49 (1967), pp. 371-84.

regarding that community.[1] There is some dispute as to Paul's specific knowledge of the congregation,[2] but the letter itself reveals a concern that the more affluent members provide for the poorer members. Paul was alert to a social stratification within the Roman community.[3] Consequently, he encourages liberality, sharing and hospitality; he calls on the wealthy to be humble and to identify with the lowly (12.3-16). This is set in a context of a strong love ethic. 'Let love be genuine...love one another with brotherly affection; outdo one another in showing honour...He who loves his neighbour has fulfilled the law' (12.9-10; 13.8-10). The letter to the Romans establishes for that community the high priority of ἀγάπη as the standard of Christian behaviour.[4] Hospitality and concern for the poor were to be essential features of that love.

Paul's letter to the Romans also introduces the rigorous view that baptism is a spiritual line of demarcation. When the believer is baptized, he is set free from sin and should never again submit to its power.

> Are we to continue in sin that grace may abound? By no means! How can we who died to sin still live in it? Do you not know that all of us who have been baptised into Christ Jesus were baptised into his death. We were buried therefore with him by baptism, so that as Christ was raised from the dead by the glory of the Father, we too might walk in newness of life...
>
> We know that our old self was crucified with him so that the sinful body might be destroyed, and we might no longer be enslaved to sin. For he who has died is freed from sin... So you also must consider yourselves dead to sin and alive to God in Christ Jesus.
>
> Let not sin therefore reign in your mortal bodies, to make you obey their passions. Do not yield your members to sin as instruments of wickedness, but yield yourselves to God as men who have been brought from death to life, and your members to God as instruments of righteousness. For sin will have no dominion over you, since you are not under law but

---

1. Cf. W.A. Sanday and A.C. Headlam, *The Epistle to the Romans* (New York: Charles Scribner's Sons, 1905), p. xiii.
2. See the discussion in Brown and Meier, *Antioch and Rome*, pp. 105-11.
3. Lampe, *Die stadtrömischen Christen*, p. 63.
4. Cf. Ignatius's comment in the introduction of his epistle to that community: 'to the church...pre-eminent in love'. See also, Eusebius, *Ecclesiastical History* 4.23.10, '...as a loving father...'

under grace. What then? Are we to sin because we are not under law but under grace? By no means! (6.1-15)

Paul himself is largely responsible for the widespread belief that through baptism the believer is liberated from the power and effects of sin. Early Christianity (and certainly the church at Rome) embraced the promise that baptism served as the 'method of entry' to eternal life, to becoming a 'new creature', gaining release from evil spirits and being washed of one's sins.[1]

The epistle known as 1 Peter in all probability was written from Rome in the second half of the first century.[2] In this letter we find further evidence that the Roman community held both a high view of baptism and a commitment to a love ethic which should govern Christian behaviour. Thus it is in Rome that the church first adopts the position that 'love covers a multitude of sins'.[3] As Paul had declared to the Romans that love for neighbour fulfilled the Law,[4] the community apparently came to regard love as meritorious and even redemptive, perhaps looking to Prov. 10.12 as a proof-text.

1 Peter calls its readers to a genuine love (cf. Rom. 12.9),[5] a love that will open hearts and homes and inspire a sharing of gifts for others. It is likely that one of the gifts the author has in mind is that of liberality (cf. Rom. 12.4-8).

> Above all[6] hold unfailing your love for one another, since love covers a multitude of sins. Practice hospitality ungrudgingly to one another. As each has received a gift, employ it for one another, as good stewards of God's varied grace (4.8-10).

1. Lake, 'Shepherd of Hermas and Christian Life in Rome', p. 27.

2. Lake, 'Shepherd of Hermas and Christian Life in Rome', p. 31; Brown and Meier, *Antioch and Rome*, p. 130 (see Eusebius, *Ecclesiastical History* 2.15.2); C.E.B. Cranfield, *The First Epistle of Peter* (London: SCM Press, 1950), p. 10; B. Reicke, *The Epistles of James, Peter and Jude* (Garden City, NY: Doubleday, 1964), pp. 72, 134.

3. Perhaps there was some attention given to Paul's earlier use of Ps. 32.1-2— 'Blessed are those whose iniquities are forgiven, and whose *sins are covered*; blessed is the man against whom the Lord will not reckon his sin' (Rom. 4.7-8).

4. This in turn can be traced to the teaching of Jesus. See Mt. 7.12; 22.39-40.

5. Rom. 12.9—ἡ ἀγάπη ἀνυπόκριτος; 1 Pet. 1.22—φιλαδελφία ἀνυπόκριτον.

6. I.e. of top priority—πρὸ πάντων.

The epistle adopts Paul's description of baptism as a participation in the suffering/death of Christ that should (because Christ is raised from the dead) free the believer from the power of sin.

> [Noah and his companions on the ark] were saved through water. Baptism, which corresponds to this, now saves you, not as a removal of dirt from the body but as an appeal to God for a clear conscience, through the resurrection of Jesus Christ... Since therefore Christ suffered in the flesh, arm yourselves with the same thought, for whoever has suffered in the flesh has ceased from sin, so as to live for the rest of the time in the flesh no longer by human passions but by the will of God. Let the time that is past suffice for doing what the Gentiles like to do... (3.21–4.3)

Sometime during the last quarter of the first century, the Roman church became familiar with the so-called letter to the Hebrews. While it is not known whether the community at Rome was the epistle's original destination,[1] *1 Clement* clearly reveals a familiarity with its contents.[2] The letter to the Hebrews must then have influenced the Roman community; the *Shepherd of Hermas* provides further confirmation of that influence.[3] The problem of post-baptismal sin is critical to the epistle. The author pronounces such a return to wickedness as 'unforgivable'[4] and warns that a second repentance is impossible (6.4-8; 10.26-29). Hermas specifically addresses this issue which troubled the Roman congregation.

Hebrews also reinforces the love ethic, calling its readers to share and sympathize with other Christians. The author implies that God acknowledges and is even appeased by such sacrifices. Despite his harsh warning against post-baptismal sin, the author writes,

> Though we speak thus, yet in your case, beloved, we feel sure of better things that belong to salvation. For God is not so unjust as to overlook your work and the *love* which you showed for his sake in serving the saints, as you still do (6.9-10; italics mine).

In his final instructions, he stresses the responsibility of helping those in need.

---

1. For a brief discussion, see Brown and Maier, *Antioch and Rome*, pp. 139-51.
2. *1 Clem.* 17.1 // Heb. 11.37; *1 Clem.* 17.5 // Heb. 3.5; *1 Clem.* 36.2-5 // Heb. 1.3-13; Brown and Maier, *Antioch and Rome*, p. 147.
3. Goodspeed and Grant, *History*, pp. 30-31.
4. Lake, 'The Shepherd of Hermas and Christian Life in Rome', p. 29.

> Let brotherly love continue. Do not neglect to show hospitality to strangers, for thereby some have entertained angels unawares. Remember those who are in prison, as though in prison with them; and those who are ill-treated, since you also are in the body...
>
> Keep your life free from love of money and be content with what you have... Do not neglect to do good and to share what you have, for such sacrifices are pleasing to God (13.1-3, 5, 16).

The beliefs reflected in 1 Peter, were strengthened in the letter to the Hebrews. The Christian community at Rome came to hold a despairing view of post-baptismal sin but found hope in the promise that God would not overlook works of love for the saints, that hospitality would be rewarded, that sharing was a sacrifice: 'Love covers a multitude of sins'.

The love ethic and the promise that love is redemptive are stressed in *1 Clement*. Indeed the ἀγάπη principle as a standard for community relationships in post-apostolic Christianity receives its 'finest testimony' in chs. 49 and 50 of the epistle.[1] As we have seen, Clement was concerned not only to restore the Corinthian presbyters to office but to reconcile the bitterly divided rich and poor factions of the church. It is his prayer that they[2] will be restored to the 'holy and seemly practice of brotherly love' (48.1). The hymn to love follows almost immediately, and even before citing 1 Corinthians 13, Clement quotes 1 Pet. 4.8—'love covers a multitude of sins' (49.5).

The use of this proof-text is intended to support the claim that love as a Christian virtue is a prerequisite condition for entering the kingdom of God. Love is redemptive.

> Let us then beg and pray of his mercy that we may be found in love, without human partisanship, free from blame. All the generations from Adam until this day have passed away; but those who were perfected in love by the grace of God have a place among the pious who shall be made manifest at the visitation of the kingdom of Christ... Blessed are we, beloved, if we perform the commandments of God in the concord of love, that *through love our sins may be forgiven* (50.2-3, 5).

The very next verse (50.6 citing Rom. 4.7) provides further proof that Clement interprets 1 Pet. 4.8 to refer to a means of redemption. 'For it is written, "Blessed are they whose iniquities are forgiven, and

---

1. G. Quell and E. Stauffer, 'ἀγαπάω', *TDNT*, I, p. 54.
2. Actually, he includes his own community, using the first person!

whose *sins are covered*"' (italics mine): love covers a multitude of (post-baptismal) sins.

While the theme of Christian love is quite broad, the practical application of this ethic—the demonstration of love—was to be found chiefly in works of compassion, including hospitality and almsgiving. The background of Romans, 1 Peter and Hebrews gives this context to Clement's remarks. More specifically, *1 Clement* is concerned that 'the strong care for the weak' and 'the rich man bestow help on the poor' (38.2). The social stratification and dissolution of the Corinthian community prompt the epistle's instruction. Emerging in the church at Rome was a doctrine of redemptive love which showed itself in almsgiving. Within Rome this was more fully developed in the *Shepherd of Hermas*, driven by an anxiety for post-baptismal sin.

The Corinthian elder, inspired by *1 Clement* understandably embraced the text, 'love covers a multitude of sins', and applied it more directly and forcefully to the crisis in his community: the (post-baptismal) sin of the wealthy and their disregard for the poor.

The homilist, however, was of course heavily influenced by the Christian tradition based in Corinth as well as by the epistle from the Roman church. Along this Corinthian trajectory we also find a prominent love ethic and attention to the responsibility of helping the poor. Paul's letters clearly authorized the priority of love (1 Cor. 13.1–14.1a) and providing for the needy was proof that love was genuine (2 Cor. 8.8, 24). Regular giving was to be practised (1 Cor. 16.2) and such charity would be rewarded by God (2 Cor. 9.6-11). Both the Roman and Corinthian communities were called by their traditions to a high standard of ἀγάπη, to a love which would show itself in good deeds, especially to the weak and the poor. Such love would reap a harvest of righteousness, covering a multitude of sins.

Paul's correspondence with the Corinthians played a major role in alerting the homilist to the danger of post-baptismal sin.

> Do you not know that the unrighteous will not inherit the kingdom of God? Do not be deceived; neither the immoral...nor adulterers... nor thieves, nor the greedy...will inherit the kingdom of God. And such were some of you. But you were washed... (1 Cor. 6.9-11).

The homilist echoes this passage when he writes, '...with what confidence shall we enter into the kingdom of God if we do not keep our baptism pure and undefiled? Or who shall be our advocate if we are found not to have pious and righteous works?' (*2 Clem.* 6.9).

The *Shepherd of Hermas* and *2 Clement* reveal that similar tensions—both social and theological—were disrupting the Christian communities in Rome and Corinth in the early second century. That these two writings come to remarkably similar solutions suggests that the two churches were in frequent contact and influenced each other's developing doctrine. Redemptive almsgiving emerged, principally from Rome, in response to the material and spiritual needs of these congregations. It was, to a large degree, the influence of the Roman church that legitimated the doctrine of redemptive almsgiving in early Christianity.

Appendix A

THE *DIDACHE*, *BARNABAS*, AND *DOCTRINA*

Concerning *Barnabas* and the *Didache*, James Muilenburg wrote over fifty years ago: 'No single question of early Christian literature outside of the New Testament has been more discussed and more controverted than that of the bearing of the one writing upon the other'.[1] While this issue has remained controversial, a consensus has begun to emerge. Recently, scholars have tended to agree that both the *Didache* and *Barnabas* are 'evolved literature', final products of several authors/editors/redactors who used recoverable (yet still hypothetical) sources.[2] The detailed history of this analysis in the interpretation of *Barnabas* has been well summarized by Pierre Prigent.[3] J.P. Audet has reviewed recent research on the *Didache*.[4]

It is common to regard the extant *Didache* as a developed merging of the 'Two Ways' material (chs. 1–6) and the 'church manual' section (chs. 7–15). The eschatological chapter (16) may have come from yet a different source.[5] Inasmuch as it is virtually certain that the document known as the *Didache* was a finished product in the second century CE, it is appropriate for us to consider the work as a loose unit.

Consistent with the New Testament and several of the Apostolic Fathers, the *Didache* promotes a love-ethic. Such is the standard of Christian living: love is *the* characteristic that defines the way of life. 'First, you shall love the God who made you, secondly (love) your neighbour as yourself' (1.2).

Almost immediately, the *Didache* identifies almsgiving (ἐλεημοσύνη) as one of the principal commandments which must be fulfilled if one is to be 'innocent' (ἀθῷος, 1.5). This text is strikingly similar to *Herm. Man.* 2.6: 'He who gives is innocent (ἀθῷος)'. This parallel tradition lends further support to the view that in early Christianity there was a widespread belief that almsgiving was meritorious. The love ethic was to be realized in an unselfish giving that would be rewarded by God.

---

1. J. Muilenburg, *The Literary Relations of the Epistle of Barnabas and the Teaching of the Twelve Apostles* (Marburg, 1929), p. 3.
2. R.A. Kraft, *The Apostolic Fathers*. III. *Barnabas and the Didache* (New York: Thomas Nelson & Sons, 1965), p. 1
3. P. Prigent, *L'épître de Barnabé I–XVI et ses sources* (Paris: Le Coffre, 1961), pp. 11-16.
4. J.P. Audet, *La Didache* (Paris: Galbalda, 1958), pp. 1-21.
5. Cf. Kraft, *Apostolic Fathers*, III, pp. 12-16.

Obedience to all the commandments was necessary if one was to achieve perfection (6.2, cf. 1.4), and the stern warning is given, 'The whole time of your faith shall not profit unless you are found perfect at the last (day)' (16.2).[1] The eschatological urgency of the final edition of the *Didache* provokes an anxiety for perfection[2] and for the innocence achieved through following the commandments. The editor is concerned with those sins committed after one has become a Christian; one still must fear the way of death. Significantly, he adapts earlier tradition that promises a reward for the giving of alms. For the *Didache*, the redemptive efficacy of almsgiving is vital for those who are not perfect. From the Two Ways source, both the *Didache* and *Barnabas* preserve and endorse the early Christian doctrine of redemptive almsgiving.

Be not one who stretches out his hands to receive but shuts them when it comes to giving. Of whatsoever you have gained by your hands you shall give a ransom for your sins. You shall not hesitate to give, nor shall you grumble when you give for you shall know who is the good paymaster of the reward. You shall not turn away the needy but shall share everything with your brother and you shall not say that it is your own. For if you are sharers in the imperishable, how much more in the things which perish? (*Did. 4.5-8*)

You shall share all things with your neighbor and you shall not say that it is your own. For if you are sharers in that which is incorruptible, how much more in that which is corruptible? You shall not be forward to speak, for the mouth is a snare to death. So far as you can, you shall keep your soul pure. Be not one who stretches out his hands to receive but shuts them when it comes to giving. You shall love, as the apple of your eye, all who speak the word of the Lord to you. You shall remember the day of judgment day and night and you shall seek each day the presence of the saints either labouring by speech, and going out to exhort, and striving to save souls by the word, or working with your hands for the ransom of your sins. You shall not hesitate to give, nor shall you grumble when you give, but you shall know who is the good paymaster of the reward. (*Barn. 19.8-11*)

The similarity of the passage in the *Didache* to that in *Barnabas* is apparent with striking parallels. Indeed, the Two Ways sections of both documents exhibit so many coincidences in theme, wording and grammar that scholars agree that some literary relationship exists between them. To trace the development of the doctrine of redemptive almsgiving in early Christianity, some conclusions (and assumptions) must be made about how the *Didache* and *Barnabas* are related. My concern is the question of literary dependence between the two documents and more particularly the relationship between *Did. 4.5-8* and *Barn. 19.8-11*.

That some literary connection exists at this point is self-evident. Yet, on the one hand, most scholars maintain that *Barnabas* could not be derived from the *Didache*.

---

1. Cf. *Barn.* 4.9.
2. Quite in contrast to 6.2: '. . . if you cannot, do what you can'!

Kraft insists that virtually all the evidence is against 'the hypothesis that *Barnabas* took its Two Ways material from the *Didache*'.[1] On the other hand, the suggestion that the Two Ways tradition in the *Didache* was taken from *Barnabas* is implausible.[2] The latter alternative is made more unlikely because *Barnabas* 18–20 is almost certainly a late addition to the original document.[3] Significantly, the Latin manuscript from St Petersburg ends with ch. 17; it does not know the Two Ways tradition in *Barnabas*.[4] Inasmuch as this material must be an editor's appendix to the epistle, the theory that the *Didache* was dependent on *Barnabas* for this tradition is forced to assume that the *Didache* was written quite late. Kraft comments on the two possibilities of direct literary dependence: 'The difficulty, if not impossibility of either of these alternatives is reason enough to invoke the aid of a hypothetical common source'.[5] The definition of a 'common source' need not refer to a document that both the *Didache* and *Barnabas*'s editors used. Kraft prefers to caution that the Two Ways material is 'common' to their traditions but seems to lie at some distance in the 'shadowy background'.[6]

E.J. Goodspeed has been more optimistic in identifying the Two Ways source common to *Barnabas* and the *Didache*. He has argued with some force that the ancient document known to us as the *Doctrina* is in fact a Latin translation of the original Greek source used in the *Didache* and *Barnabas*. A 1945 article details Goodspeed's theory. He maintains that 'a short Greek Didache' was written early in the second century CE. It is now known only in a Latin translation as *De Doctrina*. *Barnabas* 1–17 was written roughly twenty years later (130 CE), and perhaps twenty years after that our extant *Didache* was developed from the original *Doctrina* source. The last stage, Goodspeed suggests, was the expansion of *Barnabas*, the epistle being appended with the same 'primitive Didache'.[7] This hypothesis is found as well in Goodspeed's edition of the Apostolic Fathers.[8]

The possibility that the *Doctrina* is a Latin version of the common source underlying the Two Ways tradition in the *Didache* and *Barnabas* is an attractive thesis that warrants consideration. It supplies a straightforward answer to the question why the *Didache* states, 'There are two ways, one of life and one of death' (1.1) while *Barnabas* claims, 'There are two ways. . . one of light and one of darkness' (18.1). Any view of direct literary dependence between these two documents must regard the change as unexpected, even inexplicable; yet the *Doctrina*, as a common source,

---

1. Kraft, *Apostolic Fathers*, III, p. 7.
2. Kraft, *Apostolic Fathers*, III, p. 8.
3. Prigent succinctly claims, 'Barn 18-20 met evidemment en oeuvre un document particular'; *L'épître de Barnabé*, p. 12.
4. For an early interpretation of this fact, see P. Schaff, *The Teaching of the Twelve Apostles* (New York: Funk and Wagnalls, 1886), p. 227. More recently, see E.J. Goodspeed, *A History of Early Christian Literature* (rev. R.M. Grant; Chicago: University of Chicago Press, 1966), p. 21.
5. Kraft, *Apostolic Fathers*, III, p. 8.
6. Kraft, *Apostolic Fathers*, III, p. 9.
7. E.J. Goodspeed, 'The Didache, Barnabas, and the Doctrina', *ATR* 28 (1945), p. 228.
8. E.J. Goodspeed, *The Apostolic Fathers* (New York: Harper & Brothers, 1950), pp. 1-3, 285-86.

146   *Redemptive Almsgiving in Early Christianity*

would offer a remarkable explanation. It begins with the statement, 'There are two ways in the world, that of life and that of death, of light and of darkness' (1.1). If the *Doctrina* tradition were the so-called missing link between *Barnabas* and *Didache*, the difference in how the later documents begin their Two Ways sections is not a serious difficulty at all.

Goodspeed's theory has met with some approval among scholars. There has been a clear hesitancy, however, to embrace the original *Doctrina* as the common source for the Two Ways material in *Barnabas* and the *Didache*. Both Kraft and Prigent (citing Audet) prefer the more cautious hypothesis that the *Doctrina* is a version of the Two Ways tradition that is more primitive than that found in either the *Didache* or *Barnabas*. Each document offers us a 'glimpse' of the developing paraenesis.[1]

There is general agreement then that the *Doctrina* offers evidence of ethical teaching in the early Christianity which pre-dates the Apostolic Fathers. Audet claims that the *Doctrina* even preserves much of the original Jewish characteristics of its own source. Consequently, the fact that *Doctrina* advocates redemptive almsgiving is of vital significance. The doctrine of the redemption of sin through the distributing of alms can be traced to a stage in early Christianity prior to its appearance in *Barnabas* and the *Didache*. We are a step closer to the apostolic period of the church.[2]

The relevant passage from the *Doctrina* is cited here using Goodspeed's text and translation.

Noli esse ad accipiendum extendens manum et ad reddendum subtrahens. Si habes per manus tuas redemptionem peccatorum, non dubitabis dare, nec dans murmuraveris (corr.) sciens quia (quis?) sit hujus mercedis bonus redditor. Non avertes te ab egente (4.5-8).

Do not keep stretching out your hands to receive and drawing them back when it comes to returning. If through your hands you have earned a ransom for your sins, you shall not hesitate to give it nor grumble when you give for you know who is the good payer of such wages, You shall not turn away from the needy . . . (4.5-8).

Part of Goodspeed's thesis is based on his claim that the *Doctrina* ought not to be regarded as a Latin translation of the *Didache*.[3] Although brief, the passage quoted above provides evidence to support Goodspeed's contention. The Latin text does not really correspond, as a translation, to the extant Greek *Didache* although the text strongly resembles the *Didache* in content.[4]

The term *reddendum* implies repayment of giving back, which is certainly not implicit in δοῦναι of *Didache* 4.5. Yet where the *Didache* commands, 'You shall not

1. Kraft, *Apostolic Fathers*, III, pp. 9, 65; Prignet, *Epître de Barnabé* (Paris: Cerf, 1971), pp. 17-20; cf. L.W. Barnard, 'The Epistle of Barnabas in its Jewish Setting', in *Studies in Church History and Patristics* (Thessaloniki: Patriarchal Institute for Patristic Studies, 1978), p. 96; Goodspeed and Grant, *History*, p. 12.
2. Audet's claim that the *Didache* was written before 70 CE would, of course, take us back even further!
3. Goodspeed, *The Apostolic Fathers*, p. 2.
4. I gratefully acknowledge the helpful suggestions of Dr. Dwight Castro, Professor of Greek and Latin at Westminster College, New Wilmington, Pennsylvania.

hesitate to give' (δοῦναι, 4.7), the *Doctrina* parallel uses the expected *dare*. In trying to reconstruct the original text of which the *Doctrina* is the Latin translation, it is reasonable to conjecture that the Greek verb ἀποδίδωμι underlies the term *reddendum* in *Doctrina*.

While the *Didache* makes it quite clear and specific that one is to work in order to give a ransom for one's sins (δώσεις λύτρωσιν ἁμαρτιῶν σου οὐ διστάσεις δοῦναι...4.6-7), the *Doctrina* makes a subtle distinction implying that earned wages are a ransom for sin even before they are given as alms. 'If through your hands you have a ransom for (your) sins, do not hesitate to give.' The distinction is minor but nevertheless significant. For the *Didache*, wages given as charity become a ransom for sin: there should be no hesitation in giving. Yet for the *Doctrina*, one's earnings from labour are the ransom for sin which should be distributed. The emphasis placed on work and on almsgiving does not quite correspond in the *Doctrina* and the *Didache*. If the former were simply a translation of the latter, this difference ought not to exist.

Finally, it should be noted that the *Didache* (and *Barnabas*) claim that the obedient believer shall know (γνώση) who is the good paymaster of the reward. *Doctrina* regards this knowledge as a possession in the present (*sciens*). Regardless of the interpretation of the passage, the *Doctrina* version is not a translation of the *Didache*. Goodspeed's claim that *Doctrina* is not a Latin translation of the *Didache* is justified. In turn, however, the evidence for this also serves to raise questions about whether the *Doctrina* (in Greek form) was the common source of the *Didache* and *Barnabas*.[1] We are well advised by Kraft to acknowledge that too many questions remain regarding the issue of literary dependence: 'For the most part we are left to conjecture'.[2] It is sufficient for our purposes to consider the *Doctrina*, the *Didache* and *Barnabas* as three witnesses to the early Christian belief in redemptive almsgiving. Their Two Ways tradition comes from earlier sources, probably at some stage pre-Christian, and each has adopted it for a specific purpose. And each regarded almsgiving as an integral part of the ransom for sin.

The *Doctrina*, which likely preserves an early Christian (c. 60–80 CE?) manual of the Two Ways, affirms the priority of the love ethic. 'The way of life is this: first, you shall love the eternal God who made you; second, your neighbour as yourself' (1.2). A more specific list of sins follows with the constant warning, 'You shall not. . . ' Love for neighbour requires that 'you shall not desire any of your neighbour's goods' (2.2). To walk in the way of life one must not be covetous or avaricious (2.5). Significantly, love of money is also cited as a vice to be avoided (3.5).

The *Doctrina* encourages harmonious relationships by insisting on humility. 'You shall not exalt yourself or honour yourself among men, or admit arrogance to your soul. You shall not join yourself in soul with higher men, but you shall associate

---

1. Goodspeed's conclusions about *Doctrina* as a translation also bear on the question whether *Doctrina* was a source.

2. Kraft, *Apostolic Fathers*, III, p. 65.

with upright and humble men' (3.9). Here is an indication that the author/editor was aware of tensions within the community he was addressing. There was animosity between the 'higher men' and the 'humble men'. The tensions reflect the economic and social status of two groups. This seemingly inevitable stratifaction between rich and poor believers prompts the author/editor to warn against desire for a neighbour's property and against covetousness as well as avarice and the love of money. The unity of the body is at stake; love of neighbour is essential.[1]

In the context of calling for an end to factions and mistrust in the community, the *Doctrina* encourages compassion for the needy and empathy for their plight.

> You shall not cause divisions. Reconcile those who are quarreling. Judge justly, knowing that you will be judged. You shall not discourage anyone in his misfortune, nor shall you doubt whether it will be true or not. Do not keep stretching out your hands to receive, and drawing them back when it comes to returning. If through your hands you have earned a ransom for your sins, you shall not hesitate to give it or grumble when you give, for you know who is the good payer of such wages. You shall not turn away from the needy, but shall share everything with your brethren, and you shall not say it is your own. For if we are partners in what is immortal, how much more ought we to consecrate from it! For the Lord wishes to give of his gifts to all (4.2-8).

As Clement in his epistle hoped to reconcile the wealthy and the poor Christians in Corinth, so the *Doctrina*'s purpose was directed to restoring equality, justice and love in the community to which he wrote. The role of almsgiving in the 'ransom for sins' is striking. 'If, through your hands you have earned a ransom for your sins, you shall not hesitate to give it'. One's labour, with its monetary reward, merits redemption from sin as the wages are then to be given to the poor. The benefactor can be assured that his almsgiving will be of spiritual benefit: 'Do not grumble when you give for you know who is the good payer of such wages'.

While in some respects this passage is ambiguous, there is reason to believe that a strong work ethic is being advocated for the specific purpose of providing relief for those in need. Early Christianity certainly promoted labour as a means to receive wages which could be given to the poor.[2] Inasmuch as the *Doctrina* as a Two Ways manual is thought to have strong Jewish roots, it is significant that Mishnah records an interesting parallel.

> Rabban Gamaliel the son of R. Judah the Patriarch said: Excellent is study of the Law together with worldly occupation, for toil in them both puts sin out of mind. But all study of the Law without [worldly] labour comes to naught at the last and brings sin in its train. And let all them that labour with the congregation labour with them for the sake of Heaven, for the merit of their fathers supports them and their righteousness

---

1. For this theme in *2 Clement*, see pp. 104-107.
2. Cf. Eph. 4.28; Acts 20.35, see A.T. Geoghegan, *The Attitude towards Labor in Early Christianity* (Washington: Catholic University of America, 1945), pp. 115-16, 123, 125-26, 130. I. Giordani, *The Social Message of the Early Church Fathers* (Paterson: St. Anthony Guild, 1944), pp. 279-97. Cf. R.M. Grant, *Early Christianity and Society* (New York: Harper & Row, 1977), pp. 66-95.

endures for ever. And as for you [will God say] I count you worthy of great reward as though ye [yourselves] had wrought. . .

R. Eleazer[1] said. . . Know before whom thou toilest and who is thy taskmaster who shall pay thee the reward of they labour.

R. Tarfon[2] said. . . faithful is thy taskmaster who shall pay thee the reward of labour. And know that the recompense of the reward of the righteous is for the time to come (*m. Ab.* 2.2, 14-16).

It is not clear whether these texts imply that the wages earned through worldly labour were to be distributed among the congregation and so merit a heavenly reward. If so, however, the injunction to *know* the taskmaster who pays the reward of labour is a striking Jewish parallel to the *Doctrina*.

Concluding a description of the way of life, the *Doctrina* turns to an outline of the way of death. Vices which lead to divisiveness in the community are condemned: 'hypocrisies, pride, malice, willfulness, covetousness, jealousy, insolence, boastfulness, exaltation' (5.1). Characteristic of the way of death is the behaviour of the wealthy who ignore or abuse the impoverished: 'those to whom boastfulness is close, seeking those who will reward them, without pity for the poor, not grieving for one who is grieved. . . oppressing one who is afflicted, neglecting the appeals of the upright' (5.2).

The *Doctrina* provides early and valuable evidence of the socio-economic conditions which made almsgiving essential in early Christian communities. Money earned through manual labour and given to the poor is regarded as a ransom for sin. This redemptive power of almsgiving would need a theological foundation. Yet the doctrine would arise out of social conditions. The *Doctrina* is an important milestone as we attempt to map the development of redemptive almsgiving in early Christianity.

Assuming that the *Didache* is a later version of the Two Ways tradition, loosely connected to an early 'church manual', we find that certain theological concerns emerge and new community issues are raised. As was noted above, the love ethic is of high priority for the *Didache* just as it is for the *Doctrina*. While the *Didache* seemingly echoes much of the *Doctrina*'s concern for the poor and the insistence on humility and reconciliation[3] (presumably as instructions for rich and poor factions), the *Didache*'s stress on the importance of almsgiving (cf. 1.5; 15.4) is not paralleled in the *Doctrina*. In providing guidelines for how a community is to support certain members, the general principle is given, 'If you do not have a prophet give to the poor' (13.4). At the same time, however, a prophet is tested by his interest in money. 'Whosoever shall say in a spirit, "Give me money" or something else, you shall not listen to him; but if he tell you to give on behalf of others in want, let none judge him' (11.12).

The *Didache* testifies to a variety of fraudulent appeals for charity or abused hospitality. False prophets and those who 'traffic in Christ' (χριστέμπορος), living in

---

1. Circa 140 CE.
2. Circa 130 CE.
3. *Doctrina*, 2.2, 6; 3.9; 4.3-8; 5.1-2 with *Did.* 2.2, 6; 3.9; 4.3-8; 5.1-2.

idleness because they are Christians (12.4-5), have become a fairly widespread problem. Perhaps even more significantly, many are asking for alms when they are not in genuine need. The *Didache* warns, 'Woe to him who receives; for if any man receive alms under pressure of need he is innocent; but he who receives it without need shall be tried as to why he took and for what, and being in prison he shall be examined as to his deeds and "he shall not come out until he pay the last penny"' (1.5).[1]

Also lacking in the *Doctrina* are significant additions to the Two Ways tradition found in the *Didache* (and *Barnabas!*). While the *Doctrina* had characterized the way of death as being 'without pity for the poor... oppressing one who is afflicted, neglecting the appeals of the upright' (5.2), the *Didache* and *Barnabas* both report three distinctive vices which characterize those who have followed the path of wickedness. Among the many sins listed are being 'advocates of the rich' (πλουσίων παράκλητοι, *Did.* 5.2; *Barn.* 20.2), 'turning away the needy' (*Doctrina*—'turning away from good works'; *Did.* 5.2; *Barn.* 20.2), and being 'unjust judges of the poor' (*Did.* 5.2; *Barn.* 20.2). Again, these are features in the Two Ways tradition which do not appear in the *Doctrina*.

In the time between the emergence of the *Doctrina* and the development of the material or source common to the *Didache* and *Barnabas*, early Christianity became more sensitive to the dangers of wealth. Christians in social and political positions of authority were tempted to favour the rich and to abuse the rights of the poor.

For the *Didache* almsgiving is of both social and theological importance. The community is strengthened where there is mutual sharing (cf. 4.8). Almsgiving not only relieves a brother's need, it is an act of love for one's neighbour. It is evidence that one is following the way of life. Indeed, almsgiving is commanded by the gospel (15.4) and the commandments must be fulfilled if one is to be perfect (6.2). Since perfection is required of those who will survive the coming crisis (16.2),[2] it is theologically significant that almsgiving is a ransom for sin. 'Blessed is he who gives according to the commandment; for he is innocent' (1.5).

Thus the *Didache* represents a significant development of the doctrine of redemptive almsgiving from its bare form in the *Doctrina*. Almsgiving is a vital demonstration of love within the community, a work of compassion and duty. Support for the poor is virtually as important as providing for prophets. Through almsgiving, the individual is innocent; he has paid a ransom for his sins.

The *Didache* also goes beyond the tradition of the *Doctrina* rebuking those who love money, those who are advocates of the rich, those who turn away the needy. The failure to give alms characterizes the way of death.

The extant *Barnabas* almost certainly is an awkward union of an original epistle and a later appendix which includes much of the Two Ways tradition also found in the *Didache*. While the differences in these two sections are apparent, there are indications that the final editor made some attempt to bring a unity to the document.

1. Hermas issues a similar warning (*Mandate* 2.5).
2. Cf. *Herm. Vis.* 3.6.4.

Barnabas was certainly written for theological purposes, as a polemic against Judaism. This clear objective, however, ought not to conceal the editor's other intentions and motives. One consistent concern of *Barnabas* is for the unity and upbuilding of the community. As in the epistle to the Hebrews (10.25), there is a warning not to break into small groups but to continue meeting together. 'Do not by retiring apart live alone as if you were already made righteous, but come together and seek out the common good' (4.10). This caution against a pride that provokes factionalism is retained in the Two Ways material (19.3, cf. 19.10) and the injunction paralleled in the *Doctrina* and the *Didache* is made somewhat stronger: 'You shall not cause quarrels but shall *bring together* and reconcile those that strive' (19.12).[1] The editor was anxious that the several groups that were failing to meet together be brought back and reconciled.

Again, there is reason to believe that *Barnabas* is addressed to a community where animosity between rich and poor Christians has caused severe division. The editor reminds the wealthy of their obligation to help the needy. '"Behold this is the fast which I choose", says the Lord, ". . . tear up every unjust contract, give to the hungry your bread, and if you see a naked man clothe him, bring the homeless into your house, and if you see a humble/lowly man, do not despise him. . . " ' (3.3). Continuing the text from Isaiah, *Barnabas* calls its readers to 'give your bread to the poor with a cheerful heart' (3.5). This admonition to the rich is complemented by the Two Ways tradition. *Barnabas* introduces a new element into the material. Listing the sins of the way of the Black One, the way of death, *Barnabas* includes '*those who do not attend to the cause of the widow and orphan*. . . those without pity for the poor. . . turning away the needy. . . advocates of the rich, unjust judges of the poor' (20.1.-2). *Barnabas* and the *Didache* both report significant additions to the Two Ways tradition from its form preserved in the *Doctrina*. It is to be assumed that the editors of both *Barnabas* and the *Didache* regarded these 'supplementary passages' as pertinent for their own goals. *Barnabas* alone, however, includes reference to those who ignore the rights of the widow and the orphan. This category is not only lacking from the *Doctrina*, it is absent from the *Didache*. Indeed, the *Didache* makes no mention of widows and orphans.

Barnabas's inclusion of those who abuse the widow and orphan among the sinners on the way of death is consistent with the views of Ignatius (*Smyrn.* 6.2) and Hermas (*Sim.* 9.26.2). And *Barnabas* may well reflect the belief that widows and orphans can be 'purchased' so that their prayers will protect their benefactor. Two passages merit comparison.

---

1. *Doctrina* 4.3, 'You shall not cause divisions. Reconcile those who are quarreling'; *Did.* 4.3, 'Do not desire schism but reconcile those that strive'.

| This lack of sharing is harmful to you who are rich and do not share with the poor. Consider the judgment which is coming. Let therefore they who have an abundance (οἱ ὑπερέχοντες) seek out those who are hungry (*Herm. Vis.* 3.9.4-5). | I beseech those who have an abundance (ποὺς ὑπερέχοντας), if you will receive any counsel of my goodwill, have among yourselves those to whom you may do good. Fail not! The day is at hand when all things shall perish with the Evil One. The Lord and his reward is at hand (*Barn.* 21.2). |

The editor of *Barnabas* is anxious because the community is breaking into factions. Not only are theological matters in dispute, but sharp divisions have arisen between wealthy and poor members. There is a need for brothers to come together and to be reconciled. Much of *Barnabas* is a reminder and a warning to the rich to be attentive to the needs of the poor, the hungry, the widow and the orphan. A sense of eschatological urgency further prompts the reader to act.

In this context, *Barnabas* gives additional motivation for almsgiving by referring to it as a ransom for sin.

> You shall share all things with your neighbour and you shall not say it is your own. For if you are sharers in that which is incorruptible, how much more in that which is corruptible? . . . Be not one who stretches out his hands to receive but shuts them when it comes to giving. Remember the day of judgment. . . working[1] with your hands for the ransom of your sins. You shall not hesitate to give, and when you give you shall not grumble, but you shall know who is the good paymaster of the reward (19.8.11).

Whereas the *Doctrina* principally offers evidence for the social conditions which promoted a doctrine of redemptive almsgiving, the *Didache* and *Barnabas* provide testimony for the developing theological justification for the belief that giving to the poor is a ransom for sin. At the same time, however, the *Didache* and *Barnabas* are outraged at the dismal relationship between wealthy and needy Christians in their communities. Each is critical of the rich; and each levels specific indictments that are unparalleled in the *Doctrina*. Social factors shape their theology.

Also motivating the editors of the *Didache* and *Barnabas* was the expectation that Judgment Day was imminent. The need for perfection, the call to obedience, the way of life/light had become especially urgent. The necessity for a remedy for the guilt of sin was a growing concern. It is in this context that *2 Clement* makes a substantial contribution to the emergence of redemptive almsgiving in early Christianity. At the same time, however, the homily addresses significant social problems affecting the author's community.

---

1. Barnabas preserves the labour-ethic found in the *Doctrina*. Cf. *Didascalia* 2.34; *Apostolic Constitutions* 3.12.1-3. See also *Barn.* 10.4.

Appendix B

G.E.M. DE STE CROIX'S
THE CLASS STRUGGLE IN THE ANCIENT GREEK WORLD

In his *The Class Struggle in the Ancient Greek World*, Ste Croix undertakes to write the first work in English 'to analyse Greek History in terms of Marxist historical concepts'.[1] Within his extensive survey he discusses the views of property and almsgiving that emerge in early Christianity.

Ste Croix regards early Christianity as having an impact on the Greek (and Roman) world only once it had begun to spread to the urban areas of the empire. Originally the movement initiated by Jesus developed in a Palestinian world which Ste Croix describes as virtually sealed off from the influence of Hellenism. Ironically it was in the expansion of Christianity, seeking to 'save' the world, that this movement was itself Hellenized.[2]

Jesus himself, Ste Croix maintains, announced the imminent end of the 'whole present dispensation', regarded the possession of wealth as 'a positive hindrance to entering into the (coming) kingdom' and, in striking contrast to prevailing Graeco-Roman views, believed that the poor, the destitute, were uniquely privileged and blessed in God's eyes.[3]

Breaking out of its Jewish apocalyptic home, the message of Jesus was soon 'transformed' into what is known as 'Pauline Christianity', the gospel of the urban Christian movement. Ste Croix argues that in this radical transition there was 'the transfer of a whole system of ideas from the world of the χώρα to that of the πόλις'.[4] It was in this stage that the renunciation of wealth was spiritualized and the Hellenistic attitude towards private property corrupted early Christianity. Ste Croix notes that 'with hardly an exception all the orthodox writers seem to have no serious qualms in accepting that a Christian may own property. . . he must hold it as a kind of trustee for the poor, to whom he must give charity'.[5]

Ste Croix insists that early Christianity's interest in almsgiving is largely the reuslt of a concern to justify the possession of wealth and to preserve the social order. *Redemptive* almsgiving, adapted from Judaism, was intended to give greater

1. G.E.M. de Ste Croix, *The Class Struggle in the Ancient Greek World* (London: Gerald Duckworth, 1981), pp. ix, 19, 22-23.
2. *Class Struggle*, pp. 426-27, 430-34, 437-38.
3. *Class Struggle*, pp. 431-33; cf. M.I. Finley, *The Ancient Economy* (Berkley: University of California Press, 1973), p. 38.
4. *Class Struggle*, pp. 433-34.
5. *Class Struggle*, pp. 433-34.

theological prestige and value to the act of charity.[1] Consistent with his Marxist presuppositions he regards this evolution of doctrine as inevitable:

> The early Christian attitude to property ownership, then, developed into something very different from that of Jesus . . . as time went on, the eschatological nature of the concepts of Jesus gradually lost its original force, but (and this is much more important) because such a development was imposed on the Church by irresistible social pressures.[2]

Ste Croix's analysis is remarkably compatible with my own. We agree, to a large extent, on both the social tensions and the loss of eschatological fervour which affected the expanding Christian movement. Certainly wealthy Christians sought to find rationalization for their continuing affluence and the distant prospect of judgment dulled any sense of urgency in renouncing worldliness.

Still I find myself uncomfortable with Ste Croix's interpretation of the emergence of redemptive almsgiving as almost solely determined by the social forces that shaped early Christianity. In recognizing redemptive almsgiving as a distinctly *Jewish* belief adopted by Hellenistic Christianity,[3] Ste Croix, who stresses the *Jewishness* (and thoroughly *un*-Greek character) of Jesus,[4] ought to suspect that Jesus himself may have been influenced by the doctrine. The synoptic tradition (principally Luke) suggests that this was the case. I have attempted to show that the New Testament literature testifies to the primitive roots of redemptive almsgiving in early Christianity, even in its so-called 'pre-Hellenistic' stage.

Secondly, Ste Croix gives no attention to the critical theological issues which helped to promote the doctrine of redemptive almsgiving. The problem of post-baptismal sin is a crucial piece of the puzzle but Ste Croix feels able to explain the doctrine as a product of *social* pressures alone; he sees no need to attribute its emergence to any theological crisis in the early church. In the section, 'The Theological Issues', I have tried to show the significance of post-baptismal sin in the formation of the doctrine.

1. *Class Struggle*, pp. 433-35; 438.
2. *Class Struggle*, pp. 433-35; 438.
3. *Class Struggle*, p. 434.
4. *Class Struggle*, pp. 430-31.

BIBLIOGRAPHY

Primary Sources and Translations

A. *Graeco-Roman*

Aristotle, *Nicomachean Ethics* (trans. H. Rackman; London: Heinemann, 1926).

Cicero, *De Officiis* (trans. W. Miller; London: Heinemann, 1975).

Dio Chrysostom (trans. J.W. Cohoon; London: Heinemann, 1932).

Diogenes Laertius, *Lives of Eminent Philosophers*, I, II (trans. R.D. Hicks; London: Heinemann, 1950).

Epictetus, *Discourses and the Manual*, I, II (trans. W.A. Oldfather; London: Heinemann, 1967).

Hesiod, *Hesiod, the Homeric Hymns and Homerica* (trans. H.G. Evelyn-White; London: Heinemann, 1914).

Homer, *The Odyssey* (trans. A.T. Murray; London: Heinemann, 1928–30).

Isocrates, I-III (trans. G. Norlin; London: Heinemann, 1928–45).

Juvenal, 'Satires' in *Juvenal and Persius* (trans. G.G. Ramsay; London: Heinemann, 1957).

Lucian, I-VIII (trans. A.M. Harmon; London: Heinemann, 1927–67).

Musonius, in C.E. Lutz, 'Musonius Rufus "The Roman Socrates"', *Yale Classical Studies* 10 (1947), pp. 3-147.

Ovid, *Metamorphoses*, I, II (trans. F.J. Miller; London: Heinemann, 1916).

Plato, *The Collected Dialogues* (ed. E. Hamilton and H. Cairns; Princeton, NJ: Princeton University Press, 1961).

Plato, *The Republic*, I, II (trans. P. Shorey; London: Heinemann, 1930–35).

Plautus, I-V (trans. P. Nixon; London: Heinemann, 1916).

Pliny, *Letters* (trans. W. Melmoth; rev. W.M.L. Hutchinson; London: Heinemann, 1927).

Plutarch, *Lives*, I-XI (trans. B. Perrin; London: Heinemann, 1914–26).

—*Moralia*, X (trans. H.N. Fowler; London: Heinemann, 1939).

Sallust, *Conspiracy of Catiline* (trans. S.A. Handford; Harmondsworth: Penguin Books, 1969).

Seneca, *Epistulae*, I-III (trans. R.M. Gummere; London: Heinemann, 1953).

Seneca, *Moral Essays*, III (trans. J.W. Basore; London: Heinemann, 1975).

Suetonius (trans. J.C. Rolfe; London: Heinemann, 1924).

Xenophon, *Memorabilia and Oeconomicus* (trans. E.C. Marchant; London: Heinemann, 1923).

B. *Jewish*

Abot de Rabbi Nathan: The Fathers according to Rabbi Nathan (trans. J. Goldein; New Haven: Yale University Press, 1955).

Apocrypha: *The Apocrypha of the Old Testament* (Revised Standard Version; ed. B.M. Metzger; Oxford: Oxford University Press, 1977).
   The Hebrew Text of the Book of Ecclesiasticus (ed. I. Levi; Leiden: Brill, 1951).
Bible: *Biblia Hebraica Stuttgartensia* (ed. R. Kittel; Stuttgart: Deutsche Bibelgesellschaft, 1977).
   The Holy Scriptures (Philadelphia: The Jewish Publication Society of America, 1955).
Josephus, I-IX (trans. H. St J. Thackeray; London: Heinemann, 1926–65).
The Mishnah (trans. H. Danby; Oxford: Oxford University Press, 1933).
Philo I-IX (trans. F.H. Colson and G.H. Whitaker; London: W. Heinemann, 1929–41); X (trans. F.H. Colson and J.W. Earp; London: Heinemann, 1962).
Pseudepigrapha: *The Old Testament Pseudepigrapha*, I-II (ed. J.H. Charlesworth; Garden City, NY: Doubleday, 1983, 1985).
Qumran: M. Burrows, *The Dead Sea Scrolls* (New York: Viking, 1956).
   T.H. Gaster, *The Dead Sea Scriptures* (Garden City, NY: Doubleday, 3rd edn, 1976).
   G. Vermes, *The Dead Sea Scrolls in English* (Harmondsworth: Penguin Books, 2nd edn, 1975).
Septuagint: *Septuaginta* (ed. A. Rohlfs; Stuttgart: Bibelgesellschaft Stuttgart, 1979).
The Talmud: *The Babylonian Talmud*, I-XVIII (trans. and ed. I. Epstein; London: Soncino, 1961).
Tosefta (trans. J. Neusner; New York: Ktav, 1977).

C. Christian
The Apostolic Fathers (trans. E.J. Goodspeed; New York: Harper & Brothers, 1970).
The Apostolic Fathers, I, II (trans. K. Lake; London: Heinemann, 1977).
The Apostolic Fathers (trans. J.B. Lightfoot; ed. and comp. J.R. Harmer; repr.; Grand Rapids: Baker, 1980 [1891]).
Aristides, *The Apology of Aristides* (trans. J. R. Harris; Cambridge: Cambridge University Press, 1891).
Bible: *The Bible* (trans. J. Moffatt; New York: Harper, 1954).
   The Holy Bible (Revised Standard Version; New York: Thomas Nelson and Sons, 1952).
   The New English Bible (Oxford: Oxford University Press, 1970).
Chrysostom: *The Homilies of S. John Chrysostom on the Gospel of St John*, I, II (trans. G.T. Stupart; Oxford: John Henry Parker, 1848).
   The Homilies of S. John Chrysostom on the Statues (trans. E. Budge; Oxford: John Henry Parker, 1842).
Clement of Alexandria (trans. G.W. Butterworth; London: Heinemann, 1953).
Cyprian, *The Writings of Cyprian*, II (trans. R.E. Wallis; Edinburgh: T. & T. Clark, 1869).
Didascalia et Constitutiones Apostolorum, I (ed. F.X. Funk; Paderburnae: Ferdinandi Schoeningh, 1905).
Eusebius, *Ecclesiastical History*, I, II (trans. K. Lake; London: Heinemann, 1980).
Justin, in *The Ante-Nicene Fathers*, I (trans. A. Roberts and J. Donaldson; New York: Christian Literature Co., 1896).
New Testament: *The Greek New Testament* (ed. K. Aland, M. Black, C.M. Martini,

Bibliography 157

B.M. Metzger and A. Wikgren (New York: American Bible Society, 2nd edn, 1968).

New Testament Apocrypha (ed. E. Hennecke; London: SCM Press, 1973).

Tertullian (trans. C. Dodgon; Oxford: John Henry Parker, 1842).

Secondary and General Sources

Abrahams, I., *Studies in Pharisaism and the Gospels* (First and Second Series; New York: Ktav, 1967).

Achtemeier, P.J., 'An Apocalyptic Shift in Early Christian Tradition: Reflections on Some Canonical Evidence', *CBQ* 45 (1983), pp. 231-48.

Alexander, T.D., 'Lot's Hospitality: A Clue to his Righteousness', *JBL* 104 (1985), pp. 289-91.

Alfody, G., *The Social History of Rome* (Totowa: Barnes and Nobel, 1985).

Appelbaum, S., 'Economic Life in Palestine', in S. Safrai and M. Stern (eds.), *The Jewish People in the First Country*, II (Philadelphia: Fortress Press), pp. 631-700.

Arnold, E.V., *Roman Stoicism* (Cambridge: Cambridge University Press, 1911).

Attridge, H., *First-Century Cynicism in the Epistles of Heraclitus* (Missoula, MT: Scholars Press, 1976).

Audet, J.-P., *La Didache* (Paris: Gabalda, 1958).

Aulen, G., *Christus Victor* (New York: Macmillan, 1969).

Aune, D.E., *The Cultic Setting of Realized Eschatology in Early Christianity* (Leiden: Brill, 1972).

—'The Significance of the Delay of the Parousia for Early Christianity', in Hawthorne (ed.), *Current Issues*, pp. 87-109.

Avila, C., *Ownership: Early Christian Teaching* (Maryknoll, NY: Orbis Books, 1981).

Aytoun, R.A., *City Centres of Early Christianity* (London: Hodder & Stoughton, 1915).

Bammel, E., 'The Poor and the Zealots', in Bammel and Moule (eds.), *Jesus and the Politics of His Day*.

Bammel, E., and C.F.D. Moule (eds.), *Jesus and the Politics of his Day* (Cambridge: Cambridge University Press, 1984).

Banks, R., *Paul's Idea of Community* (Grand Rapids: Eerdmans, 1980).

Barnard, L.W., 'The Early Roman Church', *ATR* 49 (1967), pp. 371-84.

—'The Epistle of Barnabas in its Jewish Setting', in *Studies in Church History and Patristica* (Thessaloniki: Patriarchal Institute for Patristic Studies, 1978).

—'Hermas and Judaism', in *Studia Patristica 8* (Berlin: Akademie Verlag, 1966), pp. 3-9.

—*Studies in the Apostolic Fathers and their Background* (New York: Schocken Books, 1966).

Barrett, C.K., *The First Epistle to the Corinthians* (New York: Harper & Row, 1968).

Bartlett, V., 'The Origin and Date of 2 Clement', *ZNW* 7 (1906), pp. 123-35.

Batey, R., *Jesus and the Poor* (New York: Harper & Row, 1972).

Bauer, W., *A Greek–English Lexicon of the New Testament* (trans. W.F. Arndt and F.W. Gingrich; Chicago: University of Chicago Press, 1957).

—*Orthodoxy and Heresy in Earliest Christianity* (Philadelphia: Fortress Press, 1971).

Beare, F.W., *The First Epistle of Peter* (Oxford: Basil Blackwell, 1947).

158   *Redemptive Almsgiving in Early Christianity*

Benko, S., and J.J. O'Rourke, *The Catacombs and the Colosseum* (Valley Forge, PA: Judson, 1971).

Berger, K., 'Almosen für Israel', *NTS* 23 (1977), pp. 180-204.

—*Die Gesetzauslegung Jesu* (Neukirchen–Vluyn: Neukirchener Verlag, 1972).

Bertram, G., 'εὐεργέτης', *TDNT* 2 (1974), pp. 654-55.

Best, E., *1 Peter* (Grand Rapids: Eerdmans, 1971).

Bigg, C., *The Doctrine of the Twelve Apostles* (London: SPCK, 1922).

Billerbeck, M., *Epiktet vom Cynismus* (Leiden: Brill, 1978).

Boer, W.D., *Private Morality in Greece and Rome* (Leiden: Brill, 1979).

Boerma, C., *Rich Man, Poor Man—and the Bible* (London: SCM Press, 1979).

Bogart, J., *Orthodox and Heretical Perfectionism* (Missoula, MT: Scholars Press, 1977).

Bolkestein, H., *Wohltätigkeit und Armenpflege im vorchristlichen Altertum* (Utrecht: A. Oosthoek, 1939).

Bolkestein, H., and W. Schwer, 'Almosen', *RAC*, I, pp. 301-307.

Bonhoeffer, A., 'Epiktet und das Neue Testament', *ZNW* 13 (1912), pp. 281-92.

Brooks, R., *Support for the Poor in the Mishnaic Law of Agriculture: Tractate Peah* (Chico, CA: Scholars Press, 1983).

Bruce, F.F., *The Acts of the Apostles* (London: Tyndale Press, 1965).

—'Eschatology in the Apostolic Fathers', in D. Neiman and M. Schatkin (eds.), *The Heritage of the Early Church* (Rome: Pontifical Institutum Studiorum Orientalium, 1973), pp. 77-89.

—*Second Thoughts on the Dead Sea Scrolls* (Grand Rapids: Eerdmans, 1977).

Bruck, E.F., 'Ethic vs. Law: St. Paul, the Fathers of the Church, and the "Cheerful Giver" in Roman Law', *Traditio* 2 (1944), pp. 97-121.

Brunt, P.A., *Social Conflicts in the Roman Republic* (New York: Norton, 1971).

Buchanan, G.W., 'Jesus and the Upper Class', *NovT* 7 (1964), pp. 195-209.

—*To the Hebrews* (Garden City, NY: Doubleday, 1972).

Buchler, A., 'Ben Sira's Conception of Sin and Atonement', *JQR* 13 (1923), pp. 461-502; *JQR* 14 (1924), pp. 53-83.

—'St. Matthew VI 1–6 and Other Allied Passages', *JTS* 10 (1909), pp. 266-70.

—*Studies in Sin and Atonement in the Rabbinic Literature of the First Century* (New York: Ktav, 1967).

Buchsel, F., 'λύτρον', *TDNT*, IV, pp. 340-49.

Bultmann, Rudolf, 'ἔλεος', *TDNT*, II, pp. 485-87.

—'Das religiöse Moment in der ethischen Unterweisung des Epiktet und das Neue Testament', *ZNW* 13 (1912), pp. 91-110, 177-91.

—*Der Stil der paulinischen Predigt und die kynischstoische Diatribe* (Göttingen: Vandenhoeck & Ruprecht, 1910).

Campenhausen, H. von, *Tradition and Life in the Church* (London: SCM Press, 1968).

Case, S.J., *The Social Origins of Christianity* (Chicago: University of Chicago Press, 1923).

Chadwick, H., 'Justification by Faith and Hospitality', in *Studia Patristica 4* (Berlin: Akademie Verlag, 1961), pp. 281-85.

'Charity', *EncJud*, V, pp. 338-54.

Charlesworth, J.H. (ed.), *The Old Testament Pseudepigrapha*, I, II (Garden City, NY: Doubleday, 1983, 1985).

Chastel, E., *Etudes historiques sur l'influence de la charité durant premiers siècles chrétiens, et considerations sur son role dans les sociétés modernes* (Paris: Capelle, 1853).

Clarke, W.K.L., *Almsgiving* (London: SPCK, 1936).

Clarke, W.K.L. (ed.), *The First Epistle of Clement* (London: SPCK, 1937).

Cook, S.A., F.E. Adcock and M.P. Charlesworth (eds.), *The Cambridge Ancient History*, I (New York: Macmillan, 1936).

Corbett, J., 'The Pharisaic Revolution and Jesus as Embodied Torah', *SR* 15/3 (1986), pp. 375-91.

Countryman, L.W., *The Rich Christian in the Church of the Early Empire* (New York: Edwin Mellen, 1980).

—'Welfare in the Churches of Asia Minor under the Early Roman Empire', in *SBL Seminar Papers, 1979*, I (Missoula, MT: Scholars Press, 1979), pp. 131-46.

Cowell, F.R., *Cicero and the Roman Republic* (Harmondsworth: Penguin Books, 1956).

Cowley, A., *Aramaic Papyri of the Fifth Century, BC* (Oxford: Clarendon Press, 1923).

Cranfield, C.E.B., *The First Epistle of Peter* (London: SCM Press, 1950).

—'Riches and the Kingdom of God', *SJT* 4 (1951), pp. 302-13.

Cronbach, A., 'The Me'il Zedakah', *HUCA* 11 (1936), pp. 503-67.

—*Philanthropy in Rabbinic Literature* (Cincinnati: Union of American Hebrew Congregations, 1939).

—'The Social Ideals of the Apocrypha and the Pseudepigrapha', *HUCA* 18 (1944), pp. 119-56.

Cruttwell, C.T., *A Literary History of Early Christianity*, I (London: Charles Griffin, 1893).

Cunningham, W., *The Epistle of St Barnabas* (London: Macmillan, 1877).

Dahl, N.A., *Studies in Paul* (Minneapolis: Augsburg, 1977).

Davies, J.G., 'The Genesis of Belief in an Imminent Parousia', *JTS* (1963), pp. 104-107.

Davies, W.D., *Paul and Rabbinic Judaism* (London: SPCK, 1948).

Davis, W.S., *The Influence of Wealth in Imperial Rome* (New York: Macmillan, 1913).

Degenhardt, H.J., *Lukas, Evangelist der Armen* (Stuttgart: Katholisches Bibelwerk, 1965).

Dill, S., *Roman Society from Nero to Marcus Aurelius* (London: Macmillan, 1937).

Dodd, C.H., *The Bible and the Greeks* (London: Hodder & Stoughton, 1964).

Donehoo, J.D., *The Apocryphal and Legendary Life of Christ* (New York: Macmillan, 1903).

Donfried, K.P., *The Setting of Second Clement in Early Christianity* (Leiden: Brill, 1974).

—'The Theology of Second Clement', *HTR* 66 (1973), pp. 487-501.

Dover K.J., *Greek Popular Morality* (Berkeley: University of California Press, 1974).

Downey, G., 'Who is my Neighbor? The Greek and Roman Answer', *ATR* 47 (1965), pp. 3-15.

Downing, F.G., 'Cynics and Christians', *NTS* 30 (1984), pp. 584-93.

Driver, S.R., *Daniel* (Cambridge: Cambridge University Press, 1901).

Dudley, D.R., *A History of Cynicism* (London: Methuen, 1937).

Duncan-Jones, R., *The Economy of the Roman Empire* (Cambridge: Cambridge University Press, 1974).

Edelstein, L., *The Meaning of Stoicism* (Cambridge: Cambridge University Press, 1966).

Edmundson, G., *The Church in Rome in the First Century* (London: Longmans, Green & Co., 1913).

Enslin, M.S., *The Ethics of Paul* (New York: Abingdon Press, 1957).

Finley, M.I., *The Ancient Economy* (Berkeley: University of California Press, 1973).

Fitzmyer, J., *The Gospel according to Luke X–XXIV* (Garden City, NY: Doubleday, 1985).

Foerster, W., 'ἐπιούσιος', *TDNT*, II, pp. 590-99.

Ford, J.M., 'Three Ancient Jewish Views of Poverty', in W. Klassen (ed.), *The New Way of Jesus* (Newton, KS: Faith and Life, 1980), pp. 39-55.

Gager, J.G., *Kingdom and Community* (Englewood Cliffs, NJ: Prentice–Hall, 1975).

Garnet, P., *Salvation and Atonement in the Qumran Scrolls* (Tübingen: Mohr, 1977).

Garnsey, P., *Social Status and Legal Privilege in the Roman Empire* (Oxford: Clarendon Press, 1970).

Gelin, A., *The Poor of Yahweh* (Collegeville, MN: Liturgical Press, 1964).

Geoghegan, A.T., *The Attitude Towards Labor in Early Christianity and Ancient Culture* (Washington: Catholic University of America, 1945).

George, A., J. Dupont, S. Legasse, P. Seidensticker and B. Rigaux, *Gospel Poverty* (Chicago: Franciscan Herald, 1977).

Georgi, D., 'Forms of Religious Propaganda', in H.J. Schultze (ed.), *Jesus in his Time* (Philadelphia: Fortress Press, 1980), pp. 124-31.

—'Socioeconomic Reasons for the "Divine Man" as a Propagandistic Pattern', in E.S. Fiorenza (ed.), *Aspects of Religious Propaganda in Judaism and Early Christianity* (Notre Dame : University of Notre Dame Press, 1976), pp. 27-42.

Geytenbeek, A.C. von, *Musonius Rufus and Greek Diatribe* (Assen, 1963).

Giordani, I., *The Social Message of the Early Church Fathers* (Paterson: St. Anthony Guild, 1944).

Glover, R., 'The Didache's Quotations and the Synoptic Gospels', *NTS* 5 (1958–59), pp. 12-29.

Goodspeed, E.J., *The Apostolic Fathers* (New York: Harper & Brothers, 1950).

—'The Didache, Barnabas and the Doctrina', *ATR* 28 (1945), pp. 228-47.

—*A History of Early Christian Literature* (rev. R.M. Grant; Chicago: University of Chicago Press, 1966).

—*New Chapters in New Testament Study* (New York: Macmillan, 1937).

Goppelt, L., *Apostolic and Post-Apostolic Times* (New York: Harper Torchbook, 1970).

Grant, F.C., 'The Eschatology of the Second Century', *AJT* 21 (1917), pp. 193-211.

Grant. R.M., *After the New Testament* (Philadelphia: Fortress Press, 1967).

—*The Apostolic Fathers.* I. *An Introduction* (New York: Nelson, 1964).

—*The Apostolic Fathers.* IV. *Ignatius of Antioch* (Camden: Nelson, 1966).

—*Early Christianity and Society* (New York: Harper & Row, 1977).

—'Introduction: Christian and Roman History', in Benko and O'Rourke (eds.), *The Catacombs and the Colosseum*.

—'The Social Setting of Second-Century Christianity', in E.P. Sanders (ed.), *Jewish and Christian Self-Definition*, I (Philadelphia: Fortress Press, 1980), pp. 16-29.

—*The Sword and the Cross* (New York: Macmillan, 1955).

Grant, R., and H.H. Graham, *The Apostolic Fathers.* I. *First and Second Clement* (New York: Nelson, 1965).

Guterman, S.L., *Religious Toleration and Persecution in Ancient Rome* (London: Aiglon, 1951).

Guthrie, D., *New Testament Introduction* (Downer's Grove, IL: IVP, 1973).

Guttmann, A., 'The End of the Jewish Sacrificial Cult', *HUCA* 38 (1967), pp. 137-48.

Hagner, D.A., *The Use of the Old and New Testaments in Clement of Rome* (Leiden: Brill, 1973).

Hands, A.R., *Charities and Social Aid in Greece and Rome* (London: Thames & Hudson, 1968).

Harnack, A., *The Constitution and Law of the Church in the First Two Centuries* (London: Williams & Norgate, 1910).

—*The Mission and Expansion of Christianity in the First Three Centuries*, I (London: Williams & Norgate, 1904).

—*Geschichte der altchristlichen Literatur bis Eusebius* (Leipzig: Hinrichs, 1893).

Harrison, P.N., *Polycarp's Two Epistles to the Philippians* (Cambridge: Cambridge University Press, 1936).

Hartman, F., and A.A. DiLella, *The Book of Daniel* (Garden City, NY: Doubleday, 1978).

Haslehurst, R.S.T., *Penitential Discipline of the Early Church* (London: SPCK, 1921).

Hatch, E., *The Influence of Greek Ideas on Christianity* (Gloucester, MA: Peter Smith, 1970).

—*The Organization of the Early Christian Churches* (London: Rivingtons, 1888).

Hauck, F., *Die Stellung des Urchristentums zu Arbeit und Geld* (Gütersloh: Bertelsmann, 1921).

Hawthorne, G.F. (ed.), *Current Issues in Biblical and Patristic Interpretation* (Grand Rapids: Eerdmans, 1975).

—'πτωχός', *TDNT*, VI, pp. 885-87.

Hengel, M., *Acts and the History of Earliest Christianity* (London: SCM Press, 1979).

—*The Atonement* (Philadelphia: Fortress Press, 1981).

—*Between Jesus and Paul* (Philadelphia: Fortress Press, 1983).

—*The Charismatic Leader and his Followers* (New York: Crossroad, 1981).

—*Judaism and Hellenism* (Philadelphia: Fortress Press, 1974).

—*Property and Riches in the Early Church* (Philadelphia: Fortress Press, 1974).

Herford, R.T., *Talmud and Apocrypha* (New York: Ktav, 1971).

Heron, J., *The Church of the Sub-Apostolic Age* (London: Hodder & Stoughton, 1888).

Hiers, R.H., 'The Problem of the Delay of the Parousia in Luke–Acts', *NTS* 20 (1973–74), pp. 145-55.

Hill, D., *Greek Words and Hebrew Meanings* (Cambridge: Cambridge University Press, 1967).

Hock, R.F., 'Simon the Shoemaker as an Ideal Cynic', *GRBS* 17 (1976), pp. 41-53.

—*The Social Context of Paul's Ministry* (Philadelphia: Fortress Press, 1980).

—'The Workshop as a Social Setting for Paul's Missionary Preaching', *CBQ* 41 (1979), pp. 438-50.

Horst, P.W. van der, 'Musonius Rufus and the New Testament', *NovT* 16 (1974), pp. 306-15.

Hunter, A.M., *The First Epistle of Peter* (London: Macmillan, 1957).

Hurd, J.C., *The Origin of 1 Corinthians* (New York: Seabury, 1965).

Jackson, B., *Twenty-five Agrapha* (London: SPCK, 1900).

Jeremias, J., *The Central Message of the New Testament* (Philadelphia: Fortress Press, 1965).

—'Flesh and Blood Cannot Inherit the Kingdom of God', *NTS* 2 (1955–56), pp. 151-59.

—*Jerusalem in the Time of Jesus* (London: SCM Press, 1969).

—'Das Lösegeld für Viele (Mk 10.45)', *Judaica* 3 (1948), pp. 249-64.

—*The Parables of Jesus* (New York: Charles Scribner's Sons, 2nd rev. edn, 1972).

—'Die Salbungsgeschichte Mc. 14.3-9', *ZNW* 35 (1936), pp. 75-82.

—*Unknown Sayings of Jesus* (London: SCM Press, 2nd edn, 1964).

Johnson, L.T., *Sharing Possessions* (Philadelphia: Fortress Press, 1981).

Jones, A.H.M., *The Greek City* (Oxford: Clarendon Press, 1940).

Joseph, M., 'The Place of Charity or Almsgiving in the Old Testament', *ExpTim* (1909–10), pp. 427-28.

Judge, E.A., 'The Early Christians as a Scholastic Community', *JRH* 1 (1960–61), pp. 4-15, 125-37.

—'Paul's Boasting in Relation to Contemporary Professional Practice', *Australian Biblical Review* 16 (1968), pp. 37-50.

—*The Social Pattern of the Christian Groups in the First Century* (London: Tyndale Press, 1960).

Karris, R.J., 'Poor and Rich: The Lukan *Sitz Im Leben*', in C.H. Talbert (ed.), *Perspectives on Luke–Acts* (Danville: Association of Baptist Professors of Religion, 1978), pp. 112-25.

Käseman, E., *Essays on New Testament Themes* (London: SCM Press, 1968).

—*New Testament Questions of Today* (Philadelphia: Fortress Press, 1969).

Keck, L.E., 'The Poor among the Saints in Jewish Christianity and Qumran', *ZNW* 57 (1966), pp. 54-78.

—'The Poor among the Saints in the New Testament', *ZNW* 56 (1965), pp. 100-29.

Knox, J., *The Epistle to the Romans* (New York: Abingdon Press, 1954).

Koester, H., *Synoptische Überlieferung beiden apostolischen Vätern* (Berlin: Akademie Verlag, 1957).

Kraft, R.A., *The Apostolic Fathers*. III. *Barnabas and the Didache* (New York: Nelson, 1965).

—'The Development of the Concept of "Orthodoxy" in Early Christianity', in Hawthorne (ed.), *Current Issues*, pp. 47-59.

Kraft, R.A. (ed.), *The Testament of Job* (Missoula, MT: Scholars Press, 1974).

Lake, K., 'The Shepherd of Hermas and Christian Life in Rome in the Second Century', *HTR* 4 (1911), pp. 25-46.

Lampe, G.W.H., 'AD 70 in Christian Reflection', in Bammel and Moule (eds.), *Jesus and the Politics of his Day*, pp. 153-91.

—'Early Patristic Eschatology', *Eschatology* (Scottish Journal of Theology Occasional Papers No. 2), pp. 17-35.

—*The Seal of the Spirit* (London: SPCK, 1967).

Lampe, P., *Die stadtrömischen Christen in den ersten beiden Jahrhunderten* (Tübingen: Mohr, 1987).

Latko, E.F., *Origen's Concept of Penance* (Quebec, 1949).

Lawson, J., *A Theological and Historical Introduction to the Apostolic Fathers* (New York: Macmillan, 1961).

Layton, B., 'The Sources, Date, and Transmission of Didache 1.3b–2.1', *HTR* 61 (1968), pp. 343-84.

Leipoldt, J., *Der soziale Gedanke in der altchristlichen Kirche* (Leipzig: Koehler und Amelang, 1952).

Lightfoot, J.B., *The Apostolic Fathers* (London: Macmillan, 1926).

—*St. Paul's Epistle to the Philippians* (Grand Rapids: Zondervan, 1953).

Lincoln, A.T., *Paradise Now and Not Yet* (Cambridge: Cambridge University Press, 1981).

Lohmeyer, E., *Soziale Fragen im Urchristentum* (Leipzig: Quelle und Meyer, 1921).

Lutz, C.E., 'Musonius Rufus, "The Roman Socrates"', *Yale Classical Studies* 10 (1947), pp. 3-147.

Lyonnet, S., and L. Sabourin, *Sin, Redemption, and Sacrifice* (Rome: Biblical Institute Press, 1970).

MacKinnan, J., *The Gospel in the Early Church* (London: Longmans, Green & Co., 1933).

MacMullen, R., *Paganism in the Roman Empire* (New Haven: Yale University Press, 1981).

—*Roman Social Relations* (New Haven: Yale University Press, 1976).

Malherbe, A.J. (ed.), *The Cynic Epistles* (Missoula, MT: Scholars Press, 1977).

—'Exhortation in First Thessalonians', *NovT* 25 (1983), pp. 238-56.

—'Gentle as a Nurse', *NovT* 12 (1970), pp. 203-17.

—'Self-Definition among Epicureans and Cynics', in B.F. Meyer and E.P. Sanders (eds.), *Jewish and Christian Self-Definition* (Philadelphia: Fortress Press, 1982), pp. 46-59.

—*Social Aspects of Early Christianity* (Philadelphia: Fortress Press, 2nd edn, 1983).

Maloney, R.P., 'The Teaching of the Fathers on Usury', *VC* 27 (1973), pp. 241-65.

Mare, E.H., 'A Study of the New Testament Concept of the Parousia', in Hawthorne (ed.), *Current Issues*, pp. 336-45.

Marmorstein, A., *The Doctrine of Merits in Old Rabbinical Literature* (New York: Ktav, 1968).

—'The Treasures in Heaven and upon Earth', *JQR* 132 (1919), pp. 216-28.

Marshall, I.H., *The Gospel of Luke* (Grand Rapids: Eerdmans, 1978).

Maynard-Reid, P.U., *Poverty and Wealth in James* (Maryknoll, NY: Orbis Books, 1987).

Mealand, D.L., 'Philo of Alexandria's Attitude to Riches', *ZNW* 69 (1978), pp. 158-64.

—*Poverty and Expectation in the Gospels* (London: SPCK, 1980).

Meeks, W.A., *The First Urban Christians* (New Haven: Yale University Press, 1983).

Meier, J.P., and R.E. Brown, *Antioch and Rome* (New York: Paulist Press, 1983).

Moffatt, J., *The Bible: A New Translation* (New York: Harper & Brothers, 1935).

Montefiore, C.G., *Rabbinic Literature and Gospel Teachings* (New York: Ktav, 1970).

Moore, A.L., *The Parousia in the New Testament* (Leiden: Brill, 1966).

Moore, G.F., *Judaism*, III (Cambridge, MA: Harvard University Press, 1958).

Morris, L., *The Apostolic Preaching of the Cross* (Grand Rapids: Eerdmans, 1974).

Mott, S.C., 'The Power of Giving and Receiving: Reciprocity in Hellenistic Benevolence', in Hawthorne (ed.), *Current Issues*, pp. 60-72.

Moulton, J.H., and G. Milligan, *The Vocabulary of the Greek Testament* (London: Hodder & Stoughton, 1949).

Muilenburg, J., *The Literary Relations of the Epistle of Barnabas and the Teaching of the Twelve Apostles* (Marburg, 1929).

Mullin, R., *The Wealth of Christians* (Maryknoll, NY: Orbis Books, 1984).

Nagel, W., 'Gerechtigkeit—oder Almosen? (Mt. 6.1)', *VC* 15 (1961), pp. 141-45.

Neusner, J., 'First Cleanse the Inside', in *Method and Meaning in Ancient Judaism* (Ann Arbor: Edwards Brothers, 1981), pp. 155-64.
—*Judaism in the Beginning of Christianity* (Philadelphia: Fortress, 1984).
Nickelsburg, G.W.E., 'Riches, the Rich, and God's Judgment in I Enoch 92–105 and the Gospel according to Luke', *NTS* 25 (1978–79), pp. 324-44.
Nickle, K., *The Collection* (London: SCM Press, 1966).
Nock, A.D., *Essays on Religion and the Ancient World*, I, II (Cambridge: Cambridge University Press, 1972).
O'Connor, J.M., *St Paul's Corinth* (Wilmington, DE: Michael Glazier, 1983).
Orlinsky, H., *Ancient Israel* (Ithaca, NY: Cornell University Press, 1960).
Osiek, C., 'The Ransom of Captives: Evolution of a Tradition', *HTR* (1981), pp. 365-86.
—*Rich and Poor in the Shepherd of Hermas* (Washington, DC: Catholic Biblical Association of America, 1983).
Oulton, J.E.L., 'Second-Century Teaching and Holy Baptism', *Theology* 50 (1947), pp. 86-91.
Oxford Society of Historical Theology, *The New Testament in the Apostolic Fathers* (Oxford: Clarendon Press, 1905).
Prigent, P., *Epître de Barnabé* (Paris: Cerf, 1971).
—*L'épître de Barnabé I–XVI et ses sources* (Paris: Lecoffre, 1961).
Przybylski, B., *Righteousness in Matthew and his World of Thought* (Cambridge: Cambridge University Press, 1980).
Quell, G., and E. Stauffer, 'ἀγαπάω', *TDNT*, 1 (1964), pp. 21-55.
Rad, G. von, *Old Testament Theology*, I, II (New York: Harper & Row, 1962, 1965).
Ramsey, W.M., *The Church in the Roman Empire* (London: Putnam's Sons, 1893).
Ramsey, B., 'Almsgiving in the Latin Church: The Late Fourth and Early Fifth Centuries', *TS* 43 (1982), pp. 226-59.
Reicke, B., *The Epistles of James, Peter and Jude* (Garden City, NY: Doubleday, 1964).
—'Prophecies on the Destruction of Jerusalem', in D.E. Aune, *Studies in New Testament and Early Christian Literature* (Leiden: Brill, 1972), pp. 121-34.
Resch, A., *Agrapha* (Leipzig: Hinrichs, 1906).
Reumann, J., *'Righteousness' in the New Testament* (Philadelphia: Fortress Press, 1982).
Rich, A.N.M., 'The Cynic Conception of *autarkeia*', *Mnemosyne* 4/9 (1956), pp. 23-29.
Riddle, D.W., 'Early Christian Hospitality: A Factor in the Gospel Transmission', *JBL* 57 (1938), pp. 141-54.
Rist, J., *Stoic Philosophy* (Cambridge: Cambridge University Press, 1969).
Roberts, R., 'Almsgiving in the Apocrypha, Talmud, and Qoran', *International Journal of Apocrypha* (April, 1910), pp. 28-30.
Robinson, J.A., *Barnabas, Hermas, and the Didache* (London: SPCK, 1920).
Robinson, J.A.T., *Redating the New Testament* (Philadelphia: Westminster Press, 1976).
Robinson, J.M., and H. Koester, *Trajectories through Early Christianity* (Philadelphia: Fortress Press, 1971).
Rosenthal, F., 'Sedaka, Charity', *HUCA* 23 (1950–51), Part 1, pp. 411-30.
Ross, J.M., 'Introduction', in *The Nature of the Gods* by Cicero (Harmondsworth: Penguin, 1972).
Rostovtzeff, M., *The Social and Economic History of the Hellenistic World*, III (Oxford: Clarendon Press, 2nd edn, 1941).

—*The Social and Economic History of the Roman Empire* I, II (Oxford: Clarendon Press, 2nd edn, 1957).

Ste Croix, G.E.M. de, *The Class Struggle in the Ancient Greek World* (London: Gerald Duckworth, 1981).

—'Early Christian Attitudes to Property and Slavery', in D. Baker (ed.), *Church, Society and Politics* (Oxford: Basil Blackwell, 1975), pp. 1-38.

Sanday, W.A., and A.C. Headlam, *The Epistle to the Romans* (New York: Charles Scribner's Sons, 1905).

Schaff, P., *The Teaching of the Twelve Apostles* (New York: Funk and Wagnalls, 1886).

Schmidt, T.E., *Hostility to Wealth in the Synoptic Gospels* (Sheffield: JSOT Press, 1987).

Schoedel, W., *The Apostolic Fathers. V. Polycarp, Martyrdom of Polycarp, Fragments of Papias* (Camden: Nelson, 1967).

—*Ignatius of Antioch* (Philadelphia: Fortress Press, 1985).

Schrage, W., 'Die Stellung zur Welt bei Paulus, Epiktet und in der Apokalyptick. Ein Beitrag zu 1 Kor 7.29-31', *ZTK* 61 (1964), pp. 125-54.

Schweitzer, A., *The Kingdom of God and Primitive Christianity* (London: A. & C. Black, 1968).

Scott, R.B.V., *Proverbs Ecclesiastes* (Garden City, NY: Doubleday, 1965).

Scullard, H.H., *From the Gracchi to Nero* (London: Methuen, 1976).

Seccombe, D.P., *Possessions and the Poor in Luke–Acts* (Linz: Peeters, 1982).

—'Was there Organized Charity in Jerusalem before the Christians?', *JTS* 29 (1978), pp. 140-43.

Seitz, O.J.F., 'Relationship of the Shepherd of Hermas to the Epistle of James', *JBL* 63 (1944), pp. 131-40.

Selwyn, E.G., *The First Epistle of Peter* (London: Macmillan, 1957).

Sevenster, J.N., *Paul and Seneca* (Leiden: Brill, 1961).

—'Education or Conversion: Epictetus and the Gospels', *NovT* 8 (1966), pp. 247-62.

Shewring, W. (ed.), *Rich and Poor* (London: SPCK, 1948).

Smith, M.A., 'Did Justin Know the Didache?', in *Studia Patristica* 7 (Berlin: Akademie Verlag, 1966), pp. 287-90.

Snyder, G.F., *The Apostolic Fathers. VI. The Shepherd of Hermas* (Camden: Nelson, 1968).

Sordi, M., *The Christians and the Roman Empire* (Norman: University of Oklahoma Press, 1986).

Spence, C., *The Teaching of the Twelve Apostles* (London: Nisbet, 1885).

Stambaugh, J.E., and D.L. Balch, *The New Testament in its Social Environment* (Philadelphia: Westminster Press, 1986).

Staniforth, M. (trans.), *Early Christian Writings* (Harmondsworth: Penguin, 1968).

Stark, A.R., *The Christology in the Apostolic Fathers* (Chicago: University of Chicago Press, 1912).

Stauffer, E., *New Testament Theology* (London: SCM Press, 1955).

Stegemann, W., *The Gospel and the Poor* (Philadelphia: Fortress Press, 1984).

Stowers, S.K., 'Social Status, Public Speaking and Private Teaching: The Circumstances of Paul's Preaching Activity, *NovT* 26 (1984), pp. 59-82.

Strack, H.L., and P. Billerbeck, *Kommentar zum Neuen Testament aus Talmud und Midrasch*, I-IV (Munich: Beck, 1922–28).

Swete, H.B., *Essays on the Early History of the Church and the Ministry* (London: Macmillan, 1918).
—'Penitential Discipline in the First Three Centuries', *JTS* 4 (1903), pp. 321-37.
Talbert, C.H., 'II Peter and the Delay of the Parousia', *VC* 20 (1966), pp. 137-45.
Taylor, C., *The Teaching of the Twelve Apostles with Illustrations from the Talmud* (Cambridge: Deighton Bell, 1886).
—*The Witness of Hermas to the Four Gospels* (London: C.J. Clay, 1892).
Tenney, F., *An Economic History of Rome* (Baltimore: The Johns Hopkins University Press, 1927).
Theissen, G., *The Social Setting of Pauline Christianity* (Philadelphia: Fortress Press, 1982).
—*The Sociology of Early Palestinian Christianity* (Philadelphia: Fortress Press, 1978).
Thiselton, A.C., 'Realized Eschatology at Corinth', *NTS* 24 (1977–78), pp. 510-26.
Thrall, M.E.G., 'Agape, Caritas, Charity', *CTM* 20 (1949), pp. 861-65.
Torrance, T.F., *The Doctrine of Grace in the Apostolic Fathers* (London: Oliver & Boyd, 1948).
Troeltsch, E., *The Social Teaching of the Christian Churches*, I (London: George Allen & Unwin, 1931).
Turner, H.E.W., *The Patristic Doctrine of Redemption* (London: Mowbrays, 1952).
Uhlhorn, G., *Christian Charity in the Ancient Church* (New York: Charles Scribners' Sons, 1883).
Vischer, L., *Tithing in the Early Church* (Philadelphia: Fortress Press, 1966).
Vokes, F.E., *The Riddle of the Didache* (London: SPCK, 1938).
Watkins, O.D., *A History of Penance*, I (New York: Longmans, Green, 1920).
Weber, M., *The Sociology of Religion* (Boston: Beacon, 1942).
—'On the Date of *First* Clement', *BR* 29 (1984), pp. 35-54.
Welborn, L.L., 'On the Discord in Corinth', *JBL* 106/1 (1987), pp. 85-111.
Wengst, K., *Traditions und Theologie des Barnabasbriefes* (New York: De Gruyter, 1971).
Westcott, B.F., *The Incarnation and Common Life* (London: Macmillan, 1893).
Whittaker, J., 'Christianity and Morality in the Roman Empire', *VC* 33 (1979), pp. 209-25.
Wilken, R.L., *The Christians as the Romans Saw them* (New Haven: Yale University Press, 1984).
Williams, F.E., 'Is Almsgiving the Point of the Unjust Steward?', *JBL* 83 (1964), pp. 293-97.
Wilson, S.G., *Luke and the Law* (Cambridge: Cambridge University Press, 1983).
Windisch, H.D., *Der Barnabasbrief* (Tübingen: Mohr, 1920).

INDEXES

INDEX OF REFERENCES

OLD TESTAMENT

NEW TESTAMENT

RABBINIC WRITINGS

INDEX OF AUTHORS

JOURNAL FOR THE STUDY OF THE NEW TESTAMENT

Supplement Series